MW00532204

AGES OF THE SPIRITUAL LIFE

AGES OF THE SPIRITUAL LIFE

Paul Evdokimov

Original translation
by
Sister Gertrude, S. P.

Revised translation
by
Michael Plekon and Alexis Vinogradov

ST VLADIMIR'S SEMINARY PRESS
CRESTWOOD, NY 10707
1998

Library of Congress Cataloging-in-Publication Data

Evdokimov, Paul, 1901-1970
    [Ages de la vie spirituelle. English]
    Ages of the spiritual life.
        p.   cm.
    Includes bibliographical references (p.) and index.
    ISBN 0-88141-175-2 (alk. paper)
    1. Spiritual life—Orthodox Eastern Church.   2. Orthodox Eastern
Church—Doctrines.   I. Title.
BX382.E813   1998
248.4'819—DC21   97-29879
                                                                     CIP

Revised translation
Copyright © Michael Plekon

ISBN 0-88141-175-2

Les Ages de la Vie Spirituelle
Originally published by Desclée de Brouwer

PRINTED IN THE UNITED STATES OF AMERICA

Contents

Acknowledgements. vii

A Life in the Spirit and the Spiritual Life 1

Introduction 13

I   The Encounter

1 Atheism 21

2 Faith 49

3 Dimensions of the Spiritual Life 57

4 The Ascetic Art and the Dangers of Ignorance 61

5 Essential Elements of the Spiritual Life. 67

6 The Nature or Essence of the Spiritual Life 71

7 The Different Ages of the Spiritual Life 77

II   Obstacles and Struggle

1 Negations of Evil and Affirmations of Good 83

2 Three Aspects of Evil and the Evil One 91

3 Hell and the Infernal Dimension of the World 97
   Iconography. 97

4 Human Suffering. 103

5 The Message of Pentecost. 109

6 The Desert Fathers 115

7 Interiorized Monasticism 135
   1. *The Transmission of the Witness*. 135
   2. *The Universal Character of Monastic Spirituality* 137

3. *The Three Temptations, the Lord's Three*
   Answers, and the Three Monastic Vows 141

4. *The Vow of Poverty in the Interior Monasticism*
   of the Laity 147

5. *The Vow of Chastity* 149

6. *The Vow of Obedience* 153

7. *Christian Unity and Monastic Freedom* 155

8 The Human Being 157

9 The Asceticism of the Spiritual Life 161

10 The Ascetic Effort 165

11 The Progression of the Spiritual Life 169

12 The Passions and the Technique of Temptation 173

III The Charisms of the Spiritual Life and the Mystical Ascent

1 The Evolution of the Spiritual Life in the East and
   in the West 181

2 The Passage from the Old Testament to the New 187

3 The Charisms of the Spiritual Life 193

1. *The spirit of discernment, impassibility, silence,*
   vigilance, repentance and humility 193

2. *The charism of "joyful dying"* 204

3. *Prayer* 210

4 Lectio Divina: Reading the Bible 225

5 The Universal Priesthood of the Laity in the Eastern
   Church Tradition 231

6 The Mystical Ascent 249

Selected Bibliography 259

Acknowledgments

In our revised translation we have used that done for the Paulist Press edition titled *The Struggle with God*, by Sister Gertrude in 1966. Paul Evdokimov's widow, Mrs Tomoko Faerber-Evdokimoff of Geneva and his son, Fr Michel Evdokimov, have encouraged us and provided invaluable help. Paulist Press and Desclée de Brouwer graciously gave permission for this new edition. PSC-CUNY Faculty Research Award provided support to me for this project along with reassigned time for research from the committee and Dean Alexandra Logue of the School of Liberal Arts and Sciences, Baruch College of the City University of New York. Sarah Hinlicky did important revisions of quotations and notes and reviewed the text for us. Our families and parish, St Gregory the Theologian, made room for our work in their lives. To all, many thanks.

A Life in the Spirit and the Spiritual Life

An Introduction to Paul Evdokimov
and *Ages of the Spiritual Life*

A saint is not a superman, but one who discovers and lives his truth as a liturgical being. The best definition of a human being comes from the Liturgy. The true man or woman is the one who proclaims the *Trisagion* ("Holy God, Holy Mighty, Holy Immortal") and the *Sanctus* ("Holy, holy, holy, Lord God of Sabaoth"—"I will sing to the Lord as long as I live")...It is not enough to *say* prayers, one must become, *be* prayer, prayer incarnate. It is not enough to have moments of praise. All of life, each act, every gesture, even the smile of the human face, must become a hymn of adoration, an offering, a prayer. One should offer not what one has, but what one is. [*The Sacrament of Love*, Anthony P. Gythiel and Victoria Steadman trans., (Crestwood NY: SVS Press, 1985), pp. 61-62.]

These days the racks at book and music stores are crammed with chants and "spiritualities" of every description, from all religious sources, some authentic to their traditions, others eclectic mixtures from far and near. Similarly, we see the faces of many "teachers" of spirituality, running from DeePak Chopra, Thomas Moore, Marianne Williamson and M. Scott Peck to beloved masters such as St Seraphim of Sarov, Dame Julian of Norwich, Thomas Merton, and Fr Alexander Men.

There is not just a market but an interest, even a hunger, a passion for another way of existing, another way of thinking, feeling, acting. It would be better not to curse the passion for the spiritual life but to bless the discovery of the Kingdom and the deep desire for its Beauty.

1

In the Orthodox Church, and especially in this century, we have an extraordinary procession of eloquent teachers of the faith, insightful guides in the life of the Spirit. Many of them passed through the fire of the great turmoil of this century—the Russian revolution, immigration, the Great Depression and enormous deprivation, the unthinkable destruction of World War II, even the horrors of the Holocaust and the concentration camps. They came through these shaken, doubting, certainly challenging their Church and faith, but eventually were able to express the beauty of God and His Kingdom in ways intelligible to our tumultuous time. Sadly, most are virtually unknown outside Orthodoxy, and even within, are not familiar figures.

One such teacher of the life of faith is the Orthodox lay theologian, still remembered in ecumenical circles and among monastics of both East and West, called by his friend a "witness," a theologian of the beauty of God, Paul Evdokimov. Here we present him, something of his life and person, and a revised translation of what surely is his most important work, *Ages of the Spiritual Life.*

Pavel Nikolaievitch Evdokimov was a man of great contrasts, surprises and depths. Born in St Petersburg, August 2, 1901, his father, a lieutenant-colonel, was assassinated by one of his own soldiers in 1905. Evdokimov first was educated in a military school and later served in the cavalry of the White Army. Despite all the indications that he too would embark upon a career in military service, shortly before the Revolution he began theological studies at the Kiev Academy.

The contrasts and surprising turns were to continue for him. Fleeing the Red Army he and his family escaped from the Crimea through Constantinople, and then following a well-worn path, came finally to the émigré community in Paris. Though he revered the literature, language, culture and Orthodoxy of Russia and would pass on the treasures of her writers and theologians to the West, Evdokimov put down deep roots in his new home. Though never renouncing his Russian identity, he nevertheless wrote almost exclusively in French and never made the Diaspora community a ghetto, venturing out to the West in all aspects of life and work. While sharing the saints, monasticism, liturgy and iconography of the Orthodox Church, he appreciated and appropriated the holiness of Western Christianity. This is seen many times in the text to follow here.

A student of Nicolas Berdiaev and Fr Sergius Bulgakov, he was in the first class to graduate in theology at Saint Sergius Institute. This he accomplished while on the night shift at Citroën, as well as washing train-cars and working at restaurants, earlier having completed a degree in philosophy at the Sorbonne. Married to Natasha Brunel in 1927, he became a founding member of the Russian Christian Student Movement, took much responsibility for home and child care while his wife taught Italian, as another life-long friend, lay theologian Elisabeth Behr-Sigel remembers. Yet he also completed a doctorate in philosophy at Aix-en-Provence in 1942, excavating the problem of evil in Dostoyevski's work.

During World War II, he worked with the French Resistance in hiding and caring for those who were the targets of Nazi destruction, under the auspices of an ecumenical agency CI-MADE (Comité inter-Mouvements pour l'accueil des évacués). At the war's end, his wife having died of cancer, Evdokimov continued this diaconal service of administering the hostels, leading them at Bièvres, and ones for students, at Sèvres and Massey. He was active in the ecumenical movement from the end of the war until his death, serving on the board of the Ecumenical Institute at Bossey, as well as teaching there and at the Catholic Graduate Theological Faculty in Paris. He was an official observer at the second session of Vatican II in 1964, and his contributions are thought to have helped craft the dogmatic constitution on the Church in the world, *Gaudium et spes*. He was again married, in

1954 to Tomoko Sakai, who assisted him in the work in the hostels and later in ecumenical endeavors. From 1953 on to the end of his life he was a faculty member at his *alma mater,* the Saint Sergius Institute, and after a break during the war years resumed the publication of a rich and elegant theological authorship.

In 1958 he completed *Woman and the Salvation of the World* (SVS Press, 1995) and in 1959 his theological magnum opus, *L'orthodoxie.* He published the revision of an earlier study in 1962 as *The Sacrament of Love,* (SVS Press, 1985) an important look at the holiness of marriage and of the vocation of ordinary life in the world, the priesthood of all the baptized, both of which would be constant themes in his writing. As the bibliography here indicates, Evdokimov's work encompassed iconography and its theology, the Russian theological tradition in which he himself was formed, the liturgy, the Holy Spirit and the Mother of God. Relevant to the present text was his consistent preoccupation with bridging between the modern world and the Church's Tradition and life of prayer. Embroidered through his numerous essays in the 1960s are the names and ideas of those who shaped our age: Marx and Freud, Jung and Sartre, but especially the voices of the Fathers and those of a host of other witnesses, from St Tikhon of Zadonsk and Alexander Bukharev to Simone Weil and St Thérése of Lisieux. In his journals Thomas Merton enthusiastically noted Evdokimov's exquisite presentation of the Church's faith in *L'orthodoxie,* and copiously cites his essays on the idea of "interiorized monasticism" as a genuine resource in monastic renewal. (*Turning Toward the World,* HarperSan Francisco, 1996, 90-91, 348-349) For a man of such contrasts and surprises it perhaps should have been expected that Evdokimov would lyricize on both marriage and monasticism in the same book, *The Sacrament of Love.* For him there was a profound and common reality to both callings, despite all external differences of sexual love, celibacy, childbearing and asceticism, earning a living and poverty.

Over the years, Evdokimov's teaching, lecturing, writing and ecumenical work endeared him to Roman Catholic monastics, Protestant clergy and laity. He became a beloved figure to many Orthodox students and youth through his work at Saint Sergius, in summer theological courses and in the international Orthodox youth movement, Syndesmos. During the 1960s his writing took up themes prominent in his first articles after the war, notably his 1950 open-letter to the churches. He confronted the protests of students, even the tumult of 1968 in Paris with equanimity and understanding. He probed the challenges of a Simone Weil, a Dietrich Bonhoeffer, a John Robinson, even the "death of God" theologians. In a posthumously published anthology, *L'amour fou de Dieu*, (Éditions du Seuil, 1973) he handles issues debated in both Church and society: freedom, authority, the apparent silence of God in the face of so much evil and suffering, realities he concretely faced in the Resistance and the hostels during and after the war. It is not too much to say that the "kenotic" Christ of Philippians 2, so dear to Russian theologians of the modern era, the "divine philanthropy" of which the Eastern Church's liturgy sings, the God who empties Himself in becoming human, who suffers, allows Himself to be powerless, never forcing us to love him—this is the fundamental imagery of Paul Evdokimov's theology. It is the "absurd" or "crazy," "foolish" love of God for his creation, (mannikos eros) of which St Paul and Nicolas Cabasilas spoke who is the God of the Gospel, the crucified and the risen Lord who descends into hell to find Adam and Eve and their children, who enters the hell of the world and of the self to find and save us. Never does Evdokimov condescend to the critiques and needs of the modern heart, yet he constantly listens to these and responds, pointing to the boundless heart of God. (We hope to translate and publish a select anthology of Paul Evdokimov's best essays in the near future, those precisely dealing with the many themes of freedom and faith in the modern world noted here.)

After delivering a profound and creative paper on the relationship between the Mother of God and the Holy Spirit at the

meeting of the French Mariological Society, and returning home
to Meudon, Paul Evdokimov suddenly fell asleep in the Lord on
September 16, 1970. Later, a special number of the French Orthodox journal *Contacts* (nos. 73-74, 1971) would publish not
only an extensive biographical sketch by his friend and colleague
Olivier Clément, but numerous remembrances from family and
friends. His children, Nina Pecheff-Evdokimov and Fr Michel
Evdokimov eloquently recorded the gentleness, patience and
compassion of their father, both within their family and with an
endless stream of the residents of the hostels. Some of these,
former students who lived in the CIMADE hostels he directed,
movingly attested to his pastoral and paternal love for his charges, his
quiet listening to the many troubles of those who lived there, his
ability to lead others to prayer. Another close friend, lay theologian
Elisabeth Behr-Sigel left an unforgettable image, of the young husband and father, Paul Evdokimov, bathing and feeding his young
children while Mrs. Evdokimov was at school teaching, and all the
while introducing her to the Fathers, and to the great Russian theologians. His long-time friend Fr Lev Gillet witnessed that Paul Evdokimov was as much at home in the world of the invisible, heavenly
beings, perhaps even more so, than his lively presence here. Praying
was as natural for him as breathing, Fr Lev said. He became prayer, as
his writings taught, but he never was less than deeply human. One
catches this not only in the remembrances of Evdokimov as teacher
and father and friend, but as well in the always perceptive but
relentlessly joyful lines of his essays and books.

Ages of the Spiritual Life is not as extensive a study as the
dogmatic sweep of *L'orthodoxie,* not as specifically focused as the
studies of liturgy, of the theology of icons or the Holy Spirit, of the
heritage of Russian theology, as the explorations into the implicit
theology of Dostoyevski and other Russian writers. Though challenging, *Ages* is the book addressed to the widest readership both
inside the Church and outside. It is not the "recipe" handbook, the
"how to be spiritual" manual found in such abundance on the

bookshelves in this time of heightened interest in spirituality. However it is a persuasive argument and demonstration of how the centuries' old Tradition of Christianity can be lived out today. Evdokimov claims that the basics of the Christian life, particularly preserved by monasticism, are for all, not simply for clergy or ascetic specialists. Further, he indicates how the essentials of this life can find appropriate expression in the last years of our century and beyond in the next.

First, though, as a consummate teacher, Evdokimov makes us encounter the very points of view so ingrained in us as modern men and women that we take them for granted. We live in an era in which the principal impulse toward religion has been to criticize, moreover to be bored with it. He takes on the deep, principled challenge to faith with enormous respect for its intellectual and moral integrity. Ecclesiastical institutions and leaders have perpetrated much wrong, though they clearly can not be held responsible for the bulk of human misery in the modern era, a recognition maintained by Marx himself. Thus in the opening chapter of *Ages,* we are inserted into a demanding conversation but ultimately a rewarding dialogue between a teacher of the Church and an array of those whom Paul Ricoeur, another lay theologian, has termed the modern "masters of suspicion." We wind our way through Marx and Feuerbach, Freud and Jung, Nietzsche and Heidegger, Sartre and Camus, Malraux and Merleau-Ponty, Kierkegaard and Simone Weil. Evdokimov tracks us through socialism and psychology, existential philosophy and critical sociology, the scriptures and the Fathers. Rarely does one find as honest and surprising an engagement between a person of faith and the community of questioners as in this singular chapter.

However, as stimulating as this tour is, the goal of the book is otherwise. In *Ages* Evdokimov wants us to not just cognitively review religion and its cultured modern despisers. He also wants us to enter the living Tradition of the Church and experience the life with God lived there in our own lives, in our time. So begins a pilgrimage through the essential elements of the spiritual life, with the proviso that there are different ages, different expressions appropriate to the human situation at different times.

As he began with a contemplation of unbelief, so the second part of *Ages* commences with a discerning contemplation of the Evil One and evil. No consideration of the spiritual life in true biblical and ecclesial fashion could avoid coming to terms with that which pervades the world and its history, that which is the opposite of the One who is Love. At once the ingenuity of Evdokimov emerges, our passage into hell and its permeation of our world is accomplished, by, of all things, a probing meditation upon the feast of the Church year through their iconography and liturgical hymns and texts. Thus we see hell trampled underfoot by the God-Man crucified and risen and the breath of the Holy Spirit, of Pentecost becoming perpetual in the life of the Church.

Here we encounter for the first time that band of holy women and men who fearlessly confronted the Evil One with only the scriptures, liturgy, and the ascetical struggle in their own being. These are the desert fathers and mothers, the early monastics of Egypt, Syria and Palestine. From their "sayings" and "lives" Evdokimov draws a treasure of wisdom about the spiritual life. But as heroic, mysterious and attractive as these first ascetics are (and they have become familiar figures in the field of spirituality these "abbas" and "ammas," fathers and mothers). Their radical, maximal witness, their bloodless witness cannot be merely duplicated by us. Toward the end of our century and close the start of a new millennium, Evdokimov warns, it would be futile and very wrong to attempt to replicate their forms and methods. Rather, we must "receive" the Tradition in its basics from them, and it will be for us, in the light of the scriptures and the Fathers, the liturgy and the rest of the Church's resources, to find the ways and means of the spiritual appropriate to our time and place.

Here Evdokimov borrows a term not from Anthony the Great or Poemen or Syncletica or Sarah of the desert, but from a monk and bishop, a pastor and teacher much closer to our own time, really an inhabitant, with us, of the modern era. It is St Tikon of Zadonsk, and his notion of "untonsured monk" (*nepostrizhenniy monakh*) that every Christian can and must become. For Evdokimov this is paraphrased, echoing a long line of virtually identical insight from Basil the Great, John Chrysostom, down to the 19th century Russian monk who returned to the lay state and to marriage, Alexander Bukharev. Adapting St Tikhon he asserts: "The black monastic habit does not save a person. The one who wears the white habit, who has the spirit of obedience, humility and purity, such a one is a true monk of interiorized monasticism." The life of the monastics, summarized by the three vows of poverty, chastity and obedience is none other than the way given by Christ in his response to the three temptations of the Evil One. It is the Gospel life held out to every baptized Christian, not merely the deprivation of control, wealth or sexuality, but in all of these, the only real freedom, that by which all is lived for the Lord and in and through Him.

So, today as in the past, we must learn to pray. Like the early monastics, our brother and sister, the neighbor is for us, the face of God Himself. The unusual mortifications of the early ascetics cannot be pasted on to life in our cities and suburbs, town and rural areas. We need to find the forms of fasting, for example, distinctive to our lives—from addiction not only to alcohol and drugs—to many substances, but to wealth and security and to work itself. The goal of the spiritual life is God to be sure, communion with the Father, Son and Holy Spirit. But it is also the process of becoming truly human!

Finally, in the third and last part of *Ages*, Evdokimov pulls out from the immense history of the spiritual life some salient points of similarity and difference between the Church in the East and

the West. Always seeking the undivided Church of the first millennium, Evdokimov shows the complementarity of East and
West today. Then, he reviews the charisms or gifts of the spiritual
life, the specific tasks to which we are led as we follow Christ. In a
most practical way, he speaks about prayer, the forms and difficulties of this conversation with God, nourished by the scriptures
read daily and by the Eucharist and rest of the daily liturgical
services. Finally, in a manner astonishing for an Orthodox theologian, Evdokimov lifts up the priesthood of all the baptized without in the least pitting this or that of the ordained ministry of
bishops, priests and deacons with each other. In the end, the vision
of the spiritual life Evdokimov so masterfully sets before us here in
Ages is hardly the individualistic version marketed in such abundance
today. Rather it is sacramental: a true meeting of the divine and the
human; ecclesial, that is, always linked with the rest of the Christian
community, and last of all, diaconal, as Fr Michel Evdokimov emphasizes, both of his father's thought and his life, a seeking God in the
loving service of the neighbor. Paul Evdokimov's *Ages* is a rich contribution to our quest for a deeper spiritual life.

Michael Plekon

*That's why I
like him.

Paul Evdokimov

Introduction

Above the noise of the world, if we know how to listen, we can hear the questions put to us concerning the meaning of things. More than ever before, human existence needs clarity, placing before each person the one serious question. Beyond all catechetical literature or propaganda, and at the level of a conscience freed from every prejudice, the 20th-century believer is invited to ask: "What is God?" while the atheist, the one who denies, is invited to make clear the object of his negation.

The question elicits surprise, and while the answer is slow in coming, the silence is refreshing. This question is revealing for man himself, for it is also a way of saying: "Who are you?"

The one who would say God is creator, provider, savior, is in effect reviewing the chapters of a textbook or giving testimony to a theory, to a dialectical distance between God and himself. God, in this case, is not the All, passionately and spontaneously grasped in the immediate content of his revelation. St. John Climacus, one of the most severe ascetics, said we should love God as a smitten lover the beloved.[1] A lover who is passionately in love would say: "But that is everything. That is my life. There is nothing but that; the rest does not count, it is non-existent." At the height of his emotion, St. Gregory of Nyssa uttered these words: "Thou whom my soul loves…"[2]

1 *The Ladder of Divine Ascent,* step 30, Colm Luibheid and Norman Russell, trans. [Ramsey, NJ: Paulist Press, 1982], p. 287.)
2 *P.G.,* 44, col. 801A.

Atheism rejects only an ideology, a system, a theory, which man has too often misused; it never rejects divine reality, which is revealed only through faith.

Patristic tradition does not attempt any definition of God, for God is beyond all human words. "Concepts create idols of God, wonder alone is capable of grasping something," confessed St. Gregory.[3] For the Fathers, the word *God* is a vocative addressed to the Ineffable.

With regard to man, the difficulty is just as great. It caused Theophilus of Antioch to say: "Show me your man and I shall show you my God."[4] The divine mystery is reflected in the mirror of the human mystery. St. Peter speaks of *homo cordis absconditus,* the hidden person of the heart.[5] *Deus absconditus,* God mysterious and hidden, has created His vis-à-vis, His other self, *homo absconditus,* the human being mysterious and hidden.

The spiritual life springs forth in "the pastures of the heart,"[6] in its free spaces, as soon as these two mysterious beings, God and man, meet there.

"The greatest thing that happens between God and the human soul is to love and to be loved," affirm the great spiritual writers.[7]

"For man shall not see me and live."[8] For the Fathers, this biblical warning meant that we cannot see God with the light of our reason, and that we can never define God, for every definition is a limitation. However, he is closer to us than we are to ourselves. In the depth of his astounding proximity God turns his face to man and says: "I am...The Holy One."[9] He chooses among his

3 *P.G.,* 44, cols. 377B, 1028D.

4 *P.G.,* 6, 1025B.

5 1 Pet 3, 4.

6 St. Macarios, Homilies paraphrased by St. Symeon Metaphrastis in *The Philokalia,* vol III, G. E. H. Palmer, Philip Sherrard, Kallistos Ware, trans. (London, Faber and Faber, 1984), p. 338.

7 Kallistos, *P.G.,* 147, col. 860A-B.

8 Ex 33:20. (Scriptural citations are from the RSV)

9 Hos 11:9.

names the one that conceals him most. He is even "thrice holy," as the angels proclaim in the *Sanctus,* thus throwing in relief the incomparable and absolutely unique character of divine holiness. Wisdom, power, even love, can find affinities and similarities, but holiness alone has no analogy here below. It can neither be measured nor compared to any reality of this world. Before the burning bush, in the face of the devouring fire of "For thou alone art holy,"[10] every human being is but "dust and ashes." For this reason, as soon as the holiness of God manifests itself, it immediately arouses the *mysterium tremendum,* a sacred fear, an irresistible feeling of the "wholly other."[11] This is not at all a fear of the unknown, but a characteristic and mystical awe that accompanies every manifestation of the divine. "I will send my terror before you,"[12] God says. And again: "Put off your shoes from your feet, for the place on which you are standing is holy ground."[13]

Having thus delineated the unbridgeable abysses that separate the divine from the human, God immediately reveals their mysterious conformity: "Deep calls to deep,"[14] and "As in water face answers to face."[15] God, the lover of man, transcends his own transcendence toward us, drawing us from our nothingness, and calling us in turn to transcend our immanence toward the Holy One. We can do this because divine holiness has willed to take on our face. Even more, the "Man of Sorrows" shows us the "Man of Desire," the eternal Lover who attracts all love and enters into us in order that we may live again in him. He says to every soul: "Set me as a seal upon your heart, as a seal upon your arm; for love is strong as death...its flashes are flashes of fire, a most vehement flame."[16]

10 Rev 15:4.
11 See R. Otto, *The Idea of the Holy,* John W. Harvey, trans. (Oxford University Press, 1958), p. 25.
12 Ex 23:27.
13 Ex 3:5.
14 Ps 42:7.
15 Cf. Prov 27:19.
16 Song of Songs 8:6.

This is why Scripture tells us: "Be holy, for I the Lord your God am holy."[17] When Peter wishes to define the aim of our Christian life, he speaks of our participating in the holiness of God.[18] Likewise Paul, speaking to the Christians, addresses the "saints" of Rome or Corinth. Would he still today address the "saints" of Paris or London. Would the modern believer recognize himself among this group?

As soon as we speak of sanctity, a psychological block forms. We think of the giants of former days, the hermits buried in their caves, stylites perched on their columns. These "illuminati," "equal to the angels," no longer appear as belonging to this world. Sanctity seems out-of-date. It belongs to a past that has become strange to us, irrelevant to the disjointed forms, the broken rhythms of modern life. Today a stylite would not even arouse curiosity. He would provoke the question: "What good is he?" A saint is no longer anything but a sort of yogi, or perhaps to put it more crudely, a sick or dysfunctional person; in any case, a useless being.

Before our very eyes the world is losing its sacred character without encountering any resistance. In the past, the sacred was a sign formed by the matter of this world and reflecting a "wholly other," translating it and testifying to its presence. Does this "wholly other" speak to man today? For him the transcendent no longer transcends anything. It has lost all correspondence with the real. It is non-existent. Symptomatic of this brutal fact is the recent appearance of a form of atheism that is *organic* and *normal.* Far from seeming to be a neurosis of civilization, it appears rather to express a certain health, a psychic state free from all metaphysical unease, fully occupied with this world, insensitive to religion. Such a "profaneness," such a contented, cold skepticism neither struggles with anything, nor any longer asks a single question about God. To be intelligent today means to understand everything and to believe in nothing.

17 Lev 19:2.
18 2 Pet 1:4; Heb 12:10.

At its best, this attitude politely relegates sanctity to the cloister, far from the world, meaning that the spiritual life scarcely interests us. We consider it a useless object hampering us, fit only to be stored in the attic of history.

But there is more. Especially among adherents to established religion, anything religious provokes in sincere souls an immediate response of boredom, with services and ceremonies performed in an archaic language, or with childish hymns proclaiming a joy devoid of meaning, boredom with a closed symbolism, the key to which is lost forever.

There is also the world of black-clad clerics, sinister traditionalists, or fast-paced progressives, whether sincere or ridiculous. There is moreover the pious style of rules and restraints with their oppressive seriousness. There is the mediocrity of "the faithful," who take themselves far too seriously and impose on others their own mentality, formed by edifying discourses and sermons characterized by empty formulas and verbal axcess. A religious life that has been domesticated, socialized, democratized, has the least attractive appearance. Its intellectual content is quite low, imprisoned by old-fashioned spiritual manuals with their limited ideas and apologetics no longer accepted today. On the global level it is an enormous social obstacle, reinforcing the dominant ideologies that are hostile or indifferent to believers. Nonetheless, faced with Revelation, it is no longer a question merely concerning man. The miracle of the immanent judgment is still effective. A serious examination quickly shows that, having drawn near each other by their fundamental insufficiency and the metaphysical poverty of their respective visions, the outdated religious person and the modern sophisticated irreligious individual meet back to back in an immanence imprisoned within itself.

I

The Encounter

1

Atheism

Atheism commands attention and imposes itself on all by its universal diffusion. It is no longer the privilege of an enlightened minority, but expresses a norm common to all levels of society. A civilization has been built on the conscious rejection of God, or more precisely, on the negation of all dependence on any transcendent power. In fact, science no longer has need of God as a hypothesis. Moreover, from a moral point of view, God does not appear to be all-powerful since he does not suppress evil; and if he does not wish to do so, then he is not love.

Thus built on a negation, atheism has no metaphysical content proper to itself and no constructive philosophy. It is still rare to find it explicitly expressed. It is simply prevalent, *de facto*, spineless but practical. Philosophical considerations intervene only subsequently to justify attitudes or to provide an excuse. Its reasons are never truly rational, nor can they be, for they fall short, for being of an empirical sort, they are utilitarian and pragmatic. This explains why the problem at this level simply ceases to interest anyone. Since we are more concerned with economic and political questions, religious beliefs no longer mean anything to us. Such an attitude is reinforced by an often justifiable distrust of philosophers, who have abdicated and betrayed their social function by their own scepticism.

St. Paul knew what he was doing. He grounded his preaching on what immediately provoked a violent reaction from those who relied on discursive reason. Indeed the Incarnation is always a folly and a scandal for human thought. The latter in its historical criticism demythologizes and distinguishes between the historical Jesus and the Christ depicted in the dogmas of faith.

21

The archaic state of knowledge in past ages makes every scholar mistrustful and little inclined to take into account a so-called "revelation." He finds no assurance at the outset of the alleged event and, in every way, a truth buried in the centuries is unacceptable to the contemporary spirit interested only in the here and now. One must choose between verifiable facts and texts visibly originating in a myth. To the atheist, it is inconceivable, even offensive, that God should enter into time and confide his truth to a handful of obscure disciples and to the precarious transmission of texts, written twenty centuries ago. The life of Jesus shows only anecdotes and miscellaneous facts without any guarantee of objectivity. Can a contingent fact, scarcely observed by historians, touch the heart of today's average person? How can an event dated and fixed in time and space lay claim to an eternal value—the authority of God and the universal importance of the salvation of every person? This is monstrously out of proportion, [1] even unbearable for critical reason. The man Jesus could very well have lived in Palestine. It is not so much his divinization by his disciples as the *humanization of God* that is declared impossible. A moral ideal, a philosophical concept could, if need be, receive the title of divine, but the philosopher rejects the God-man, rejects a God speaking as a human being and taking on the face of a man. Thus the authority of the apostolic witness crumbles, and with it, that of the Word. With no one to hear it, it is more than ever a voice crying in the historical wilderness. Like the wise men of Athens in former times, the man in the street now repulses all discourse with "We will hear you again about this."[2]

We must pay attention to this very real difficulty and be clear about what faith requires of us and the reason for this require-

---

1 The man who declared himself God is insupportable for the Jews, and God-become-man is a scandal for the Greeks. The Old Testament knew God but was closed to the idea of a suffering God; the Greek mysteries knew the image of a suffering God, but they did not know God. The New Testament reveals both.

2 Acts 17:32.

ment. Unfortunately, believers and unbelievers are profoundly ignorant of each other. They do not understand one another, for they belong to different anthropological types. Even for St. Gregory of Nyssa, one who is not moved by the Holy Spirit constitutes a separate species, a humanity apart.

Believers naively advance arguments drawn from a fear of judgment or from a metaphysical disquietude in the face of death. On the present level of evolution, the resurrection of the dead and all the traditional problems of the religious man do not even graze the conscience of a certain type of atheist, for in this case of advanced degeneracy, even the subconscious does not bear any trace of them. We are witnessing a profound change in the substratum of our consciousness.

It is important to understand this, for above the always amorphous crowd, the existence of a real spiritual life, the existence of a saint, would constitute a kind of insufferable "thorn in the side" of an atheism that wishes to be systematic, moral and totalitarian. Sooner or later the reciprocal ignorance of dynamic faith and militant atheism, as well as their peaceful coexistence, will be shown to be impossible. Messianic mandates reach a point where they not only exclude one another but are violently opposed. In fact, there already exist a lucid and serenely authoritarian manner of posing the problem of faith by putting atheism in question in a direct confrontation that permits no cheating, no loophole, no "asylum of ignorance."

Atheism can be explained by the simple fact that God does not impose himself on anyone and that his existence is not immediately evident to all. In the mind of the masses, religious faith is reduced to exploitation, alienation, or compensation. But if we pass beyond this demagoguery, a relatively simple task, such a critique comes up against a real difficulty. It is not a question of those who are indifferent. They do not concern us here. The most surprising thing is the existence, even the possibility, of a conscious atheism. How can one be an atheist?

The word atheism, by its negative "a," denies theism, denies God. Now the real problem is to show how it can really do this but, first of all, we must specify what it denies. How does atheism define the complex "God" before denying him? The whole question lies here. At most it is the negation of a certain type of theology, of an anthropomorphic and human conception of God. This in no way goes beyond the human and in no way does it touch God in himself. On the other hand, philosophically speaking, one can deny a thing only by affirming another. In denying God, what does one affirm in his place? If it is a crude protoplasm already bearing within itself its future prophets, we must confess that this is a more problematic hypothesis than the very simplistic and reasonable idea of a creator God.

To deny, and to be ignorant of, are two very different courses of reasoning. An agnostic affirms nothing and is ignorant of everything. Conversely, he can deny only proved errors and evident impossibilities. Atheism claims that God is evidently impossible. Now science teaches us to be extremely prudent when we make hypothetical judgments, especially in considering what is impossible. The boundary between the possible and the impossible is changing so constantly that one no longer knows where to place it. What if the science of tomorrow should demonstrate that atheism is an impossible deception, an untenable ignorance, a survival of scientistic obscurantism worse than the so-called darkness of the Middle Ages?

Such a complete change of ideas will certainly not take place today. But the flagrant absence of a sufficiently consistent and constructive atheistic philosophy obliges academic atheism in its recent forms to place itself beyond the problem of God. This is no longer the end of reflection but its point of departure. That the existence of God is not a philosophical problem is a gratuitous, simplistic and uncritical postulate.[3]

Atheism thus simplified pervades the masses. It no longer comes from the minds of philosophers and is thus freed from any exercise

3 The term atheism "is more fitting for religious polemics than for philosophical discussions, from where, moreover, it tends to disappear" (de Lalande, *Voc. phil.,* p. 88). For neopositivism, there is no knowledge corresponding to the word God; metaphysical problems are devoid of meaning.

of the intelligence. Imperceptibly it identifies itself with the historical situation, setting itself up as a consequence of political and economic conditions. It claims and appropriates all efforts against famine, war and injustice. It does this more easily than organized religion, compromised by having been associated with an order that has passed, now sharing its fate, seeing itself thrust aside.

After all, there is no dispute about God as such. "Let us leave the heavens to priests and sparrows," Heine said. It is his presence in the world, his rooting in humanity that are passionately denied, negations made easier by God who reveals but does not give proof of himself. To speak empirically, it is evident that one person can find another and even become passionately involved, without the intervention of the gods. Consequently, at least in appearance, the more human a person becomes, the less religious he or she is and the more one can feel oneself the sole maker of one's destiny and the master of history.

Atheism does not appear anymore as a chance by-product of our human condition; it has become essential, for example, to *Marxist doctrine.* Communism only exists as a function of an integral humanism. According to its assumptions, man is the only reality in history. He bears within himself the principle of his own genesis, the creation of man by man. The dialectical relation constitutes history, the relation of human production and of the transformation of nature into human nature. Man exists, therefore, only because he has produced himself. From having (the non-plenitude of possessions) he passes to being (ontological plenitude). He appropriates the whole of his being; he creates himself. "Human meaning" applies only to man and arouses man's passion for man. At the height of his consciousness, freedom is revealed and imposes itself in the "understood necessity" of the creation of its own substance, the production of the total and universal social man.

What is important to understand is that militant atheism is pre-Communistic. It is clearly defined by its own limits. The denial of God, the proofs for his non-existence, the philosophic exposé of the contradictions inherent in religion, constitute the preliminary dialectic, the praxis or action. Over against this *praxis* there is inevitably a sphere of abstraction. Man in the period of militant atheism, even the one who expresses it the best, is still an abstract man, for criticism, though Marxist, is a purely intellectual operation.

At such a time as all forms of alienation are radically suppressed, religious alienation will automatically be suppressed, without the need for any further act. Absolute humanism is effectively atheistic: this is a matter of fact.

At the end of historical evolution there will be no place for a militant and critical atheism, for once its objective—the *telos*—is attained, the religious question of the existence of God will not even arise and, at the same time, the period of abstract and theoretical atheism will have been definitively completed. Religion, theism and atheism will share the same lot. They will become museum pieces. Indeed, in such a golden age, the act of individual conception would be an act of total genesis. It would be self-sufficient and in it the whole law of the species would be concentrated and totally present to such a degree that the question of the first ancestor would be meaningless. Every question on the subject of origins turns aside from experience, takes a step backward toward a prior reflective stage. It puts man and matter again in question and, in so doing, renders them fully non-existent. It is the avowal of their non-essential character. Communism is not a philosophical postulate but an act that completes history. The advent of socialist man is its sole proof. Being irrefutable, it will be more than a proof, it will be a revelation. This is why Communism begins *after* atheism. It is the *praxis,* the transformation of the world. The practical denial of God completed *in actu* is situated once for all at the beginning of the new era.

The denial of God has thus permitted the affirmation of man. Once this affirmation is effected, there is no longer anything to be denied or subordinated. The psychological state of socialist man suppresses the speculative atheism of negation, and the circle is closed on man who is everything, and on his substance that has been made absolute and divine. On this level total man will not be able to ask any questions concerning his own reality, just as God does not put a question to himself.

As one immediately perceives, the method is simplistic and pre-philosophical. The invisible transcendent is decreed to be non-existant, not directly, but as a function of matter, because it would otherwise diminish the reality and integrity of material fact. It would escape the essential objectivity of consciousness. Furthermore, and this is most serious, once established, integral Communism, in suppressing critical atheism, would suppress the very conditions that permitted its access. Therefore, it would suppress all possible verification of its own foundation. Critical atheism is merely the affirmation of a truth which undermines its own premise without any possible reversion. Its final act contro-verts the conditions of its own actualization.

Before the advent of the whole man, denial of God is not sufficient, it is only pragmatic. After his advent, it is non-existent. Therefore, at no moment is it valid in itself. Right and fact are on two different planes, and the split between them makes it impos-sible to appeal from one to the other. This flagrant lack of dialec-tical connection renders the Marxist atheistic demonstration extremely weak, incoherent and untenable in the face of serious philosophical investigation.

Effective atheism is thus more than atheism. It is an entirely different thing, for it rests on something beyond atheism and its problems. It is accessible only to future man. Therefore, it does not yet exist, and it will not until there is a fully developed Communism. *A fortiori* it is not accessible to a non-Communist. It is clearly the fetishism of matter that leads the god-man to rise from its depths.

This vision explains the present [1964] situation in Russia where a certain place is left to the Church as well as to the virulent criticism of religion. These are facts inherent in the pre-Communist stage. There is a desperate struggle from which critical atheism can extricate itself only by projecting the incredible fabrication of a future myth.

The stronger Marxism is politically and economically, the weaker it is philosophically. The matter of Marxism has nothing in common with that of modern physics. When Marx says, with a certain lyricism, that the spirit is "the torment of matter," he is dating and manifesting an outmoded romanticism. A sharply defined intellectual regression forces Marxism to be only a very archaic form of pancosmic monism. Indeed, it presents an emanativist philosophy of the totality of matter. The social collective is the only concrete thing of organized existence. Whatever deviates from this "general line" that marks the contours of the socialist *pleroma* (fullness)—an individual, for example, or a person wishing to detach himself from it, or worse still, to oppose it—immediately becomes a heretical abstraction. Not being able to become one of the elements of the socialist whole, God hinders totalization, and thus reveals himself as the abstraction *par excellence*.

The Marxist totality expels God's being, but lays claim to the possession of all divine attributes. We recognize here most paradoxically the ontological argument of Marxism: one might even say that, in the state of divinized primal matter, perfection and existence coincide.

This totalitarian character of Marxism makes it a substitute religion. Marx created the myth of the collective proletariat-messiah, the only class free from the original sin of exploitation. By its sufferings this chosen people expiates and saves humanity, leading it toward the promised land of the kingdom.

Matter attains its peak in the infallible consciousness of Karl Marx. His doctrine is immutable and universal truth. It applies to this earth but also to the innumerable worlds in the universe, for matter is everywhere identical. The Marxist metamorphosis asks a question that has no possible answer: How did matter evolve toward consciousness, how did it become capable of feeling itself and knowing itself as above and beyond matter, as super-matter? What kind of mind did that astonishing first ape have who discovered himself to be human, and what was his spiritual condition?[4] Here "the more comes forth from the less," and the effect contains that something, that "indefinable something" of which there is no trace in the premise. This is characteristic of a miracle. Matter endowed with self-movement, the cause of which no one can determine, directs itself relentlessly not toward the absurd but toward the *logos* of super-matter.

In its self-critical impulse, Communism today confesses that it has neglected the individual and his solitude. This is the favorite subject of present-day Soviet novels. Whitehead, a great mathematician, said precisely that "God is what man makes of his solitude..." Slowly but surely, the surprising idea strikes this man: to be opposed to someone is to recognize his existence.

In the light of serious analysis, dialectical materialism appears anti-dialectical, retrograde and anti-modern, for it solves the problem of God without having propounded it correctly. It solves it against man, against a fundamental fact of his being. It is a frustration and an alienation in reverse. God is deprived of the human, he is disincarnated. One wonders what man has gained in exchange and what is going to happen when reversing the view of Feuerbach, God will become conscious of his impoverishment and will definitely appropriate for himself the human—the *totus Christus*, the total, whole Christ—and that will be the Judgment.

"Give man this world and the need for another will disappear," is the expression of the demagogic pretension of the atheist to lay hold of this world. *Praxis*, substituted for the truth, emphasizes

---

4 One may suppose that those who affirm that man is descended from an ape really do come from one, and those who claim they are children of the heavenly Father are the children of God. One can suppose also that at the lowest point to which he fell, man had engendered the ape.

efficiency and production in technical areas. It explains its momentary successes, which are always possible, but always provisory, being suspended in the "pauses" of history and in the balance sheet of its failures.

In Soviet Russia, the Church declares that it accepts science and its techniques in their totality, the existence of God and the atheist mystique not being scientific questions. The Church theoretically admits the full agreement of religion and science and accepts without any objection the community of goods, preoccupation with one's neighbor, and peace on earth—all these as truths of the Gospel. Such an attitude disarms and disorganizes critical atheism, which no longer has any valid arguments. The bishops refer calmly to history and say: "In spite of the faults and errors of Christians, Christianity still exists. It will always exist, for eternity works for us, for every man, and for time."

Scientism represents a rather widespread form of methodological atheism. However, its simplistic vision risks making the soul sterile, incapable of any religious fruitfulness. This danger comes from the cultural and technical context of present-day life. In the long run it exerts a pressure and a hold on persons who are unaware of it. They inhale it, as it were, in all public places.

The sectarian and semi-scientific mentality of scientism permeates the popular press. Closed to all ideas that go beyond it and to all transcendence, scientism, by its methods, makes an effort to account for the world without the intervention of the gods. The universe is formed by the groping expansion of life. Man is a being constantly in a state of "becoming." Starting from the initial facts, everything can be explained, and every existent being is only a partial accomplishment of the possibilities inherent in things. In penetrating the secrets of nature, man does not in any way prove that God does not exist; he simply ceases to feel the need for doing so.

In spite of its apparent optimism, scientism today has singed its wings in reaching its own limits too quickly. It is no longer dogmatic nor does it promise man happiness. It has shown that it is powerless to resolve conflicts, to console suffering, or to say: "Rise up and walk." It has lost its seductiveness. In the place of truth, it offers only solutions that are momentarily practical, or it hypnotizes the crowd for a few seconds by the distracting range of its techniques. Like the sorcerer's apprentice, it is outstripped by the famous "possibility inherent in things." It is by no means master of the future, and is anguished in the face of the unknown. Its adherents, being warped and narrow in their views, have difficulty understanding why a surgeon in operating discovers no trace of the soul, or why an astronaut does not see angels passing by him in the sky. That souls and angels are spiritual realities, invisible by their very nature, does not even cross their minds. Can a being living in three dimensions deny the existence of one which transcends these, precisely one that shows the "possibility inherent in things"? The adventurous minds of mathematicians are fortunately not hampered by such limitations.

The causalist vision considers the interior of a being no different from what is seen on its exterior. Thus it misunderstands the irreducible newness of spiritual activity. Even Marxist dialectics goes beyond simplistic causality for it shows the interdependence of human consciousness and history. One acts on the other, and their reactions are never passive. Depth psychology complements this vision by showing that the biopsychological is not solely a product of factors at work but a reaction and a *creative human expression*. Besides an external causality, there exists an internal dynamism, a finality sought by the intelligence, a conscious and reasonable intentionality. To all that is "by," there is added a "for." To every affirmation "This is not that" is added "This is that, and more than that." A statue, for example, is only marble, but it is also beauty and harmony. A human being is only a biochemical process, but also has a mind, is a spirit and a child of God. Motivation is always grafted onto a cause. The causal vision explains man as the product of biological, psychological and sociological structures, but these are ambivalent. They explain but also *express* man, speak of his aspirations and of his projects which go beyond him and transcend the scientistic vision.

Science today no longer assimilates the higher to the lower but recognizes the thresholds of different constitutions, levels and planes. When phenomenology inclines toward the affirmation of the continuity of planes, implied one in the other and reducible one to the other, when it affirms "that is that and nothing but that," it goes beyond the descriptive method and passes on to the ontology of pure contingency and of a closed world. Now the radical distinction of orders, in Pascal's meaning of the word, remains unmistakably evident. It is not in the concept of matter that materialism can find sufficient reason for a denial of God and of the transcendent. The converse is also true. It is not on matter that a believer bases his faith in God. No scientific method, not even that of materialism, is opposed to the superior that is different in nature and radically irreducible. It thus leaves the metaphysical plane entirely open.

True science affirms soberly and honestly that it offers only a hypothesis, giving a satisfactory interpretation of the known facts, an interpretation that is provisory and in need of constant revision. The scientific rationalism of immanence alone is never sufficient or decisive. In an atheistic scientist, the current objections against religious faith are mingled with affective motivations. The so-called "objectivity" of a scientist is a myth. He always has his human reactions and, at most, his attitude can be reduced to agnosticism. Science does not at all value the reason of the heart or metaphysical choices.

For a scientist like Einstein, the study of life suggests the irresistible idea of order. "I have met nothing in my science that I could oppose to religion," he said. True science is humble. It knows that each of its explanations only places the difficulty elsewhere. "The greatest mystery is in the very possibility of a little science."[5] All of science is a great mystery. "The greatest emotion that we can experience is mystical. This is the seed of all true science."[6] Lavelle[7] speaks of "the total presence" that awakens the attitude of prayer, and for René LeSenne,[8] philosophical meditation is transmuted into prayer.

The so-called *ex officio* atheism of scientists is definitely outmoded. The more scientific we are, the more repugnant we find the absurd and the more we posit a meaning for the world, even if we cannot formulate it scientifically. We leave this task to other competencies while maintaining a profound respect for Mystery. To quote Einstein once again: "The most incomprehensible thing in the world is that the world is comprehensible." What the intelligence grasps can never be God. At most it is only the imprint of his glory, the luminous traces of his Wisdom. The intellect can embrace what is intelligible in the mystery. It can never elucidate the mystery itself. When the resources of the intellect are exhausted, when its last arrow—that of myth—is shot to the very heart of being, the mystery, without allowing its nature to be penetrated, can become enlightening.[9] It can arouse in us the presentiment of something of immense importance. The mystery is not what we understand, but what understands us.

Existentialist philosophy appears more nostalgic than aggressive. Its pessimism seems to be deliberate. An aphorism of Heidegger expresses a certain strength in despair: "Man is a powerless god."

Unquestionably it all goes back to Kierkegaard and to his violent reaction against Hegelian rationalism. Hegel's panlogic speculation introduces no harmony into the real, and it offers no salvation. Kierkegaard's genius was the centering of his very personal and most

5 P. Franck, *Einstein, sa vie et son temps.*
6 L. de Broglie, *Continu et discontinu*, p. 98
7 *Présence Totale.*
8 *Obstacle et Valeurs; Le Devoir.*
9 Gabriel Marcel.

concrete reflection on the religious question: What must I make of myself. In other words, what must I do to be saved?

He constructed a most penetrating vision of self-knowledge and anticipated depth psychology. In the depths of the soul he discovered anxiety and a feeling of *a priori* guilt which divide a human being and instill an infernal element in him. It is at this level that a thirst for salvation springs up. The ultimate alternative sets the choice between nothingness and the absolute. It offers the exploit of faith contemplating Christ, who has made himself the contemporary of every soul. On the other hand, to flee idealistic metaphysics is to flee the judgment of God.

Reason can function only between the beginning and the end, therefore it is placed between the two. This is why the intermediary sphere of the immanent has no ontological foundation. Only anxiety in the face of nothingness can shatter the immanent and lead toward the religious "wholly other." It is because he is "other" that he requires the crucifixion of reason and appeals to "the crucified judgment." The case of Abraham illustrates how the ethical is transcended by the foolishness of the cross. Since then the only true witness to the truth is the martyr. Man in himself is nothing except a passover. Now the Paschal resurrection-passage of the *transitus* brings about the transcendence whereby death is made Christian. It is no longer an intruder, but the great initiator into the mystery of eternity.

However, dialectical theology, the theology of the cross, is not yet a theology of the *Parousia* (Second Coming). The God of Kierkegaard, like the God of Jaspers, remains an absolutely transcendent God. Man is not in God and God is not in man. Man stands *before* God. His tragic thirst is not assuaged. He does not yet know all the mystery of the immanent God and the mystical marriage of every soul with God. Kierkegaard did not know that in marrying Regina Olsen his soul could have married Christ.

Heidegger took up the formula: man is the existing ego. Existence precedes essence, which means that man creates him-

self, that no essence determines his destiny; consequently he has
no nature but he has a history.

Thrown into co-existence with others, finding himself always
"in a situation," the average individual makes a fatal mistake in
not opposing the world. Now his cares, an immediate element of
life, disperse his attention, direct it toward "non-being," and
conceal what is real. Alienated from himself, he loses his true ego
and veers toward the impersonal and anonymous —expressed by
"one," *das Man.* Constructed by our cares, the world is illusory,
deceitful, ghost-like, for cares make us forget the real, namely, the
ego and its freedom. That is why the ego does not emerge except
on the background of nothingness, on that crude screen where the
inevitable experience of death is projected. This is the tragedy of
man.

By themselves nothingness and freedom are without reason
and without foundation. They are *limitless* and therefore correlative. In fact, freedom is limited only by nothingness; it experiences
its bounds only in the feeling of death which is essentially concrete, personal and inevitable. Only by transcending our anxiety
about death are we offered the experience of absolute freedom.[10]
Furthermore, and this is essential, awareness of death gives rise to
and imposes the decision to realize all the possibilities of freedom
and thus to assume the full responsibility of the ego faced with its
own destiny.

In the metaphysical emotion caused by anxiety in the face of
death we experience the finiteness of our temporal being, but we
grasp above all our "non-being," evident as soon as it was founded
on our cares and preoccupations. We understand then the fundamental thesis of Heidegger, which can be reduced to the celebrated formula, *Freiheit zum Tode,* freedom toward death. Man's
tragic grandeur reveals to him his *Sein zum Tode,* his "being
toward death."

10 See the dialectic of Kirilov in *The Possessed* by Dostoyevski.

Our ethical task consists in transcending the world of our cares toward the heroism of that freedom which is responsible for his destiny. This ethical teaching is that of the Stoics. Powerless, mortal man is declared to be god. Not responsible for the being imposed upon him, he assumes his freedom of evaluation and thereby assumes his destiny, whatever the final results may be. He imposes on himself the duty of judging. His freedom is not then purely arbitrary, but he remains a powerless judge through want of an objective criterion of judgment, that is, an axiology of values in function of the Absolute. Is this not the penitent judge of Camus' *The Fall*?

Only an extreme and profound subjectivism, one that is serious and truly tragic, can condition such a vision. The philosophy of nothingness is a theology without God, the place of God being granted to nothingness, and the character of nothingness is to annihilate. Such an impasse, however, could become salutary. Heidegger will never write the second volume of *Sein und Zeit* (*Being and Time*), for he has noted that his philosophy is not an explanation but a description, and that it is not a denial of God but a certain expectation.[11]

Sartre continues Heidegger's theses. His existential psychoanalysis constructs a mythology of the *en-soi* (in-itself) and the *pour-soi* (for-itself), of being and nothingness. The vision is complicated because being is divided and nothingness is multiple. On the plane of being, the *en-soi* is irreconcilable with the *pour-soi*. They establish and destroy each other. The union of these two realities, or the convergence of essence and existence, is declared impossible. This is a radical denial of the idea of God, who is this very union.

The *pour-soi* (conscience, idealism), dynamic and changing through its choices, appears as a fissure in the static *en-soi* (being, realism). To establish oneself means to deny the static order, to deny above all, one's own immutability. In affirming its freedom

---

11 See Holzwege, *Ist Gott tot?*

as independent from the world and of the *en-soi,* the *pour-soi* effects negation, annihilates ceaselessly and thus enlarges the gap of nonbeing in the static being of the *en-soi* and places it at the limit of nothingness.

The denial of a beginning and of an end, both transcendent, renders freedom tragic, places it outside redemption, which is possible at the beginning, and outside justification, which is possible at the end. Between the massive existence of a world deprived of meaning, where every value is artificial and irremediable, and the human mind inhabited by the exigency of its reason, the rift is inevitable. There remains for man only the freedom to deny a world that denies him.

Man is terribly alone in his fearful and absolute freedom for which, as in Heidegger's philosophy, he experiences full responsibility. In thus making freedom the formal element of truth (when it is a condition of it) he arrives logically at the affirmation: "Man is condemned to freedom." He is condemned because he is not the creator of his being, and free because he is wholly responsible. Sartre clearly belongs to the great French school of moralists.

The analysis of bad faith (*mauvaise foi*) shows the failure of communication. This is because each *pour-soi* tends to transform another *pour-soi* into an *en-soi,* to make of a subject an object. In the end, one risks transforming onelf into an *en-soi,* to petrify onelf in a stasis by one's memories and projects. Either we take possession of another or we are possessed by him. Our relationship to another is always deceitful, and that is why other people are hell for us.

While Marxism is a philosophy of totality, Sartrian existentialism is just the opposite. It is the philosophy of what cannot be made whole: totality expresses the ultimate abstraction. Conversely, the concrete is the individual. Its reality is in function of the gap, the discontinuous, the absurd and free will. We can understand how the whole idea of God, of the one who fills in the gaps, who makes unity out of plurality and gives meaning to things, would diminish the tragedy of existence, suppress solitude, limit the arbitrary and lessen the sense of autonomous responsibility.

We must be attentive to this existential inquiry, which, from a philosophical point of view, is very powerful. It overthrows the smug optimism of religious philosophies according to which evil serves the good and in so doing ceases to exist as evil. This renders the death of God on the cross incomprehensible. Quite rightly for Sartre, God would diminish the radicalism of evil, of misfortune and of guilt. We can recognize here Kantianism become a religion, but having lost the postulate of practical reason. It is a Kantianism without God. Kantian rigorism would here attain its climax. The idea of God would contradict the absolute of ethical exigency, and it is this absolute character that requires an ethic without the Absolute. The greatest paradox is that despair at its depths necessarily refers to the Absolute that has been declared impossible. Tacitly, in order to retain its grandeur, existence is an accomplice of value, and thus the ontological argument is denied and described simultaneously. In the final analysis, it is the absence of God that makes the world absurd and hopeless. Therefore, this absence alone justifies the extreme positions of existentialism. Certainly there is no answer to the question asked by this relationship. There is not even a question, for there is no "judge" in this world without finality. Nevertheless, although negatively, God serves here as a point of reference, *all is thought of in relation to the absence of divine meaning.* Dostoyevski has shown that suffering in its extreme forms can turn into complacency in suffering, and that from this state no return is possible. The pleasure of suffering suppresses every solution capable of transcending it.

The more free a man is the more he is alone and a stranger to the world. In the rarefied air of the heights, the permanent act of establishing himself, of inventing himself, dominates man's fear and despair. Does it give him the right to be the supreme arbiter? If God does not exist, is everything permitted? For Sartre, who understands this formidable question of Dostoyevski, the suffi-

cient reason for ruling out crime resides in the absolute of freedom, which is related to values, even if the latter are contingent
and contrived. Because being is to be-with, it has a side that
touches the existence of others. When a man posits himself, he at
the same time posits others. To be free and to remain upright and
sincere, is to posit oneself morally; it is to be of good faith. A
criminal, on the contrary, destroys the integrity of his being and
of his choice. He is in bad faith.

The situational reality of existence is inserted into history, and it is
Marxism that offers the meaning of history in its theory of social
evolution. Sartre seeks in it the possibility of human communication.
The abyss of freedom, very strangely, produces dizziness, disgust,
nausea. One could say that the deception pays off. This is what
Dostoyevski has indeed foreseen, saying that man will never be able
to bear the yoke of freedom and that Marxism offers the greatest
possibility for getting rid of this royal gift. Sartre confesses: "I lead to
nothing, my thought does not allow me to construct anything; then
there is no other solution but Marxism" (*La critique de la raison
dialectique*—Critique of Dialectical Reason). The difficulty, however,
remains without a solution. Marxism exaggerates the importance of
matter in order to make it creative. Existentialism, on the other hand,
makes it blind in order better to fight against it and to hold man in
check.

Nietzsche, and Sartre in his wake, have proclaimed the death
of the adversary without ever succeeding in definitively eliminat-
ing him. His shadow pursues them. The "flip-side" of God is
indeed present in man's every thought. Man's drive toward the
superman is thwarted by his impotence and is defeated. Freud
correctly identified the mysterious original fault, the "death of the
Father." The man who brought it about could never overcome his
remorse, and this is the origin of collective neurosis. The profound pessimism of the last works of Freud comes from his
ultimate disillusionment. His utopia of human happiness had

crumbled away, and his resignation was bitter. Moreover, the superman led to nothing, while the closed humanism of the atheists was doomed to failure.

Malraux in his *Métamorphose des dieux* (*Metamorphosis of the Gods*) declares that in order to invent and to start his own divinization, man has to conquer his obsessive complex of the Absolute. Can he do this? Freud, as a psychotherapist, answers negatively. According to Sartre, man kills God in order to say: "I am, therefore God does not exist." But even for Sartre, this power of freedom manifests its own emptiness and the vanity of nothingness. Gide wished his ethics to be more consistent. His only principle was that a man should go to the limits of the self, to conform *sincerely* to his own norms which each one would give himself according to his free choice.

However, the impunity that every atheist enjoys during his earthly existence is not the last word. Death jealously hides its mystery. The devil told Ivan Karamazov the story of an atheist who after death perceived that reality was different from his advanced ideas. "I do not accept it, it contradicts my convictions," he cried, and lay down across the road. He was condemned to walk until his chronometer would fall apart.

In answering Sartre, Merleau-Ponty[12] said that man is not condemned to freedom. He is condemned to meaning. In other words, he is called upon to decipher the meaning of existence and, above all, the meaning of freedom itself.

We must recognize the grandeur of existentialism that has centered all its reflection on freedom. As fundamental evidence for the human spirit, freedom constitutes the creative activity of man. Now in this function, unless it contradicts itself, it cannot come from the world with its system of dependencies and con-

---

12 *Phenomenology of Perception*, Colin Smith, trans. (London, Rutledge and Kegan Paul, 1962) p. xix. According to the Gospel, it is the truth, the *meaning* that makes man free.

straints. It is evident that freedom is transcendent in relation to the world, has its origin elsewhere, and is offered as a *royal gift.* That is why in his profound philosophy Jaspers designates clearly the *Giver* and bears powerful witness to the existence of God. Jaspers' great merit is his discovery of a proof of divine existence in freedom. We find there the fatherland of freedom, its roots, and an opening toward God. God inspires it to be truly free. This renders it different in every respect from the type of dependence found in the Kantian idea of God's rule. God has created a *"second freedom."* To this gift of God man answers by the gift of himself. He dies and rises in the convergence of these two freedoms, and by this experience he has access to the meaning of his existence. For man, freedom is never considered an object. It is not even action, but rather a creative reaction to the Giver, to his invitation to become   freedom in service and in witness to its heavenly origins.

There still remains a rather widespread form of atheism: *psychologism.* This perspective tends to regard every religious sentiment as a function of the soul, a subjective psychological given. It thus reduces religion to a causality which produces particular ends or to the sublimation of an instinct. Every expression of man brings us back to our present reality, but it also expands it and leads to what will make us more fully ourselves. It breaks the vicious circle of immanence and refers to the transcendent. Here the role of depth psychology and the genius of Jung are decisive. Jung has demonstrated that the religious symbol testifies to a reality that is at the same time intra-human and trans-human. Even in clinical cases, the symbol always bears traces of trans-subjective archetypes. The judgment of truth refers not only to the causal order but to the order of meaning. Disorders come from meanings that have been imposed on a man but which he himself has not assumed. Normally, one ought to discover freely *what he is* and to give himself his own proper meaning. This is why, according to Jung, the fundamental problem for all the sick is their *religious attitude.* "All have become sick from the fact that they had lost what living religions have always given to their faithful."[13] Jung declares as a certainty that every life has a meaning, and the task of the doctor is to lead his patient to this discovery. This entails a clear religious awareness. "The one who has passed through this can calmly say: 'It was a grace of God'."[14] "The man who has experienced it possesses an inestimable treasure and a source that provides a meaning to life."

It may be that modern atheism is providential in showing us the urgent need to *purify our idea of God,* and to raise the dialogue to a biblical and patristic plane, above all scholastic systems, all purely academic theology. Here Jung's message takes on breadth and importance. The future depends on the trans-subjective spiritual content of the human psyche: *With what and by what* will man live his destiny? The quaternity of which Jung speaks is an application of the dogma of Chalcedon ("without confusion and without separation") to the mystery of the eighth day, to the *apocatastasis* or final restoration of all beings to God. The consubstantiality of all creatures is opposed to fragmentation. The saints and martyrs before the throne of the Lamb await the final conversion of dissimilarity into resemblance. Origen[15] insists on this, saying that Christ is waiting for his glory to shine forth in the totality of his body. While this still remains a mystery, it is clear, however, that only love can break the infernal monad from within. But to do this, it must, following the example of Christ, descend to our hell.

Jung tells us this as a psychologist.[16] It is his last word, his final testament. Here he goes beyond science, suppresses psychologism,

13 "Psychotherapists or the Clergy," in *Psychology and Religion: West and East,* Bollingen Series XX, vol. II, Collected Works, (New York, Pantheon, 1958), pp. 327-347. See p. 331.

14 *"Psychology and Religion,"* in *Psychology and Religion: West and East,* p. 105.

15 *In Levit., hom. 7, n. 2.*

16 "Answer to Job," in *Psychology and Religion: West and East,* pp. 355-474.

and attains the grandeur of a prophet of the last days. By his words, Job gives us the answer that he finally received. It is for Job's friends, believers and atheists, to listen.

By the absence of a positive content, all forms of atheism lead to a systematic deception. The existence of evil keeps atheism from becoming a solution. The irrational character of suffering and of death keeps reason in check and shows its failure. Nature is indifferent to good and to evil, as she is to man and to his destiny. She crushes him by her absurdity. The sole efficacious solution would be to postulate ignorance of freedom. Only on this condition would evil and suffering be suppressed since one would suppress consciousness of them. A puppet has no right to tragic tears, but every form of resignation is felt to be nothing but an unendurable abdication of man.

Father Valensin[17] carries his reflection to its extreme. If, by an impossibility, evidence were given that there is no God, "I would think I would be honoring myself in believing it, for if the universe is something idiotic and despicable, it is so much the worse for him. The wrong was not in me for having believed that God is, but in him for not existing." At this higher plane, the absence of God for man is infinitely more important than the presence of the world, meaning that his absence is unthinkable. This is not due to mere longing, neither is it a solution out of anguish, nor Pascal's wager. It is evidence for every *adequate reflection*. The problem of evil was a stumbling block to Jewish theology. Christ did not suppress evil, therefore he is not the true Messiah. This is also the argument of atheism: Christ has not realized the Kingdom of God on earth. But the Gospel has never promised any material happiness on earth. It is profoundly pessimistic with regard to history, for if freedom is real, it is so also for evil. The deliverance of which the Gospel speaks is never the mechanical destruction of evil, but a *healing,* and Christ "has risen from the dead, trampling down death by death." As long as the

17 *Autour de ma foi* (1948), p. 56.

last human being has not freely participated in this victory, evil will continue to condition history. God could take our place in order to suffer and to die, but he cannot do so *for our acts* of freedom, of choice and of love. Freedom comes only to the one who desires it. That is why the one who desires nothingness will have it in his own way, at least for a fleeting moment. No human necessity equals the divine demand for man's freedom. This is what forms God's hell before forming man's hell, and that is why God descends there.

The Christian position is decisive here. Apologetic pragmatism does not treat the problem of evil in itself, but as a necessary component of the world. Now evil has an astonishing power. It has drawn God forth from his silence and has made him pass through death and Resurrection. And it is still the existence of evil that is the most striking proof of God's existence. The world that put to death the just and innocent Socrates[18] calls for another world, and bears testimony to a greater reality where Socrates reappears and the risen Christ will inaugurate eternity. "Atheism inevitably affects the spirit, but only to a certain degree," Pascal noted.[19] No denial of God reaches him, for it is situated outside him. It is a negation of a false god or of an abstract conception of God. No one can ever invent God, for no one can ever go toward him unless he starts from him. Ontological truth precedes noetic truth and is presented under the form of experimental evidence.

The error of every criticism of the ontological argument for the existence of God is to see in it a deduction of being from the content of thought. St. Anselm never meant this. It is a question of intuition seizing the impossibility of thinking certain contents as pure contents of consciousness.

The idea of the absolute is *inalienable.* Every philosophical thought has as its object and reflects upon the absolute. God

18 Justin Martyr sees in the trial of Socrates a prefiguration of the trial of Jesus.
19 *Pensées,* n. 225.

thinks God. If we think God, we are already within the divine thought about God, and we are in the evidence that God has of himself.[20] The content of the thought about God is not a content that is only thought. In every thought of God, it is God who thinks himself in the human mind and who constitutes immediately the experience of his presence. We cannot yet say anything concerning God, but we can invoke him and cast ourselves into his presence.

Between the impossibility of denying and the impossibility of proving is situated this irrefutable experience, with its unshakable evidence. If every thought is always in relation to God and is directed toward him, every thought on existence that becomes an argument affirms the existence of God. As Péguy said: "One must do violence to oneself not to believe."[21] An interiorized conception of the ontological argument[22] could indeed trace the path of every modern man toward God.

It may be that the world is now more than ever near religious faith. Science no longer presents any difficulty, and atheism can advance no serious argument. However, there is a considerable obstacle that comes from Christianity itself. It is the *latent atheism of ordinary believers,* drowsy in their own inspired good conscience, which out of thrift, avoids conversion of the heart. This unreal manner of living an abstract faith profanes the name of God. A *Mishna* or teaching in the Judaic tradition clearly states it: "You act as if I [God] did not exist." For Jean Rostand, the nostalgia for God on the part of non-believers is infinitely deeper than every "satisfaction" of a believer. It is time for the religiosity of Christians to cease being as easy for them as atheism is difficult for atheists.

On the threshold of faith, the enduring freshness of words such as: "I have set before you life and death, blessing and

20 "In a saint it is God who speaks from his depths" (*Philokalia*).
21 *Porche du Mystère de la deuxième vertu,* Oeuvres complètes, p. 175.
22 See our study, "L'aspect apophatique de l'argument de saint Anselme," in *Spicilegium Beccense* (1959).

curse,"[23] invites us to most serious reflection. It is a question of choosing our destiny. At the opposite pole from *no,* which produces endless heterogeneous groups and infernal separations, there is the unconditional *yes* which turns all things into an infinity of unions. St. Paul says: "But in him it is always yes."[24] In this *yes* our *fiat* (let it be done) answers the *fiat* of the Creator, and since Pentecost, it is directed toward the last day. On the clock of history, the hour of messianic restoration may sound at the most unexpected moment as the Gospel tells us. To hear it, and more especially to be able to listen to the interior march of history, we must attain that depth of silence below which, according to Kierkegaard, "man has neither eyes nor ears." For this reason the Gospel ceaselessly returns to the warning: "He who has ears let him hear."

Simone Weil noted that there are two kinds of atheism, one of which is a purification of the idea of God. In a certain sense this is a grace. The Church is invited to present to the world a "showing" of the true God. It can begin an "ecumenical" dialogue with the atheist, because atheism is clearly a Christian heresy. It has never approached faith in its essence, and has never contested it in its mysterious reality as a gift of God. Believers and historic expressions of faith are in question.

If empirical conditions favor unbelief, it is because in our day we no longer tolerate any abdication of our rights nor any mandate over us. Here is a most positive element that we must take seriously, namely, the refusal of any recognition of God that would not be at the same time recognition of man. Atheism obliges Christians to correct the flagrant faults of the past and to recognize man and God at the same time, to show in God a *human epiphany.* Abraham's faith made him confess that with God all things are possible. The Christian's faith implies that with man also all things are possible.

23 Dt 30:19.
24 2 Cor 1:19.

For the apostles and saints, the relationship of man with God was always concomitant with that of man with man. In the modern dialogue between atheists and Christians, the Marxist atheism of solidarity must be answered by the member of the ecclesial community, and atheistic existentialism of solitude must be answered by the monastic.

It is necessary to remove the Gospel message from all dated historical and social contexts that imprison it. Our age, as Simone Weil has said, is in need of "a sanctity that has genius."

It would be a grave error to assign only negative characteristics to our age. We grow in relation to our needs. Religious ideas are deepened in the same proportion. History moves toward an ultimate inquiry on God and on man, and these two form a single mystery of divine love. The tensions can end in an apocalyptic outburst. In the worst case, there will resound the *maranatha* ("Amen. Come Lord Jesus"), and the awesome prayer of those in agony which the stones will cry out as an accompaniment to the last martyrs.

2

Faith

Faith bears within itself an obstacle, inherent in its very enigmatic nature, one in exact proportion to its grandeur: "God is in heaven, and you are on earth."[1] This unbearable distance wrenched from Isaiah the profoundly human cry: "O that thou wouldst rend the heavens and come down."[2] The often forced optimism of our hymns does not resolve the secret feeling of an absence we fear to admit.

How can we move from an abstract, distant and catechetical knowledge to a personal encounter, to a living communion? How can the presence of God enter our lives? "Why does God make faith so difficult?" we ask in our doubt. The Resurrection inaugurated "the eighth day," yet in appearance nothing has changed. The new world has been inserted into the old, and the eighth day exists only in the seven others. St. Peter knew the skeptical and mocking spirit that asked: "Where is the promise of his coming? For ever since the fathers fell asleep, all things have continued as they were from the beginning of creation."[3] Likewise the Jews wished a clearcut answer, without any possible equivocation: "Tell us whether thou art the Christ."[4] They asked for an even surer guarantee: "Show us the Father, and we shall be satisfied."[5] Certainly such a *proof* would be more than sufficient; but proofs wound truth, and the Lord's refusal was immediate and categori-

1 Eccles 5:1.
2 Is 63:19.
3 2 Pet 3:4.
4 Mt 26:63.
5 Jn 14:8.

cal: "Why does this generation seek a sign? Truly, I say to you, no sign shall be given to this generation."[6]

God has come, but it seems he does not want us to perceive his divinity. In the rare cases of his miracles, Jesus commanded: "Go and tell this to no man." Pascal observed: "Revelation means that the veil has been removed. Now the Incarnation veils the face of God even more."[7] God hides himself in his very manifestation, and this is the great mystery of the hidden God.

Reason, even at the moment when "all is consummated," lays down its conditions. "He is the king of Israel; let him come down now from the cross, and we will believe in him."[8] God answers by his silence, but for the one who knows how to listen, it is in this silence that "he declares his love to man."[9] This is the "divine foolishness" of which St. Paul speaks, the incomprehensible respect that God has for our freedom.

Every compelling proof violates human conscience and changes faith into mere knowledge. That is why God limits his almighty power, encloses himself in the silence of his suffering love, withdraws all signs, suspends every miracle, casts a shadow over the brightness of his face. It is to this kenotic attitude of God emptying himself that faith essentially responds. It keeps and will always keep an element of darkness, a crucifying obscurity, a sufficient margin to protect its freedom, in order to guard its power to say *no* at any moment and to build on this refusal. It is because a man can say *no* that his *yes* can attain a full resonance. His *fiat* is then not only in accord with, but on the same exalted level, of free creation as the *fiat* of God.

Faith is a dialogue, but the voice of God is almost silence. It exerts a pressure that is infinitely delicate and never irresistible. God

6 Mk 8:12.

7 *Lettre à Mile de Roannez* (Oct. 1656).

8 Mt 27:42.

9 Nicholas Cabasilas, *The Life in Christ*, C. J. deCatanzaro, trans. (Crestwood, SVS Press, 1974), pp. 162ff.

does not give orders. He issues invitations: "Hear, Israel," or "If thou wouldst be perfect..." The decree of a tyrant is met by a hidden resistance, but the invitation of the master of the banquet is answered by the joyful acceptance of the one "who has ears to hear," who makes himself the chosen one by receiving the offered gift.

More profoundly than the divine reserve with regard to our freedom, "Before the foundation of the world...the Lamb...was slain"[10] points to the ineffableness of the "suffering God."[11] In creating a "second freedom," God elicits a relation of reciprocity. The Father is father without imposing his fatherhood. He offers himself in his Son, and every person is a son of God. "You are gods,[12] sons of the most high," "gods" on the condition of recognizing ourselves as sons in Christ and of saying with the Holy Spirit: "Abba, Father." The freedom of sons is identified and coincides with the gift of God, the Holy Spirit.

That is why God consents to be unappreciated, refused, rejected, expelled from his own creation. On the cross, God took the part of man against God.

The Christian may be miserable, but he knows that there is someone still more miserable, the beggar of love at the door of man's heart. "Behold, I stand at the door and knock; if anyone hears my voice and opens the door, I will come in to him and eat with him, and he with me."[13] The Son came down to earth to sit at "the table of sinners."

From all eternity, God has thought only of our salvation. We ought to leave this care to God, and not seek it before all else. We ought even to forget it. We ought to think of the salvation of divine love, for God has been the first to love. We do not know why.

10 Rev 13:8.
11 The expression is that of St. Gregory Nazianzen, who contemplates the Lamb immolated *before* the Incarnation, and who speaks with insistence of the *passion* of the Being *impassible* by definition.
12 Jn 10:34.
13 Rev 3:20.

The attitude of God becomes clearer if we understand what is mysterious about love—*all love is always reciprocal.* Love is possible only because it is miraculous, because it immediately engenders reciprocity, even if the latter is not conscious, refused or perverted. This is why every great love is always a crucified love. It produces a gift equal to its own grandeur, a royal gift because it is free. In awaiting a *fiat*, a "yes" of equal vastness, love can only suffer and be a pure oblation until death and the descent into hell.

John of Saroug, a Syrian writer, raises human love to the level of Christ. "What man," he asks, "has ever died for his spouse, and what woman has ever chosen as her spouse one crucified? The Lord has espoused the Church, bestowed upon her a dowry by his blood, and forged for her a ring from the nails of his crucifixion."[14]

Our sin is not disobedience. Disobedience is only an inevitable consequence of it. Sin is the repudiation of the gift of communion, the refusal of freedom, the giving up of filial love. God died that we may live in him. "It is no longer I who live, but Christ who lives in me."[15] Paul dies and Christ lives in him. This is the full adult development of the person of Paul, his entrance into the nuptial *pleroma* (fullness), the communion with Christ that the Bible describes as marriage.

Science imposes its vision of visible and verifiable things and forces me to accept them. I cannot deny an earthworm, nor a virus, but I can deny the existence of God. This is because faith, according to St. Paul, is "the assurance of things not seen."[16] It transcends the order of necessity. "Blessed are those who have not seen and who have believed" means blessed are those who are not compelled, forced, constrained.

Faith thus appears as a step beyond reason, commanded by reason itself when it reaches its limits. Faith says: "Give up your

14 *Sur le voile de Moïse,* quoted by Dom O. Rousseau in A. Raes, *Le Mariage dans les Églises de l'Orient* (Chevetogne, 1958), p. 15.
15 Gal 2:20.
16 Heb 11:1.

puny reason and receive the Word." It is a transcendence toward evidence, toward the hidden reality that reveals itself. It suppresses all demonstration, all intermediaries, all abstract notions of God, and it makes that Someone who is the most intimately known immediately present.

The insufficiency of the proofs of God's existence is explained by a fundamental fact: God alone is the criterion of his truth, God alone is the argument of his being. In every thought concerning God, it is God who thinks himself in the human mind. That is why we can never prove his existence rationally nor convert another by arguments, for we can never do so in the place of God. We cannot submit God to the logic of demonstrations nor enclose him in a chain of causes.

If God is the sole argument of his existence, this means that faith is not invented. It is a *gift*, and it is to its royal and gratuitous nature that man must bear testimony, for faith is given to all in order that God may effect his *Parousia*, his coming again, in every human soul.

In accordance with his desires, the Word has chosen so strange a form that it constitutes a stumbling block. The Gospel is a chronicle of the life of Jesus, a collection of his words. However, there exist so many texts: there are the apocryphal gospels, the prophets of Pepuza, the wonderworkers and the messiahs even to our days. How can we choose?

The testimony of the apostles? Yes, but it is not absolutely convincing. It leaves a sufficient margin for doubts. There is a difference between a state of doubt and the difficulties of faith, but a thousand difficulties do not make a single doubt, as Newman so profoundly stated. Historical criticism has dealt hard blows to all naive beliefs. There is a lack of irrefutable historical documentation to prove even the earthly life of Jesus, much less his heavenly life. This is very good. It is perhaps the best proof of the truth of the Gospel, for Jesus never imposed himself, never directly proclaimed his divinity. He asked only: "Do you believe this?" He never addressed himself to reason, never set forth proof or argument, never asked: "Do you know? Are you convinced? Are you won over?" God's desires converge on the heart in the biblical sense, and this focal point overthrows man's wisdom. Here the Holy Spirit rights the scales of justice and a careful man, like Job, weighs the proofs and the evidence, gives up the phantoms of doctrines and receives revelations. From this depth the words of St. Paul sprang forth: Nothing "will be able to separate us from the love of God in Christ Jesus our Lord."[17] Here the famous paradox of Dostoyevski is verified: "If one were to prove to me as a + b that truth is not on the side of Christ, I should remain on the side of Christ." This means that the truth that one proves as a + b can never be all the truth, that the truth of Christ is not commensurable with the truths of reason, that God is not only the object of faith but also the means by which he is revealed. The expressions, "the divine eye," "the eyes of the dove," mean that it is God who looks at himself in us. Invisible to creatures, God is not invisible to himself, the Fathers say. "What is born of the spirit is spirit" means that man lives by the divine life. We see God by God, and it is this mystery that conditions and safeguards the mysteries of faith. God, affirms St. Gregory of Nyssa, remains always the "one sought for," the mysterious one. And St. Gregory of Nazianzen declares: "You have all names and how can I name you, you the only one that cannot be named?"

Man asks himself at least once in his life: "Where do I come from; where am I going?" This question is as old as the world itself. It seems that Christ had heard it when he said: "I come from the Father and I am going to the Father." This answer is echoed in the Creed. Between the atheist's limitations and the agnostic's abdication, the symbol of faith points precisely to the abyss of the Father.

Here the inspired argument of Dostoyevski has its place. Man is defined by his Eros. "For where your treasure is, there will your

17 Rom 8:35.

heart be also."[18] If love, in the image of God, is the formula of man, it is evident that one can love only what is eternal. God and man are correlative, as Father and Son. "The abyss of the heart yearns for the abyss of God."[19] "You have made us for yourself, and our heart is restless until it rests in you."[20] "It is according to Christ that the human heart has been created; like an immense jewel case, it is vast enough to contain even God. That is why nothing here below can satisfy us... For the human soul thirsts for the infinite...everything has been created for its end and the desire of the heart is to run toward Christ."[21] "The light of Christ," says the First Hour of the Daily Prayer Office, "enlightens every man who comes into the world," echoing the prologue of St. John. Is there a single person to whom the faith has not been offered?

According to the Fathers, the Holy Spirit is the very essence of the gift of God. That is why there is one prayer that has never been refused, one which the Father always answers immediately, and that is the request for the Holy Spirit, the *epiklesis*. The one who seeks honestly and sincerely, who knows how to listen to the silence of his mind, can formulate the prayer of his heart in a conditional form: "If thou art, answer me, and send the Holy Spirit." "O God, if there is a God, enlighten me." Thus prayed a great Englishman who found both faith and a vocation to the office of bishop. This is also the "if" of the inquiring and sincere Thomas to whom, however, it was given to say: "My Lord and my God!" Between the saddle and the ground, the rider may find grace, says an English proverb.

The Church cultivates the faith of martyrs and glorifies their confession: "It is You whom I desire; in seeking You, I struggle and I crucify myself with You, in order to live in You."[22]

18 Mt 6:21.
19 Angelus Silesius, cf. Ps. 42:8: "An abyss calls to another abyss."
20 St. Augustine, *Confessions.*
21 Nicholas Cabasilas, *The Life in Christ,* p. 96.
22 Troparion of the virgin martyrs in the Greek liturgy.

The martyr and the confessor, the believer and the witness are synonymous. The *homologia,* or proclamation, is inherent in faith. Every believer tells what he has seen in God. He confesses publicly during the liturgy: "We have seen the true light; we have received the heavenly Spirit." He is a truthful eyewitness. From the depth of the eucharistic chalice, his faith can repeat the words of St. John: "I write...what we have heard, what we have looked upon and our hands have handled: of the word of life."[23] For faith, what is invisible is more intimate and better known than the visible. According to the beautiful words of Tauler: "Certain ones undergo martyrdom once by the sword; others know the martyrdom of love that crowns them interiorly,"[24] invisibly for the world.

However, the confession of the martyrs is given to all in their last hour. In the face of the violence of death, the Creed resounds, and at the moment of death, it suppresses death. "Whether...life or death...all things are yours."[25] Thus even death is a gift, according to St. Paul. The believer is born, lives and dies in the miraculous, permanent dimension of his faith.

God remains hidden, but he offers his saints and martyrs as "a spectacle" to men and angels. The pure of heart see God and by them God allows himself to be seen.

23 1 Jn 1:1.
24 Quoted by Arnold, *La Femme dans l'Église* (Paris, 1955), p. 59.
25 1 Cor 3:21.

3

Dimensions of the Spiritual Life

The religious life of many believers is limited to "practicing the faith": going to services, "doing one's Easter duty," fulfilling one's religious obligations, without forgetting charitable activities. While such a life quite full and positive in many respects, nonetheless it runs the risk of having no connection at all with an authentic spiritual life. Furthermore, the common sense of the honest believer, set up as a reasonable system, can be like a formidable suit of armor which nothing extraordinary can penetrate, not even a miracle, nor anything that might impinge upon a man of the 20th century. Could he even catch the hidden irony in Pascal's wager instead of retaining a calm assurance: ...what if...?

Moreover, there are those who have an interior life that is very rich but not religious. Thinkers, artists, theosophists also, live an intense and profound psychic life and are able to go quite far in cosmic mysticism or spiritualism without God.

Therefore one can observe that of these two forms of life, "religious" and "interior," the first always entails a relation of dependence on a transcendent and personal Absolute. The second is autonomous and penetrates its own psychic richness.

The spiritual life alone integrates these two dimensions and shows them to be complementary. Essentially interior, it is also the life of man facing his God, participating in the life of God, the spirit of man listening for the Spirit of God.

Considered on the vast plane of the world religions, the spiritual life represents the Christian synthesis between the anthropocentric inwardness of the Oriental religions without God, and the transcendental and theocentric personalism of the biblical religions,

Judaism and Islam. In combining the marvelous penetration of Hinduism into the abyss of human inwardness with the sacred fear of Jewish and Islamic monotheism before the absolute transcendence of the creator, the Christian, nevertheless, creates an entirely new element. The divine "I" has spoken to a human thou. His word has established the one who listens to him, has brought him into existence in his image, and he continues to create and fill him by keeping him in living communion with the *Word made flesh*.

The new tone of the Gospel is overwhelming. The God of the Christians is most strange. He does not in any way resemble human ideas concerning God, and this unheard of characteristic shapes the spiritual life. The Creator of the world, in order to create it, made himself "the Lamb immolated since the beginning." And on the cross, God took our part against his own Godhead. For our benefit, God is no longer all-powerful. He dies to himself that we may live. He transcends his intra-divine silence toward another You, and introduces him into his mystery, into the sacred circle of the trinitarian communion. Since then we can say with St. Augustine: "You were at the same time more inward than my inmost self and loftier than the highest of myself."[1]

God desired to become man, and it is the Incarnation that structures the divine and human nature of all spiritual life. In living it, we are never alone. We live it with God and God lives it in and with us. This participation of God in the human is decisive. The spiritual life does not come from below, from human fabrication, from our desires or longings. We do not invent it for our consolation. Such a romantic mythology would never resist the trials of time and of death. The spiritual life comes from above. God inaugurates it by the gift of his presence. We receive this revelation-event and answers by our act of faith. We formulate and confess the Creed, the saying of the Father's You with his Son and his Spirit. A liturgical dialogue, leading to unity, is begun.

1 *Confessions*, III, vi, 11.

The spiritual life is an event within the spirit. Seen from the outside, it easily lends itself to misunderstandings and to frequent confusion with psychic phenomena and activities. Thus psychology formulates this classic yet pointless question: "Is there a connection between the subjectivity of religious experience and the objectivity of its object?"

Thus formulated, the biased question produces its own simplistic solution: the object of the experience—God—is only an aspect immanent in the soul, *esse in anima*. We enter into dialogue with the elements of our own psyche, romanticize and make them a mythology.

The error lies in introducing a speculative distance between the experience and its object; *religious experience is inherently the manifestation of its object.*

It is not a question of conformity between the experience and the spiritual reality, for the experience is this reality. The experience of the saints and mystics is the coming of the Spirit. The idea of God is not anthropomorphic. We do not create God according to our own image. We do not invent him. However, the idea of man is theomorphic. God has created us in his image. Everything comes from God. The experience of God also comes from God because God is closer to us than we are to ourselves. As soon as God manifests his presence, we see it. That is why nothing can be proved one way or another, but one who denies the reality of experience can at best only prove that he has not lived it. The person of Christ is the place where once for all the experience of man by God and that of God by man have converged. It is this Christic reality that precedes every religious experience and actualizes it in Christ: "You are in me and I am in you." This reality interiorizes religious experience even to the point of divine intimacy.

One could almost say that the marriage-like possession of man by God attains a kind of reciprocal substitution. The Holy Spirit utters in us and with us, as a single being: "Abba, Father." At his crucifixion, the Islamic mystic Al Hallaj said: "I am the one whom I love and the one whom I love has become me."[2] "It is no longer I

2   See L. Massignon, *La passion d'Al Hallaj* (Paris, 1922).

that live but Christ lives in me," St. Paul declared. Meister Eckhart and St. Symeon the New Theologian describe in an identical manner this nuptial and eucharistic transmutation: "You become a single spirit with me, without confusion, without alteration."[3]

God cannot be made an object. He is radically interior. "God is the more invisible the more his burning intimacy radiates in man's spirit." The spiritual life and religious experience are likewise incapable of being made objects. The very artificial psychological question, nevertheless, disturbs man and arouses a useless battle of words which is not fought on the level of evidence. It takes place on the exterior. Bergsonian intuition, in accordance with Oriental philosophy, permits us to affirm that every thought rendered too adequate to its verbal expression loses something of its dimension of depth. This is also the profound experience of L. Lavelle who wrote: "The word takes from the thought its purity and its secret." On the other hand he says: "Silence does not differ at all from the inward word."[4] The more this interior thought-word matures in its silent depths the more it becomes inexpressible, ineffable. It is transformed into *evidence* that is as irrefutable as it is unprovable. The final logic of all revelation is evidence. The God of the Bible is above all else self-evident.

Another error is shown by syncretism. A psychologist easily crosses the frontiers of the various confessions, and supposes that all religions converge. Nothing is comparable, however, to the truth of the Gospel offered and lived in the Eucharist. It bears in Christ the accomplishment of the aspirations not only of men and angels, but of the three divine Persons, for according to Nicholas Cabasilas, the Incarnation is the "pouring of God outside himself."

3 *P.G.*, 120, col. 509.
4 *La Parole et l'Écriture,* pp. 133, 144.

4

The Ascetic Art and the
Dangers of Ignorance

In our day psychiatry recognizes that the origin of many organic illnesses lies in psychic disorders and in the ignorance of the elementary principles governing the economy of the soul. Jung goes so far as to think that the fundamental problem of all the sick has its origin in the ambiguity of their religious attitudes.[1]

Our great malaise as modern individuals comes from our feeling a secret dependence on the elements we bear within the depths of our souls and which we no longer know or understand, or which we fear to understand. Whatever our awareness, it makes our psychic equilibrium most precarious and unstable. Although the rapid evolution of psychology has unsettled our knowledge of the human soul, this science has refused to define clearly the changing border between health and sickness.

How much more vulnerable is the one who is totally ignorant of his interior life. In moments of solitude or of suffering, he has no social formula to protect him or to solve the conflicts in his soul.

Freud saw in mental disorders a diversion or an escape from conflicts that had grown unbearable. In extreme cases, the instinct of self-preservation makes one prefer madness to suicide.

Analysis does not stop at the level of the psyche. At a deeper level, psychiatrists who are believers discover spiritual disorders. According to Jung, except in clinical cases, we suffer from the fact that our life is deprived of meaning and of any positive and creative content.

1 "Psychotherapists or the Clergy," in *Psychology and Religion: West and East,* p. 331.

Man is bored by his own indigence and is so worn out by his worries that, according to Jung: "His complexes very much resemble demons." This is the threshold of temptations, and ascetics know well the abyss of "sinful sadness" which ends in *accedia*, in dereliction or the extreme dejection of despondent souls.

Most believers, even when they are interested in psychology and know something about psychiatry or have submitted to it, are most superficial in the spiritual life. Lived according to the inspiration of the moment and with a total lack of appreciation for its nature and its laws, the religious life of the majority of believers fails since it offers only a feeble resistance to indifference and to the feeling of emptiness.

The simplifications of the positivists reduced sin to ignorance, crime to the influence of the social environment, evil to imperfection, and asceticism to hygiene. The notion of "sin" gets no hearing today. We no longer know its meaning. According to the definition of the Sixth Ecumenical Council, sin is a sickness of the spirit. We know, on the other hand, that according to P. Janet: "Insanity is the loss of the function of the real." One who is insane no longer perceives reality as others do. Thus, since we are unable to form an idea of sin and of its opposite, holiness, we become afflicted with a functional disorder, a form of spiritual madness.[2] When St. Paul asked for the spirit of discernment, he desired to find the norm, spiritual health, a function of total reality that comprises the earthly and the heavenly.   *Definition*

"Man," says Pascal, "is the meeting between nothing and everything." He vacillates between nothingness and the absolute. The ambivalence of his situation leads to an acute sense of his own limits. Even when he has arrived at the summit of his genius, man remains like Job: "I cry for help but there is no redress."

At a certain level, this reflection borders on the pessimism that gnaws at the roots of life. Civilization is evolving and is destroying

2 "The fool says in his heart, 'There is no God'" (Ps. 13, 14:1).

the equilibrium of the human spirit. It is striking in its methods and at the same time astonishingly superficial in its pragmatic philosophy. The universe is becoming a vast workshop where everything is expressed in numbers and is governed by the principles of production and of curiosity. In the face of the inhuman anonymity of the enterprises, our anxiety drives us to hyperactive, erratic rhythms, toward an "atomized" style of activity. The more the necessities of life weigh us down with all their constraints, the more society frees itself from all taboos, and the more the atmosphere is one of a secret revolt, we ask: is the modern world for or against man?

The biological rhythm of rural civilizations regulated by the solar cycles gives way to the technical rhythm of invasive and massive urbanization. Life in a world of factories and laboratories is no longer organic. It is organized. Its reinforced concrete very rapidly kills the sense of living nature. Even the simplest materials used in the sacraments—water, bread, wax, fire—are disappearing from natural use in homes, or are so falsified as to be no longer the familiar and known representation of the cosmos. Thus liturgical symbolism is not appreciated. Ritual no longer says anything spontaneously. It requires a very laborious initiation. The coming generations are more and more strangers to symbols of the sacred.

Modern symbolism takes refuge in acronyms and the corporate logo. Words are dessicated and the most familiar objects seem to have lost their original meaning. We even see in contemporary churches candles topped with electric bulbs, a hybrid which we are at a loss to name.

Nevertheless, it is this world that is the object of God's care. He calls Christian thought to a creative effort, asks it to translate into modern terms the immense heritage of the past, the precious experience of the great spiritual teachers of former times, all to be put in perfect harmony with our most adventurous life, thought and art.

It is not a question of modernism, but of a vision of that which remains above time and by that fact directs human history and destiny. It is on this level that the spiritual life can be offered again to our wonder, to our searching and our openness to its signs.

In present conditions, under the burden of overwork and stress, our sensibility is changing. Medical treatment protects and prolongs life, but at the same time it lowers resistance to suffering and privations. Christian asceticism is only a method in the service of life, and it will seek to adapt itself to the new needs. In the desert of the Thebaid, extreme fasts and constraints were imposed. Today the combat is not the same. We no longer need added pain. Hair shirts, chains and flagellation would risk uselessly breaking us. Today mortification would be liberation from every kind of addiction—speed, noise, alcohol, and all kinds of stimulants. Asceticism would be necessary rest, the discipline of regular periods of calm and silence, when one could regain the ability to stop for prayer and contemplation, even in the heart of all the noise of the world, and above all then to listen to the presence of others. Fasting, instead of doing violence to the flesh, could be our renunciation of the superfluous, our sharing with the poor and a joyful balance in all things.

The forms of ascetic endeavor, like the faces of the saints, mirror the age. How symptomatic it is that in a world bowed down under the weight of cares, St. Thérèse of Lisieux speaks of spiritual childhood, traces her "little way," and invites all to sit down at "the table of sinners." Depth psychology, for its part, draws attention to the transcendence of humility and to the incarnations of the spiritual in social life. Modern asceticism serves the humanity that God assumed in the Incarnation. It is violently opposed to any diminution or abandoning of one's neighbor.

"No longer do I call you servants...But I have called you friends."[3] These words of the Lord announce our adulthood, our transcending human limits. The spiritual life is oriented toward

3 Jn 15:15.

material

divine friendship. Asceticism will rid itself of a penitential mentality and will become a preventive therapy. Almost everywhere monasticism seems to be seeking, beyond the somatic and psychological asceticism of the Middle Ages, the eschatological asceticism of the first centuries, that act of faith which kept the Christian in a joyful expectancy of the Parousia, the second coming of Christ. *doctrine of final things*

Experienced spiritual guides such as the "startsy," the elders of Russian, Greek and other monasteries, are rarer than ever. However, there is a vast ascetic literature that offers us a very precise knowledge of the human soul. If Freud and Jung professed their admiration for the psychological insight of Dostoyevski, it was because he had been nourished by the works of the great spiritual writers.

From the time of Clement of Alexandria and Origen the spiritual life bears the name of asceticism. This signifies diligence, training, practice. The negative asceticism of suppression is allied to the positive asceticism of acquisition and growth of charisms. In a broader sense, an ascetic is a Christian who is keenly aware of the call of the Gospel, of the beatitudes, and who seeks humility and purity of heart in order to help his neighbor to do the same.

5

Essential Elements of the Spiritual Life

The word "spiritual" refers to the Holy Spirit and designates the level of being proper to "birth from on high," to "the nuptial mystery," the soul's union with God. It reveals the fundamental phenomenon of every human person heedful of his heavenly origins.

Not only in history but also in the depths of the human soul Christ is born, dies and rises; baptism reveals this. It is in this inwardness that the bonds between God and man are forged and that the itinerary of the spiritual life is formed. The latter is always an encounter. God comes from himself towards us, and we leave our solitude to meet his Otherness. "No, You have never hidden Yourself from anyone, but we are the ones who always hide from You by refusing to go to You," said St. Symeon [Introduction to *Hymns of Divine Love,* George A. Maloney, trans. (Denville, NJ: Dimension Books, 1975), p. 9].

Thus, the constitutive elements of the spiritual life go beyond the human. Dante speaks of the three partners in the divine game —God, man, and Satan. The ascetic masters specify the three wills that confront one another. (1) That of God, salvific and working within us under the form of appeals and invitations is *theonomy.* We may adhere to it and make it our own. (2) Then there is that of our humanity, unstable and uncertain. Our *autonomy* encloses us within ourselves. (3) Finally there is that of Satan, hostile to humanity, and which draws us out of ourselves without preparing any encounter. This is *heteronomy*—submission, slavery, perdition.

There is very little to say about the *divine element* in the spiritual life. It is more proper to be silent and to venerate it through silence. God is the initiator who in his presence is yet radically transcendent. "Flesh and blood have not revealed this to you, but my Father heaven,"[1] "and that not from yourselves, for it is a gift of God,"[2] it is a free gift. By his love alone, God makes us his trinitarian abode. "We will come to him and make our home with him."[3] This act in its incomparable grandeur is not matched by any human effort. The three divine persons dwell in our souls according to our capacity to receive them, as St. Macarius says.

A contemporary spiritual writer admirably expresses this idea. "God gives himself to men according to their thirst. To certain ones, who could not drink any more, he gives only a drop. But he would love to give an enormous drink in order that Christians could in their turn quench the world's thirst."[4]

It is evident that on this level of the divine initiative, there is no technique or method of the spiritual life. Grace grants its gifts and we simply receive them, though with the angels we are astonished and lost in wonder.

The *demonic element* is the obstacle. "He was a murderer from the beginning, the father of lies."[5] This adversary wages a relentless battle. "Be watchful. For your adversary the devil, as a roaring lion, goes about seeking someone to devour."[6] "Put on the armor of God, that you may be able to stand against the wiles of the devil."[7]

It is on this level of struggle that man is an active agent. This highly refined strategy of "invisible warfare" constitutes our asceticism.

Finally, there is the *human element* aspiring to lift itself beyond all struggle. It is expressed essentially in the liturgical attitude of adoration. "I will sing to the Lord as long as I live."[8]

1 Mt 16:17.
2 Eph 2:8.
3 Jn 14:23.
4 *Revue Contacts,* no. 35-36, p. 248.
5 Jn 8:44.
6 1 Pet 5:8.
7 Eph 6:11.
8 Ps 103:33.

An anonymous mystic of the Middle Ages has expressed it in humble but beautiful words: "I am an ass, but I carry my Lord."

"Behold, I stand at the door and knock. If anyone hears my voice and opens the door, I will come in to him and eat with him, and he with me."[9] The initiative of God who knocks is answered by the eagerness of the human being who waits with all his heart for this to happen. We hear and open the door of our soul, prostrate ourselves before this Visitor, and sit down with him at the banquet table. The Fathers loved to comment on the parable of the Prodigal Son, which emphasizes the decision, the act that places human action within the divine. "When he *came to himself,* he said... *'I will arise* and go to my father...' And he *arose* and *came* to his father."[10]

According to St. Cyril, it is this decision that makes the invited person one of the chosen, and this is precisely the creative effort of positive asceticism. If this positive form is not present at the very beginning, St. Macarius teaches, if it does not precede negative, normative and disciplinary asceticism, the latter is of no use.

On the eve of Lent, a wise saying warns: "The devil does not eat, he does not drink, and he does not marry, and this great ascetic in form is no less a devil...Let us always relate the nonessentials—fasting, vigil, solitude—to the principal end, the purity of heart that is love,"[11] as Cassian teaches in quoting Abba Moses.

9 Rev 3:20.
10 Lk 15:17-20.
11 *Confessions,* I.

6

The Nature or Essence of the Spiritual Life

In the beginning," at the time of the decisive testing of man, the resounding failure of his choice made him fall *below* the level of his being and immersed him in the life of the senses and of matter. We became carnally and sensually enveloped in darkness, but the economy of salvation lifted us *above* the level of our being even to that of *new creatures*. St. Paul's dialectic takes its point of departure here. "Though our outer nature is wasting away, our inner nature is being renewed every day."[1] "Strip off the old man...and put on the new."[2]

The spiritual life is oriented toward this metamorphosis, "putting on the new man." What makes us new is the fact that we are no longer alone. At the heart of our transformation, we have "put on Christ." We are Christ-like.

The Fathers take almost literally the fact of putting on Christ and see in it a projection or, more exactly, a continuation in the human person of the Incarnation of the Word, perpetuated especially in the Eucharist. That is why they teach us not to "imitate" but to "interiorize" him. This inwardness is not a simple metaphor of forced meaning. It has its roots deep in God himself. While the Incarnation reflects a certain anthropomorphism of God (a mysterious primordial conformity), it reveals above all and undoubtedly the *theomorphosis* of man, our transformation in

1 2 Cor 4:16.
2 Col 3:9-10.

God. From the biblical point of view, the Incarnation brings to perfection our nature, which is made in the image of God, and it reveals the manifestly Christological structure of the spiritual life.

Man then crosses an immense distance to the interior of his being. St. Paul quotes an ancient hymn charged with almost explosive dynamism. "Awake, O sleeper, and arise from among the dead, and Christ shall give you light."[3] A variant reinforces its meaning: "And you will touch Christ." This passage from the state of death to the state of life, from hell to the kingdom, is precisely the path of the spiritual life.

Moralizing spirituality reduces salvation to the forgiveness of disobedience. Now biblical ontology, vigorous and exacting as it is, leads from a moral catharsis (purification) to an ontological catharsis. This represents a very real change in the whole human being—body, soul and mind. It is the strongest affirmation of patristic exegesis, stressing the Gospel's call to *metanoia* or conversion. "Repent, for the kingdom of heaven is at hand."[4] It would be more exact to say: "Change yourself," become a new creature, for it is a question of a repentance in the full meaning of the word—a complete turning about of the mind and of the whole human being.

The encounter with God could not be made in the state of fallen nature. It presupposes a previous restoration of this nature in the sacrament of Baptism. For Baptism, according to the Fathers, is a true re-creation of the redeemed being. Repentance, *metanoia* in its strongest sense, goes to the root of all our faculties, volitional and affective, and even to the heart of one's entire being, body and spirit. St. Irenaeus, in his celebrated doctrine of the recapitulation of all of nature in Christ, closely follows St. Paul. St. John's Gospel emphasizes it in speaking of the "second birth." The two terms, *metanoia* (transformation, conversion, repentance) and birth, clearly express that profound transformation of

3 Eph 5:14.
4 Mt 3:2.

the human being and mark his entrance into the spiritual world, whose principles are the opposite of those of this world. Between a baptized and an unbaptized person there is an abyss, the infinite difference of the two natures. To stress this absolutely new character, the Fathers chose by preference the miracle of the changing of the water into wine at the wedding feast of Cana. The symbolism of this image makes Baptism and the Eucharist converge. In fact, the baptismal water has the value of the blood of Christ, declares Nicholas Cabasilas: "It destroys a life and produces another...we leave our garments of skin to put on a kingly mantle."[5]

We can now understand the extent to which the spiritual life at once effects a *break*. It is not the same life to which are added some religious devotion, reading and pious attitudes. It is essentially a rapture, a combat, a violence that takes heaven by assault and seizes the kingdom. On the threshold of this life are the resounding words of St. Paul: "Behold, the new has come."[6]

The Gospel emphasizes the formidable power of the prince of this world. St. Paul, in calling him "god of this world,"[7] underscores the state of alienation of man by the diabolic powers, and it is from this power of Satan that a complete break is required. We find it in the most expressive symbolism of Baptism. The total immersion, or descent into the water, signifies real death to a guilty past, and emerging, or being raised, the definitive victory, the resurrection to a new life. The "promise" of Baptism, however, the great baptismal profession of faith in the Trinity, presupposes a radical intervention of purification and a personal act of the human spirit. Indeed, the Church takes very seriously the power of evil and its murderous ravages. This is why the ancient rites placed before baptism the *lavacrum*, the rite of exorcism and the solemn renouncing of the Evil One.

The priest reproduces the divine act. He breathes on the face

5 N. Cabasilas, *The Life in Christ*, pp. 71-72.
6 2 Cor 5:17.
7 2 Cor 4:4.

of the "dead" the breath of life, analogous to the breathing of life into man when he was created. Facing West, the kingdom of the prince of this world, where the light of day disappears, the neophyte renounces his past under the power of the enemy. Symbolically imitating the struggle he must sustain all the length of his spiritual life, he turns toward the East, where the day appears, confesses his faith and receives grace.

This ritual contains the seed of new existence. Negatively, it is unceasing combat. Positively, it is the metamorphosis asked for in the final baptismal prayer with its Pauline accents: "O God, put off from him the old man, renew him and fill him with the power of your Holy Spirit, in the union of Christ."

This is a most succinct summary of the spiritual life. Its progression never stops. "No one who puts his hand to the plow and looks back is fit for the Kingdom of God."[8] Every pause is a regression. The total character of the consecration of every baptized and confirmed person, stressed in the rite of tonsure, places such a one in extreme tension every instant, in one's yearning for the ultimate, the impossible. This rite of tonsure,* an organic part of the sacrament of Chrismation/Confirmation in the Eastern Church, is identical to that of entering monastic life. The prayer of the rite asks: "Bless your servant who has come to give you as his/her first offering the tonsure of the hair of his/her head." Its symbolic meaning is very clear. It is the total offering of one's life. In undergoing the rite of tonsure, every lay person becomes a monastic of "interiorized monasticism," submissive to all the absolute demands of the Gospel. The faithfulness of the newly baptized will resist the trials of time and the assault of temptations, for Christ is going to fight in him and with him.

*clipping of the hair

8 Lk 9:62.

7

The Different Ages of the Spiritual Life

Poets sing of the miracle of a glance, always unique. Unique as well is the destiny of each person also seems unique. There exists, however, a certain correspondence between the phases of each spiritual life as in the rhythm of different ages. One enduring element remains, around which the destiny of each human life is formed. The circumstances change, but the spiritual theme, personal for each one, remains identical through all disguises. Its call and the unavoidable exigency of an answer, a combination of what is given and what is desired, constitute what the Gospel calls the personal cross of each person. It is inscribed within us at birth. No power can change it. "Which of you by being anxious can add one cubit to his span of life?"[1]

Whether in the heart of a great city or in the depths of a desert, we cannot flee from this personal theme of our life. It accompanies us and speaks to us at every turn on our way. We can respond differently and each time change our course in one direction or another. We can marry or become monks. We can polish lenses, like Spinoza, or repair shoes like Jacob Boehme. The question, our question, remains identical and fixed in us as an integral element of our being. It is no longer a question, it is we ourselves who are called into question.

To understand our "cross" is to foresee the facts of our destiny, to decipher its meaning. It is to understand ourselves. The spiritual life does this. It introduces order, reveals the rhythm of its own growth, and requires a progressive march.

1 Mt 6:27.

Religious psychology traces the outline of this evolution in three stages: (1) the preliminary unity of the human being, precarious and unstable; (2) the sharp conflict between the spiritual and the empirical; (3) and at the last, the final integration.

With rare exceptions, the spiritual life comes into being in an event that is called "conversion." Its precise content is of little importance. It is a remarkable event, a shock followed by a sharply defined passage from one state to another. Just as light reveals shadows, it suddenly unveils the inadequacy of the unstable present and leads us to doors opening upon a new world. This beginning of an untried promise leads to decisive actions and entails the joyful commitment of our whole being. Even those who have inherited the faith in their childhood pass sooner or later through this by a conscious discovery of their faith, and by appropriating it to themselves personally. This is always an overwhelming experience.

Something we have read, an encounter, a reflection causes a light to break forth suddenly, brilliantly. In its brightness, all is seen in its true order as in an inspired poem that gives to everything a new and inestimable value, as in the music of Mozart. It is a religious springtime, full of joy and enthusiasm. Like the buds filled with sap, the human being feels uplifted in a surprising joy and a spontaneous sympathy for everything and everyone. This is an unforgettable time. Like a feast illumined by a thousand lights, it makes one see in God the smiling countenance of the Father coming to meet his child.

This time, however, is brief. The face of the Father takes on the face of the Son, and his cross casts its shadow within us. Our own cross stands out clearly, and there is no possible return to the simple and childlike faith of former days. Sorrowful discords tear our soul in its clear-sighted vision of evil and sin. There is an extreme tension between two states that are mutually exclusive. The brutal experience of our falls and weakness can fling us to the edge of despair.

We are strongly tempted to cry out that it is an injustice, that God expects too much from us, that our cross is heavier than that of others. An old story tells of a simple and sincere man who experienced this. An angel led him to a pile of crosses of different sizes and told him to choose. The man chose the lightest, and at once discovered that it was his own! We are never tempted beyond our strength.

God is watching for us at this decisive moment. He expects from our faith a vigorous act, the full and conscious acceptance of our destiny. He asks us to assume it freely. No one can do it in our place, not even God himself. The cross is made of our weaknesses and our failings. It is constructed by our enthusiastic impulses and especially by the dark depths of our heart where a secret resistance and a shameful ugliness lurk, in short, by all that complexity which is at this precise moment, the authentic *I*.

"Love your neighbor as yourself," allows a certain love of self. It is a call to love our cross. It means perhaps the most difficult act of all—to accept ourselves as we are. We know that the proudest beings, those full of self-love are the ones who most feel ill at ease with themselves and who secretly hate themselves. It is an infinitely serious moment when we encounter ourselves, for this requires a baring of ourselves, an immediate and total vision of ourselves even in our most secret recesses.

"He who sees himself as he is, is greater than the one who raises the dead,"[2] spiritual masters say, thus stressing the importance of this act. This vision is always frightening. We must therefore look at Christ. This is the experience of St. Paul and of every Christian. "When I wish to do good, I discover this law, namely that evil is at hand for me...Wretched man that I am! Who will deliver me from this body of death?...Jesus Christ our Lord."[3]

In moments of crushing solitude, only humility can help us in recognizing the radical powerlessness of human nature. It inclines

2 St. Isaac the Syrian, *Sayings.*
3 Rom 7:21-24.

us to cast our whole being at the foot of the cross, and then suddenly our heavy burden is lifted by Christ: "Learn of me...For my yoke is easy, and my burden light."[4]

"Thy will be done," the *fiat*, or word of assent—"Let it be done"—springs forth. I accept it as my own. I read in this burden what God has thought of me, and I recognize in it my destiny. We are no longer self-centered, but made joyful and lighthearted. "Behold the handmaid of the Lord."[5] "The friend of the bridegroom, who stands and hears him, rejoices exceedingly at the voice of the bridegroom. This my joy, therefore, is made full."[6]

According to our spiritual teachers, the art of humility does not at all consist in becoming this or that, but of being exactly as God made us. Dostoyevski describes this vivid moment through what the pilgrim Macarius says in *The Adolescent*. With a single glance, this man envelops the universe, his life, time and eternity. He can only say finally, "All is in you, Lord; I am yours; receive me." Without being yet able to understand it all, we seize more than we need at the moment. It is our destiny to find the freshness of a passionately loved existence. It is only after this "second birth," this personal Pentecost, that the authentic spiritual life begins.

4 Mt 11:29-30.
5 Lk 1:38.
6 Jn 3:29.

II

Obstacles and Struggle

* I have experienced this glimpse of infinity (with mirrors) when ill as a teenager. Odd that he uses just this example.

My spiritual question has always been: Does my health problem come from the devil?

1

Negations of Evil and
Affirmations of Good

In Greek the words "symbol" (*symbolon*) and "devil" (*diabolos*) come from the same root, and thus all the more forcefully express two opposed realities. The devil is a divider, one who separates and cuts off all communion, reducing a being to ultimate solitude. On the other hand, a symbol binds together, builds a bridge, reestablishes communion.

The story of the possessed man of Gerasa[1] clearly shows the nature of evil. Christ asked the devil a formidable question: "What is thy name?" To the Jewish mind the name of an object or a being expresses its essence, and the old adage, *nomen est omen*, sees in the name both the expression and destiny of a person. Christ's question meant therefore: "Who are you; what is your destiny, your secret being?" The demon answered "My name is legion, for *we* are many."

This abrupt transition from *my* to *we* reveals the action of evil in the world. The innocent being created by God in its unity, at once fragile and unconscious, is broken, splintered into isolated particles, and this is hell. Both the Greek *Hades* and the Hebrew *Sheol* refer to a place of darkness where solitude reduces a being to the extreme impoverishment of demonic solipsism. We can represent hell as a cage made of mirrors in which one can see only one's own face multiplied to infinity, without a glimpse of anyone else's.

1 Mk 5:9.

That self is the only existent thing, can know nothing but its own modifications and states

81

To see only oneself is to be satiated with oneself even to the point of nausea. The Coptic Sayings (*Apophthegmata*) of Macarius the Elder give a striking description of this solitude. The captives are tied to one another by their backs, and only great prayer by the living can bring them an instant of rest. "For the time of a twinkling of an eye, we see one another's faces."

Conversely, confronted with this action of evil, St. Paul[2] shows us the action of good, of Christ: "Because the bread is one (Christ), we though many, are one body, all of us who partake of the one bread."[3] In eucharistic communion we find the one of all who are recapitulated in Christ in the image of the trinitarian communion, God who is one and at the same time three, unity in multiplicity.

It is natural then that the Eucharist is the very heart of the Church and reveals itself as productive of the unity that is proclaimed, offered and lived. Like a golden block without the least fissure, it constitutes the *esse,* the very essence of the Church. The most ancient invocation, *Marana tha* (Come, Lord),[4] completes a liturgical prayer and refers to the *Parousia* (the Second Coming), to the eucharistic coming of the risen Lord.[5] God comes to offer himself as nourishment, and we consume his substance, the *agapé,* "incorruptible love."[6] Eucharistic communion effects a substantial participation in the total Christ, and this work, unitive by essence, makes the communicants, according to St. Athanasius, "beings transformed into the Word, Christified." St. Ignatius of Antioch sees in the Eucharist a "medicine of immortality," that cures death.[7] Furthermore, "in consuming the flesh and blood of the Spouse, we enter into a *koinonia* (communion) of marriage

2 1 Cor 10:17; 12:12.
3 Cf. Rom 12:5. The apostle here repeats the devil's expression; the being decomposed by evil into many, into a legion, a wicked multitude.
4 1 Cor 16:22, Rev 22:20; the *Didache,* chapter 16.
5 See O. Cullmann, *Early Christian Worship* (Philadelphia, 1953).
6 St. Ignatius of Antioch, Rom 7, 2; Eph 14, 1.
7 Eph 13.

with him," says St. Theodore of Cyrus.[8] This communion fills us to such an extent that one "can go no further nor add anything."[9]

The *hénosis,* "union with Christ," lived in the Eucharist, determines the eucharistic character of the spiritual life. Communion with Christ and his body—human beings—becomes entirely positive growth: "Between the body and the head, there is no room for any interval, for any negation."[10] All who participate in God "in whom there is only yes," profess a complete yes to life, to being. On the other hand, in Satan, there is only no, and this refusal marks the limits of the place from which God is excluded, negation, nothingness, hell.

St. John[11] recognizes this "no" in sin: "transgression," going beyond the ontological limits set by God and delineated by his name: "I am the one who is." The third prayer of the *Didache* speaks of it: "We give you thanks, O Holy Father, for your holy name that you have made to dwell in our hearts. It is you, almighty Master, who have created the universe in your name."[12] "I am a great King, says the Lord, my name is praised among all the nations."[13] To go beyond this limit is to break the original bond, to renounce the King, to claim autonomy and to place oneself outside the name.

Atheism suppresses this limit of created being in its radical denial of all dependency. In place of the human thirst for "the wholly other," it substitutes the decision to live "as if" this limit had been rendered forever non-existent. Such is Western atheism. The atheism of the anti-God militants of the Soviet world is, in a certain sense, more consistent and radical. Remaining faithful to the historical interest inherent in Russian thought (Chadaaev, Berdyaev), it is centered in only one negation since this is historical: "Christ has not risen."

8 See J. Daniélou, *Eucharistie et Cantique des Cantiques* (Irenikon, 1950), p. 275.
9 N. Cabasilas, *The Life in Christ*, p. 114.
10 St. John Chrysostom, *P.G.*, 62, 26.
11 1 Jn 3:4.
12 X, 2.
13 XIV.

It is fitting to mention here the name of St. Isaac the Syrian. In the seventh century, he formulated a synthesis of patristic thought. As an ascetical master, he also shaped a phenomenology of sin. Without attaching much importance to the multitude of sins which are minimal in the sight of God since he forgives them, Isaac points in his Sayings to the unique sin, the sin, which is indifference to the Resurrection! A moving prophecy of Soviet atheism. To be efficacious, it attacks only the irrefutable argument of the Cross, and this is a question of life and death not only for man, but for God. Indeed the denial of the Resurrection attacks, beyond the creative act, the Creator himself. Mystically this denial effects deicide, the murder of the Father. Nietzsche had formulated it well in speaking of the death of God. "Where is God? I am going to tell you. We have killed him." The conscience of atheists culminates there, according to Dostoyevski: "There was once on earth a day when three crosses were lifted up in the center of the world...toward the end of the day they died...but they found neither paradise nor resurrection...That is the idea, the whole idea. Outside it, there is no other."[14] This is the very heart of atheism. It is the secret source from which comes the Freudian complex of universal guilt—the death of the Father—and the inclination of a being toward death, *Todestrieb*, and likewise Heidegger's formula, *Sein zum Tode,* being toward death.

"Alea jacta est" : the die is cast, the choice is made, the atheist's Credo is proclaimed *orbi et urbi,* everywhere: God is dead and he does not arise. "The Lamb slain from the foundations of the world" means the Lamb immolated and truly dead, annihilated, non-existent. In the beginning there was the death of God and his silence.

Since his destiny is at stake, man is driven to choose between the alternatives of *yes* and *no.* There is no third choice. Nietzsche expressed this in his correspondence. There are two madnesses, he says, that make men live. One, Nietzsche himself chose: that of

14 *The Possessed.*

the superman, surviving in the eternal return. The other, which to him was unacceptable, is that of St. Paul, the madness of the cross, of the risen God and of immortal man.

The atheistic argument was foreseen by St. Paul.[15] If Christ is not risen, our faith is in vain, nothing has meaning, and all is nothingness. There are no half measures, no intermediary formulas. We are in the presence of the fundamental evidence of Jesus risen from the dead. A God who is not the lover of mankind, a God who is not love crucified in order to radiate "Life, the death of death," as St. Augustine says, is not really God. In following St. Paul's thought to its conclusion, we could say that all religion exists only by the Resurrection of Christ and is mystically supported by this event. If Christ is risen, this fact concerns all of humanity. If the Christian witness to the risen Lord is suppressed, no religion will survive in the modern world, for outside the Gospel every religious message stops halfway. The Gospel's transcendent end is God become a risen man. This fact does not concern only a few witnesses. The risen Christ as the contemporary of all means that every person is a contemporary of the eternal Christ. This makes all the events of history essentially christological. Christ is risen as head of the human body, and now all religions and all people can and ought to seek their life in him. This testimony alone determines the ecumenical mission of the Church in the midst of all religions and in the great meeting between East and West. History places the Christian faith in the risen Christ at the crossroads of all ideologies that now reformulate the only important question—the one asked by Pilate—"What is truth?" It obliges faith to say its "yes," even at the cost of martyrdom, the unique answer that resounds universally. Christ is in agony, and eternity is impatient to hear the answer.

The apostolic kerygma announces the Paschal event, the intervention of God in raising up Jesus. This alone gives a definitive

15 1 Cor 15:14.

meaning to human existence in history. We find its central focus in 1 Corinthians 15:3-4, in Romans 4:24-25 and Acts 2:36. The Resurrection of Jesus is God's "Amen" to his promise, an "Amen" full of the Holy Spirit who manifests it. "Amen" comes from the Hebrew *heemin*, which means an unshakable foundation. Those who proclaim the Resurrection—the apostles and martyrs—claim the right to proclaim the event before the rulers of the earthly city. Likewise the *Apologies* of Justin, Athenagoras, and Aristides present to emperors the same decisive message and warn them of the imminent judgment. Their kerygma concerns everyone. It is preached in the presence of angels and relates to the whole of creation: the Kingdom of God has already come. We are contemporaries of the One who sits at the right hand of the Father. Here is the Lamb immolated and risen and here is his Kingdom. He is here and it is the fullness of time. All religions are ways by which humanity seeks God. They are numerous. However, the Christian revelation is unique for in it, it is God who finds man. The preaching of St. Paul is of the utmost importance for the theology of religions. In deciphering the monument to the unknown God and in giving him the name, Jesus Christ, the apostle integrated into Christ the religious aspirations of all times and gave them value in Christ.

Our transgression confines us to a state that is closed to all that is not of this earth. The more material it is and the more it is made a thing, the more it appears deprived of reality and of any substance. This is the world of finance, with its temple, the Stock Exchange, and its devotees of luxury. It is the political world of ambition and covetousness, a collective neurosis of mad passions and unfaithful erotic love. It is a world vacillating above an abyss, without any consistency, vaporous, peopled with phantoms, and which at any moment can vanish "as smoke in air and as wax melted by fire." On the other hand, Origen compares the efforts of desert hermits, in their march toward perfection,[16] to the slow departure of the inhabitants of Plato's cave. Leaving the silhouet-

---

16 A group of ascetics used to be designated by the name of *synodia* or caravan.

ted shadows for a vision of reality, where nothing is interposed between a person and the truths of the divine life, the monk of the desert kept firmly on the way back to the Kingdom.

We find a vigorous and complete vision of human destiny even in the beginnings of Christian thought. St. Gregory of Nyssa[17] mentions the celebrated teaching of the two ways. It is clearly described in *The Testament of XII Patriarchs*: "God has given two ways to the son of man and two inclinations, and two manners of acting, and two ends." This is the doctrine of the two *yeser*, of the two inclinations of the heart, in conformity either with the action of the angel of light or with the action of the angel of darkness. The *Didache*, the *Epistle of Barnabas*, and other writings draw from the same source, and this theme was to have a great influence on early Christian letters. It goes back to the choice offered by God, "I have set before you life and death."[18] It is always the same choice between *yes* and *no*.

According to the Bible, the fool is free to say in his heart: "There is no God." (Ps. 14) However, the meaning of the negation changes according to the level of depth and suffering in the one who denies. That is why "perfect atheism (perfect here means lived even unto suffering) is at the top of the ladder, on the next to last step before perfect faith," as Dostoyevski affirms.[19] When, far from formless indifference, atheism and faith are carried to "perfection," they can meet together above senseless talk, in the silent combat of the angel with Jacob, and of grace with despair. Consistent atheism, burning with suffering, knows its own paradoxical cross. At the end of his life, in notes scribbled at the height of his strange madness, Nietzsche wrote his definitive name—the Crucified. Likewise the atheistic Grand Inquisitor[20] scoffed at

17 *Life of Moses*, II, 45, Abraham J. Malherbe and Everett Ferguson, trans. (Mahwah, NJ: Paulist Press, 1978), p. 64.
18 Deut 30:19.
19 "Confession of Stavrogin," in *The Possessed*.
20 *The Brothers Karamazov*, Richard Penear and Larissa Volokhonsky, trans. (New York: Vintage, 1990), pp. 246-264.

materialism and positivism, but he attained his true grandeur in
his passion for humanity. His no in spite of himself, would almost
participate in the love of God for humanity, though he is not
conscious of this. Perhaps human passion, at a certain level, goes
beyond the merely human. Is the essence of divine love not this
very same passion, and is this not one of those mysterious "liminal
stages?" Perhaps it is necessary to be a saintly "philanthropist," just
like God, to feel the deep correlation. There is a purifying atheism,
according to Jules Lagneau, "that salt which hinders belief in God
from corrupting itself." In this role of protection and safeguard, this
unbelief cooperates with grace. That is why the Christ of Dostoyevski's *Legend* is silent, and kisses the suffering face of the
Grand Inquisitor.

2

Three Aspects of Evil and the Evil One

Among the multiple manifestations of evil are discernable three symptomatic aspects—parasitism, imposture and parody. The Evil One lives as a parasite on the being created by God, forming a monstrous excrescence, a demonic swelling. As an impostor, he covets the divine attributes, and substitutes equality for likeness. "You will be as God," as his equals. Finally, as a jealous counterfeiter, he parodies the creator and constructs his own kingdom without God, an imitation with an inverse sign.

The philosophers have never succeeded in elucidating the problem of evil. Rather, they have complicated and entangled it. Conversely, evil was never a problem for the Fathers of the Church. For them it was not a question of speculating about evil, but rather of fighting the Evil One. The prayer of a saint would be: "Preserve us from all vain speculation on evil and deliver us from the evil one." Likewise, the Bible does not speak of ethical principles concerning good and evil but it reveals God and mentions the adversary. The Bible denounces also "the man of sin" of the last days, "the son of perdition" who...proclaims himself to be God.[1]

From the very heart of his being, "from the beginning," the devil has been a murderer, according to the words of Christ.[2] A spirit of negation, he is above all a murderer of his own truth, that of being Lucifer, a bearer of divine light. Thus, he consummates his own metaphysical suicide, and sets himself up in universal denial of the imprint of God. He thereby attains at the same time *homicide* and *deicide*.

1   2 Thess 2:3-4.
2   Jn 8:44.

While for Plato the opposite of truth is error, for the Gospel, at its deepest level, it is the lie. "Liar and father of lies" by essence, the Evil One has taken upon himself a frightful vocation, that of knowingly altering truth. The initial perversion of his will has made it possible for him to usurp whatever he can in order to fabricate an existence with spurious materials. Isaiah clearly describes this enterprise: "We have made lies our refuge, and in falsehood we have found a hiding place."[3]

To lie in the face of heaven is to oppose God's truth and to impose one's own version on the world. The devil sets himself up as a counterpart in order to dislodge God from his creation, rendering it indifferent to the divine presence, and thus he effects a gigantic substitution. Disdainfully proud, he says: "I, and no one else," "A god am I."[4]

"When he tells a lie, he speaks from his very nature."[5] This judgment of the Lord contains a whole philosophy of evil. Every lie by its nature originates in what is false, that is to say, the non-existent. The "very nature" of the evil one, from where he draws his lies, is then nothingness. Thus St. Gregory of Nyssa could define evil as having a phantom-like substance. God, by his *fiat*—his *yes*—creates likeness and fills all in all. The evil one, by his anti-*fiat* expels and completely empties all things, constituting "a place of dissimilarity."[6] On the other hand, "the saints are those who do not speak from their own nature, but it is God"[7] who speaks in them, and thus they form "the place of likeness." The dreadful secret of Satan conceals the absence of any metaphysical foundation, and this emptiness obliges him to borrow, to usurp the being founded and rooted in the creative act of God. Evil, as a parasite, adheres to being, sucks its blood and devours it.

3 Is 28:15.

4 Ezek 28:2; Is 47:8.

5 Jn 8:44. The Samaritan Torah codex in Gen. 3, 2 in place of "serpent" reads *the liar,* which puts it in harmony with Jn 8:44.

6 see *L.* Ouspensky, *Theology of the Icon,* vol. I, Elizabeth Meyendorff, trans. (Crestwood, NY: SVS Press, 1992), pp. 156-159.

7 Barsanuphius, *Lettres,* 885.

The Scriptures do not teach philosophy. The Bible does not see in evil a simple lack of good or of perfection, a non-fulness, but a freedom that has failed and has turned into an evil will. In adding the non-existent to the existent, it has perverted it, turning it into a malevolent being. However, this perversion, or evil, is not materialized and personalized in the Evil One except under certain conditions. We must furnish him with ontological "bed and board" which means that, thanks to our freedom, we can be conscious or unconscious accomplices in serving a lie. In this real ministry of those "possessed" by evil, beings are diminished so that the Liar may swell and grow. The devil's tragedy is that he lacks the nourishment of the gods, "the bread of the angels...eaten by men,"[8] for the heavenly bread is the fulfillment of the Father's will. This will is the substance of all things, St. Irenaeus teaches. Thus in the world of God, the phantom-like Evil One, famished for what is real, must become an ontological parasite. He feasts on our captivity, and his horrible carousels, by increasing the emptiness caused by the absence of God, are for us the beginning of hell here below.

Where there is no God there is no humanity either. The loss of the image of God entails the disappearance of man's image, it dehumanizes the world, and multiplies the "possessed." The absence of God is replaced by the burdensome presence of obsession with oneself, self-worship.[9] In the long run our sad utopias risk modifying our anthropological type. We lose our dimension of depth, the dimension of the Holy Spirit. In the bold words of St. Gregory of Nyssa, the one whoever is not moved by the Holy Spirit is not a human being.

Every passion bears within it the seed of death since it dulls the spirit of discernment. Likewise every bad means is never justified

8 Ps 78:25.

9 St. Andrew of Crete, the Canon read during Lent. See *The Lenten Triodion,* Mother Mary and Kallistos Ware, trans. (London and Boston: Faber and Faber, 1984), pp. 370-414.

by a good end for it is already negation. One can say just the opposite: the good means to a bad end may change into good. It is entirely a question of its root and its source. Temptations never fulfill the expectations they arouse, for evil possesses no source of life within itself. It satiates without ever satisfying or quenching thirst. It is not in its power to repeat the words of the Lord: "Who drinks of the water that I will give him shall never thirst."[10] The one who seeks other springs in the passions imposes on himself unquenchable thirsts.

At the root of every passion, be it ambition, eroticism, gambling or narcotics, there is a simple mechanism of possession which, once broken, strikes us by the infinite dullness of its meager content, leading to boredom. As the oyster sheds its shell, every ideology which makes atheism its passion ends sooner or later by secreting boredom. Perceptive observers note this as a symptomatic state of mind. It is especially true of the ponderous dogmaticians, busy creating "the new man." Such a creature must be "machine-made" in the factories of the social sciences. In order to survive, the power ruling the masses, now saturated with graphs and statistics,[11] galvanizes and excites them by presenting lunar landscapes, fantasies of space exploration, a most ambiguous peace, and five-year plans for a paradise here on earth. But now, instead of this "new being" is the same old humanity, forever bored. Dostoyevski and Baudelaire said that the world would perish, not by wars but by a gigantic and unbearable boredom when, from a yawn as wide as the world, the devil would come forth.

Dostoyevski attentively studied this phenomenon which is rapidly becoming universal. He found that the most efficacious method against every evil enterprise is to identify its purest essence, which is immediately shown to be ridiculous. Everything that is manifestly and evidently ridiculous unfailingly cuts right to the heart. Is not the devil himself always somewhat ridiculous?

10 Jn 4:14.

11 The good sense of Disraeli distinguished three degrees of lies: lies, preposterous lies, and statistics.

Dostoyevski has drawn largely from the humor of the "fools for Christ," so greatly loved by the people. Protected by their apparent madness, concealing great humility and love of neighbor, during the day they set themselves against guilty silence and fearlessly denounce every hypocritical profanation with stinging irony and irresistible humor, and during the night they pray for everyone. They throw stones at the houses of "the good," and kiss the thresholds of the houses of sinners.

During recent times of bloody persecutions, it was these "poor in spirit" who at the crossroads of cities preached the Gospel and the Kingdom of God.

Humor, like laughter, has a liberating power. It frees us from the weight of social conventions, from every temptation to take ourselves too seriously. It also frees us from excessive suffering in the spiritual life. Open and childlike joy is typical of great saints; they enjoy themselves as children of God, and divine wisdom takes delight in their play.[12]

12 Prov 8:31.

3

Hell and the Infernal
Dimension of the World

Iconography

The icons of the Orthodox Church echo the depths of the liturgical texts and present a contemplative reading of them. As theology expressed in images, they are related in their function of revelation to the light of Tabor.[1] This explains the constant contrast they evoke between light and darkness, the confrontation of heaven and hell.

Among its charisms, the Johannine Eastern Church, so conscious of the Resurrection, is most attentive to the theme of hell, a theme that St. Paul treats in a concise and striking way in Ephesians 4:9-10: "Now this, 'he ascended,' what does it mean but that he also first descended into the lower parts of the earth? He who descended, he it is who ascended also above all the heavens, that he might fill all things." We see the astonishing range of the itinerary of Christ, the winged Lamb between the two extremes, the descent to the lowest point—hell—and the ascension to the highest point—heaven. The Orthodox Church in wonder contemplates "the height and the depth" of the mystery of salvation. She sees in it the dimensions of the love of Christ and his triumphal message: "Ascending on high, he led away captives" (Eph 4:8).

On Holy Saturday the Church sings: "You have descended on earth in order to save Adam, O Master, and not finding him there, you have gone even into hell to look for him." The *icon of the Nativity* reflects to this text showing the thick obscurity of a cave,

---

1 The light of Christ transfigured on Mount Tabor.

a black triangle where the child Jesus is lying as in the dark bowels of hell. In order to place himself "in the heart of creation," Christ *mystically* situates his birth in hell, the point of final despair. Since the time of Adam, humanity has ended up in Sheol, the dark abode of the dead, so it is there that Christ will go to seek it.

In its eschatological aspect, the icon of the Nativity, like every icon, summarizes in a prophetic way all the events of salvation. By his immobility the Child has already entered into the great silence of Holy Saturday, the great Sabbath. "Life has gone to sleep and hell shakes with fear."[2] The swaddling clothes of the infant Jesus have the exact form of the winding cloths that the angel will show to the myrrh-bearing women on the morning of the Resurrection. The luminous Child stands out in sharp contrast to the black background and anticipates the descent into hell. He is himself "the light shining in the darkness." "The sun has set with him, but the flesh of God under the earth dissipates the darkness of hell."[3] "Light battles with darkness; life annihilates death."[4]

From the beginning of his mission, Jesus confronted the cosmic elements that conceal dark powers—water, air, the desert.[5] A liturgical text of the Epiphany feast has the Lord saying to John the Baptist: "Prophet, come to baptize me...I hasten to destroy the enemy hidden in the waters, the prince of darkness, in order to deliver the world from his nets and grant it eternal life."[6] In speaking of unsanctified waters, the image of the death-deluge, the liturgy calls them a "watery grave."

In fact, the *icon of the Epiphany,* the baptism of the Lord, shows Jesus entering into the waters of the Jordan as if he were entering into a watery grave. It takes the form of a cave, containing the

2 Office of Holy Saturday.

3 *Ibid.*

4 St. Gregory of Nyssa, *P.G.,* 45, 65A.

5 See O. Rousseau, "La descente aux enfers," in *Mélanges Lebreton.*

6 See *The Festal Menaion,* Mother Mary and Kallistos Ware, trans. (London and Boston: Faber and Faber, 1984), p. 380.

entire body of the Lord (an image of burial reproduced in the sacrament of Baptism by *total immersion*—a figure of the Paschal *triduum*), in order "to snatch the head of our race from the dark abode."[7] In following the anticipatory symbolism of the Nativity, the icon of the Epiphany shows the pre-descent into hell. "Having descended into the waters, he bound the powerful one."[8]

St. Ephrem of Syria compares the Epiphany to the cross and the ladder "as the ladder that Jacob saw reaching the gate of heaven; light descended on it at baptism..."[9] And James of Saroug writes: "Christ on the cross stood upon earth as on a ladder with many rungs."[10] The cross is "the tree of life planted on Calvary,"[11] "the place of the great cosmic struggle."[12] The *icon of the Crucifixion* shows in the vertical branch of the cross, the descent and the ascent of the Word. The *Acts of Andrew* declares: "One part was planted on the earth in order to unite the things on earth and in hell to heavenly things."[13] That is why on the icons, the foot of the cross is sunk into a black cavern where the head of Adam lies; this is hell.[14] Also on the Orthodox cross, the third bar, under the feet of the Lord, is slightly inclined. The *scabellum pedum*[15] inclined downward represents the destiny of the thief on the left, and the other, inclined upward, represents the destiny of the thief on the right. The "scale of justice"[16] and an opening into eternity, the cross in the middle is like a connecting link between the Kingdom and hell.

The icon of the Resurrection is that of the "descent into hell."[17] According to St. Peter, Christ as liberator proclaimed to

7 St. Cyril of Jerusalem *P.G.,* 33, 1079.
8 St. Cyril of Jerusalem *P.G.,* 33, 441B.
9 *Hymn,* XI, 11.
10 *Homily on the Vision of Jacob at Bethel,* n. 95.
11 Office of the Exaltation of the Holy Cross, *The Festal Menaion,* pp. 156-158.
12 *Pseudo-Hippolytus,* n. 55.
13 See Daniélou, *Théologie judéo-chrétienne,* p. 312.
14 Origen, *On Matthew; P.G.,* 1309s.
15 Acts 2:35, Ps 109.
16 Troparion of the Ninth hour.
17 The Gospel says nothing about the time of the Resurrection.

the captives the Gospel of salvation.[18] "You have broken the eternal bars holding the captives."[19] In the silence of Good Friday, the Eucharist is not celebrated, for Christ is in hell. For earth it is a day of sorrow, but in hell this Holy Friday is already Pascha-Easter. Death is vanquished and eternal life is proclaimed. The icon shows Christ, "the Living One who holds the keys of death and of hell."[20] He is surrounded by a mandorla, the luminous halo of glorified bodies. His left hand holds a scroll, the proclamation of the Resurrection to those who are in hell: "With my right hand I have given them the baptism of life."[21] He tramples under foot the broken gates of hell. "And the Lord extended his hand, made the sign of the cross on Adam and all the saints, and holding Adam's right hand, he ascended from hell and all the saints followed him."[22] It is not from the tomb that Christ is coming, but "from among the dead," "coming forth from the former hell as from a bridal chamber."

Primitive catechesis drew attention to an aspect of the sacrament of Baptism that has been forgotten in the course of history: Baptism by immersion reproduces the figurative curve of salvation, and every baptized person follows the same itinerary in the footsteps of the Lord. The sacrament of Baptism is then a real descent with Christ in his death. It is also a descent into hell. St. John Chrysostom clearly says this: "The action of descending into the water and then coming out of it symbolizes the descent into hell and the coming out from that abode."[23] The Light on the Jordan shines in the baptismal light[24] and signifies the illumination of hell's darkness. Once enlightened, the baptized person is

18 1 Pet 4:6.
19 Pentecost Sunday, third kneeling prayers at Vespers. See *A Book of Prayers*, (Cambridge NY: New Skete, 1988), p. 227.
20 Rev 1:18.
21 *Testament en Galilée.*
22 *Gospel of Nicodemus.*
23 Hom. 40, on 1 Cor. 15:29. Quoted by O. Rousseau, *op. cit.,* p. 273.
24 Justin, *P.G.,* 6, 421.

sacramentally united with the souls who have risen with Christ from hell toward eternal life. Thus Baptism is not only dying and rising with Christ, but also descending into hell and coming out from there, following him. This is because hell is more frightful than death. Consider of the words of a Father of the Church: "And the nothingness that they seek will not be given to them." It is here that the definitive victory has been won.

Christ descends there, laden with the sins of mankind, and bearing the stigmata of the cross, of crucified Love. We must forcefully emphasize the ultimate and immediate consequences of this act. Every baptized person, risen with Christ, also bears the stigmata of the priestly cares of Christ the Great High Priest, the stigmata of his apostolic anguish for the destiny of those who are in hell. "There are places in our hearts which do not yet exist, and it is necessary for suffering to penetrate there in order that they may come into being," Léon Bloy reminds us. In a vivid image, this care appears in the early Christian text, *The Shepherd of Hermas*[25] and in the writings of Clement of Alexandria:[26] the apostles and teachers descend into hell after death in order to announce salvation and to give Baptism to those who ask for it.

Finally the *icon of Pentecost* shows the apostolic college, seated in a luminous circle, receiving the tongues of fire. The contrast is stark. Below, in an arch and coming out from darkness, is an old king, holding in his hands a linen cloth. On this linen are placed twelve scrolls. Often the arch is separated by a prison grill that stresses the state of captivity. It is the cosmos personified as an old man satiated with the days from the Fall, the universe held captive by the prince of this world. The obscurity that surrounds him signifies "darkness and...the shadow of death,"[27] the hell from which the non-baptized world stands out and which, in its more enlightened portion, aspires to the apostolic light of the Gospel.

25 IX, 16, 5-17.
26 *Strom.* II, 9, 43.
27 Lk 1:79.

He holds out his hands to receive grace, and the twelve scrolls symbolize the preaching of the twelve apostles, the universal promise of salvation.

The content of this icon is found in the liturgy of Pentecost. The Vespers that follow the Liturgy of Pentecost Sunday contain three great prayers of St. Basil, which the priest reads before the people, all on their knees, a sign of particular attentiveness in prayer. The first prayer presents the Church to the Father. The second asks the Son to protect all the living. The third prays for *all* who have died since the creation of the world and thus refers to the descent of Christ into hell. "You who on this final day of Pentecost have revealed the mystery of the Trinity; you who have sent the vivifying Spirit...true knowledge of God...you who deign to listen to our prayers of expiation for those who are imprisoned in hell, and who give us the great hope of seeing you, grant them deliverance from their torments...give (them) rest in a place of refreshment...make them worthy of deliverance, for it is not those who are in hell who will have the boldness to confess you; but we the living, we bless you and supplicate you and offer you our prayers and sacrifices for their souls."[28] The abundant grace of the feast removes all limits. Once a year, on the day of Pentecost, the Church prays even for those who commit suicide. We see once more the breadth of the feast—from heaven to hell, and from hell to heaven.

28 Kneeling service, Pentecost Sunday.

4

Human Suffering

Although it has never been given a dogmatic definition, the theme of hell and of its destiny, continually present in the Liturgy, is becoming universal. Evil is not a substance. A perverted will, conscious and jealous of its autonomy, dynamic in its transgression of rules, multiplies distances and absences. An evil being lives as a parasite, metastasizing as a cancer. What one steals from a being, one returns as disease. We are able to do this, for God has created "another freedom," and the risk that God has taken already proclaims Christ, "the Man of sorrows" and predicts the shadow of the cross. According to the Fathers, God can do all things, except force us to love him...In awaiting his beloved, God relinquishes his omnipotence and empties himself (*kenosis*)[1] as "the Lamb who has been slain from the foundation of the world."[2] His destiny among us depends on our *fiat*, our "yes." To assure the freedom of this *fiat*, Christ gives up even his omniscience. The apparent passivity of God conceals, according to St. Gregory of Nazianzen, "the suffering of God who cannot suffer." God foresees the worst, and his love does not remain the less vigilant on this account, for we can refuse God and build our life on this refusal. Which one will win, love or freedom? Both are infinite, and hell asks this question.

The Eastern Church rejects every juridical or penitentiary principle. Her understanding of sin and attitude toward the sinner is essentially therapeutic, evoking not a courtroom but to a

---

1 Kenosis: humiliation, abasement, veil of humility hiding the divinity of the Word in his Incarnation. Cf. Phil. 2:7.

2 Rev 13:8.

hospital. Without "prejudging," the Church abandons herself to God, the lover of mankind, and doubles her prayers for the living and the dead. The greatest among the saints have had the audacity and the charism to pray even for demons. Perhaps the most deadly weapon against the Evil One is precisely the prayer of a saint, and the destiny of hell depends also on the love of the saints. We create our own hell in closing ourselves off from divine love that remains unchangeable. "It is not right to say that the sinners in hell are deprived of the love of God...But love acts in two different ways, it becomes suffering in the damned and joy in the blessed."[3]

Every faithful member of the Orthodox Church, in approaching the Holy Table, confesses: "Of sinners I am the first," which means the greatest, or more exactly, without any possible measure or comparison, "the only sinner." St. Ambrose, as a pastor and a liturgist, explains this in a concise and striking expression: "One is at the same time condemned and saved."[4] St. Isaac, as an ascetic, gives another: "The one who sees his own sin is greater than the one who raises the dead to life." Such a vision of naked reality leads to a final and paradoxical conclusion. A very simple man confessed to St. Anthony: "In watching the passers-by, I say to myself, 'All will be saved, I alone shall be damned.'" St. Anthony concluded: "Hell really exists, but for me alone." This love of men is answered by the magnificent words of a Muslim mystic: "If you place me among those in Gehenna (hell), I shall spend eternity speaking to them of my love for you."[5]

In repeating St. Ambrose's words, we can say that the world in its totality is "at the same time condemned and saved." Even more, perhaps hell in its very condemnation finds its own transcendence. It seems that this is the meaning of the words of Christ to St.

3 St. Isaac the Syrian, *P.G.,* 34, 5440. Cf. Origen, *De Prin.,* III, 6, 5; St. Gregory *of Nyssa, Catech. Discourse, XXVI,* 5, 9: *Comment on Eph.,* III, 10 of Ambrosiaster.

4 *P.L.,* 15, col. 1502, quoted by O. Clément, *Notes sur le Mal,* in *Contacts,* no. 31, p. 204.

5 René Khawam, *Propos d'amour des mystiques musulmans* (Paris, 1960).

Silouan of Athos, a contemporary elder: "Keep your mind in hell but do not despair."[6]

Péguy reproached Dante for having visited hell "as a tourist." The great spiritual masters have another way of descending there.[7] "The light of Christ enlightens every man coming into the world," says the prayer of the First Hour of the Daily Office. Even unconsciously, all bear the light mysteriously. It is not for Christians to despair then, but to hear Christ saying to the Church these most serious words given her to hear for her mission: "He who receives you, receives me..." The fate of the world depends on the art of our being witnesses of Pentecost, on our creative love in the face of hell in our world.

All that theology teaches about the condemnation of the world is in the phrase: "Cain, where is your brother Abel?" Then there is the mystery of the Church in the light of the priestly prayer of Christ (Jn 17): "Abel, where is your brother Cain?" The love of God was "from the beginning" (1 Jn 4:9-10) as an event transcending every response to it. The two Paracletes, Christ and the Holy Spirit, come to save. Love, in its depths, is unselfish like the pure joy of the friend of the Bridegroom, like the joy that subsists by itself, a joy intended for all.

In John 14:28, Jesus asks us to rejoice with a great joy, the reason for which is beyond us, namely, the objective existence of God. In this radiant and royally free joy lies the salvation of the world. John 13:20 invites us to discover the manner in which we can be accepted, "received" by the world. It is now the hour for the Church no longer just to speak of Christ, but *to become Christ.* The heavenly mansion extends its walls even to the confines of the world, even though the world is in revolt, in opposition to God. *God loved the world even when it was in sin.*[8] The bride takes on the face of her Spouse. She is the eucharistic bread, communion,

6 See Arch. Sophrony, *Wisdom from Mount Athos* and *The Monk of Mount Athos,* Rosemary Edmonds, trans. (Crestwood, NY: SVS Press, 1975), p. 119, pp. 115-118.

7 See Arch. Spiridon, *Mes missions en Sibérie* (Paris, 1950), p. 44.

8 Jn 3:16; 12:32.

friendship. Her light shines not merely to shine but to change the night into the day that never ends.

More than ever before, the world seeks something that would unite people. It seeks "the truly human: the brother and sister" in each of us. It is here that Christian love alone—the kind that neither calculates nor measures nor limits—can cause the light of the still enclosed Christian world to shine on the one most distant from Christ, for it is in this one that Christ is waiting to be received. St. Symeon called himself "the poor brother of all men," and he really was. The "new man" is not being fabricated in the Marxist factories of social discipline. The "new creature" originates in the Holy Spirit, who forms "apostolic souls." Such a one takes faith seriously and does things that are very simple when seen in the light of Gospel faith—raising the dead when the Lord commands. This moment in history is so fearful that it calls upon all the powers of faith, and that is why St. Peter quotes the prophecy of Joel and announces an abundance of gifts, with Pentecost redoubling its outpourings in the time before the Apocalypse, the Revelation.

Every baptized person is invisibly *stigmatized*, bearing withinhimself the deep wound of the destiny of others, of all others. Each of us adds something to the suffering of Christ who is in agony until the end of the world. To "imitate" Christ is to follow him in his descent to the depths of our world. "Imitation" is conformity to the total Christ. It is martyrdom, according to Origen,[9] for "the love of God and the love of man are two aspects of a single, total love."[10] My personal attitude, always unique, is to fight against *my hell,* which threatens me if I do not love enough to save others. He who saves shall be saved. Still, an almost imperceptible sliding toward activism leads me to say: "I love you in order to save you." The truly apostolic soul says: "I save you

9 *Exhortatio ad martirium.*

10 St. Maximus, *P.G.,* 91, 409B.

because I love you..." During each Liturgy we sing: "We have seen the true light, we have received the heavenly Spirit." Every Sunday is a renewal of Pentecost. This liturgical verse expresses the truth, but in giving its gift, it makes an urgent appeal: how do we spread this overwhelming experience of light into the hell of today's world?

5

The Message of Pentecost

"The Kingdom of God is within you." The Gospel's heart-beat can be heard in these words. Two worlds draw near each other, the borders are blurred, the beyond becomes the here and now. Every believer, taking part in the Liturgy, has this experience: "Now all the heavenly powers invisibly with us do serve." However, these eruptions of "the wholly other" mean that hell is also in our midst. In spite of the clarity of this idea,[1] the same term is applied to many situations in life. We hear of the hell of an unhappy love, the hell of married life, the hell of the presence of others, the hell of oneself. Hell in a human face forces itself upon our intimacy, becomes a familiar element, well-known but terrifying. Certainly, while different from the image presented by the masters of the Middle Ages, of Bosch, Goya, or the *danse macabre*, the "dance of death," it is nevertheless real. The devil sets aside his romantic mask and becomes as familiar as Ivan Karamazov's devil decked out in a business suit, or as anybody else, and as such we perhaps meet him every day. He is no longer disguised as an archangel with burnt wings. Quite human, and for that reason more to be feared, he resembles us. Marcel Jouhandeau has expressed it well: "By myself, I can set up in the face of God an empire over which he can do nothing; this is hell...man does not understand hell because he does not understand his own heart."[2]

The titanic power of rejecting God is the ultimate human freedom. Freedom has been willed as such by God, that is, without limits.

---

1 See von Balthasar, *Dieu et l'homme d'aujourd'hui* (Paris, 1958).
2 Quoted by von Balthasar, *op. cit.,* p.245.

one scarcely dares to say it, is the hell of his love, the heavenly dimension of hell, the desolate vision of our endless repetition of the action of Adam or of Judas, fleeing into the darkness of solitude. Hell is nothing but the separation of man from God, our autonomy excluding God's presence, and we know this hell very well. It is the hell of all those who in despair, explore Satan's depths. Not all the wrong is on Adam's or Judas' side. They have acted thus because of their ignorance of the graces of Pentecost and because of the lamentable absence of true witnesses. An acidic pessimism eats into the roots of their lives, making them indifferent and impermeable to grace. From the hell of their hearts they hurl toward an empty heaven their despair and blasphemies. The satanic paradise of the proletarian regime produces the poison of an enormous boredom. This technologically sophisticated empire abandons us to ourselves, an abandonment equal in vastness to interplanetary space where rockets take the place of angels and where the thunder of God's wrath is beginning to rumble.

It is no longer possible to reduce faith or atheism to a "private affair." Our time is indeed the age of universalism—the catholicity of the Kingdom or of the anti-Kingdom. The beyond, sacred or secularized, is posited in the apocalyptic dimensions of our existence. It excludes any middle ground and implacably obliges us to choose between two totalitarian systems—"God is all in all," or "God is nowhere." The intermediate type, that of Max Stirner, for example, that (*Kleinbürgerlich*) petty bourgeois Prometheus, who stole fire from heaven to heat his coffee and to light his pipe, is disappearing from the world scene. For the religious needs of the human spirit, the dominant new philosophies offer their own absolutes, their stimulants and their mystic intoxications. "Certainly," wrote Simone Weil, "there is an intoxication in being a member of the mystical body of Christ. But today many mystical bodies, which do not have Christ as their head, procure for their members intoxications that are, in my opinion, of the same nature."[3]

3 *Waiting for God,* Emma Crawford, trans. (New York: Harper & Row, 1973), p. 81.

Present-day science is no longer a dream. As a dream, it has been magnificently realized, and beyond all expectations. Its rapid progression is becoming unpredictable. It is going beyond the laboratories of scientists, and it is indispensable in any meditation on being, the existence of man and his destiny. It is neither theology nor philosophy that is changing the face of the world. It is science. Cybernetics and automation are providing the human brain with a marvelous complement. They allow very exact forecasts to be made which concern us all. Power over biological processes and over space, plant in human consciousness the seeds of a new spirit of prophecy. By an effective solidarity, all men find that they have a common destiny with its own risks. Scientists cry out to us in their anxiety: "I am a man," said Harold Urcy, "who is afraid and who wishes to share his fear."[4] This is because science and technology intervene in a *political context*, bringing to it a power over men that is almost unlimited, as in George Orwell's *1984*.

Humanity risks being reduced to rationally conditioned, predictable gestures, with its critical faculties, cunningly controlled or inhibited. A balanced interaction between material progress and spiritual growth seems more and more problematic. An existence that has broken away from God is built on the refusal of God. Science, good in itself, risks finding itself set up entirely against God. The Antichrist of the *Legend*, by Vladimir Soloviev, presents himself as a great benefactor of humanity, as an accomplished scientist, offering as bread the miracles of technology and peace.

The situation of the modern world calls upon the Christian conscience, questions it and accuses it. If Communism exists, it is because Christians, unfaithful to the Gospel, have not been able to bring about the Kingdom of God on earth. If present-day thought has such an accent of despair and emptiness, it is because Christian hope has lost "the consolation afforded by the Scrip-

---

4 *Sommes-nous en révolution?* (1958), p. 45.

tures,"[5] and is no longer on the plane of the divine promise. If
abstract art exists, it is because figurative art no longer represents
anything, for it incarnates no spirit and radiates no light. Surrealism
arises only where we have lost the flame of things and the secret
content of simple reality. The feats of technology, according to Revelation 13:13, only parody the flames of Pentecost. In the midst of an
infernal existence, man feels himself abandoned in complete solitude.
Sheol signifies a place of darkness, and hell, in Greek, the place where
one does not see, where no glance meets that of another. Hell knows
no vis-à-vis, no meeting face to face. It is a place where there are "the
tears of the victims with *no one to comfort* them."[6]

Here the message of Pentecost is seen in all its breadth. Speaking
for all, Christ cried: "Why hast thou forsaken me?" This cry shook
the foundations of hell and moved the heart of the Father. But the
Father who sent his Son knows that even hell is his domain and that
"the door of death" is changed into a "door of life." Even infernal
despair is touched by a hope that it formerly contained, and it is not
for Christians to despair. The hand extended toward Christ never
remains empty. The fourth Gospel shows us Judas holding out his
hand. In placing in it the eucharistic bread,[7] Christ made his last
appeal to evil, to night at its darkest. Judas' fingers closed over the
immolated Lamb. Judas went out and "it was night." St. Augustine
has this to say: "He who went out was himself night."[8] The night
received him and hid his terrible communion with Satan. Satan is
in Judas. But Judas carries away in his hand, which is that of Satan,
a fearful mystery. Hell keeps in its heart that morsel of bread. Is this
particle of light not the faithful and exact expression of the words,
"the light shines in darkness"? The gesture of Jesus shows the last
mystery of the Church: she is the hand of Jesus offering the

5 Rom 15:4.
6 Eccles 4:1.
7 This is the opinion of St. Ephrem, St. John Chrysostom, St. Ambrose, St.
Augustine, St. Jerome.
8 See Lelong, *Saint Jean parmi nous* (Paris, 1961), p. 138.

eucharistic bread, addressing her appeal to all, for all are in the power of the prince of this world. The Light has not yet dissipated the darkness, but the darkness has not overcome the invincible Light.[9] We are all in the ultimate tension of divine love.

On this level we find not the denial but the exigency of hell, which comes from human freedom. Confronted with God, who forces no one to love him, hell bears witness to our freedom to love God. This freedom engenders hell, for we can always say: "May thy will not be done," and even God has no control over this decision.

God is a *mysterium fascinosum,* absolutely and for all eternity. He is not a clever architect with perfectly balanced plans. The cross is planted at the threshold of a new life. It is folly and a scandal. It upsets every design that is too geometrical, or "Euclidian," as Dostoyevski would say. Through the reasoning of our heart, we feel that our image of God would become disturbing if God did not love his creature even to the point of withholding punishment. It would also be disturbing if God did not save his beloved, neither touching nor destroying his freedom.

"Hell is other people," Sartre declares. A Christian can say: "The destiny of others is my hell." The Father has given all judgment to the Son of Man, and it is "the judgment of the judgment,"[10] the judgment crucified. "The Father is crucifying love, the Son is crucified love, the Holy Spirit is the invincible love of the cross."[11] This invincible power shines forth in the out-pouring of the Holy Spirit whom every baptized person receives. While those in despair explore the depths of Satan, the Gospel calls upon believers "to move mountains." Perhaps this means for us to move the infernal

9 Jn 1:5. The Vulgate translates "the darkness did not receive him"—*non comprehenderunt.* The Eastern Church follows Origen and translates: "the darkness did not conquer him." Both are true: the resistance of the darkness and the invincibility of the light.

10 St. Maximus, *P.G.,* 90, 408D.

11 Metr. Philaret of Moscow, *Oraisons, homélies et discours,* translated into French by A. Sturdza (Paris, 1849), p. 154.

mountain of the modern world and its nothingness toward the dazzling light of Pentecost and its new life: "I have *today* set before you life...and death." The "night" of the Western Church's mystics, and "the abandonment by God" of the Eastern Church's spiritual teachers, refer to the descent into hell. For the one who is attentive to the world, the experience of hell is immediate.

In the Orthodox Church services of Matins, during the Easter Vigil, in the silence of the end of Holy Saturday, the priest and people leave the church. The procession stops outside, before the closed doors of the church. For a brief moment, this door symbolizes the Lord's tomb, death, hell. The priest makes the sign of the cross on the door, and under its irresistible force, the door opens wide and all enter the church, which is flooded with light, singing: "Christ is risen from the dead, trampling down death by death, and upon those in the tombs bestowing life." *The gate of hell has become again the door of the Church.* One can go no further in the symbolism of the feast. Yes, the world in its totality is at the same time condemned and saved. It is at the same time hell and the Kingdom of God.

When we confess in the Creed that "I believe in the Holy Spirit, in the Holy Catholic Church," we mean "in the Holy Spirit who descended on the Church at Pentecost," and this is Pentecost perpetuated and the *Parousia* begun, in action in history. This time does not withdraw us from the world but it lightens the weight of the world, making us more joyous by the breath of the Spirit. It is in our world of television, guided spacecraft, supersonics, interplanetary journeys, in this world that is at once atheistic and believing, heavenly and infernal, but always loved by God, that we are called to the miracle of faith. Like Abraham of old, we start out without knowing where we are going or why; but we knows that we bear in our hearts a flame of fire, and we can only repeat the spirited words of St. John Climacus: "I go forward singing to you..."

6

The Desert Fathers

In the unending struggle against evil, the Evil One and hell, the remarkable effort of the desert Fathers and later of monasticism has played a decisive role in the destiny of Christianity. Following them, today's believer takes up the same task that has been enormously lightened, and lives in the heritage of this glorious and highly instructive past.

The eschatological texts of scripture place history between the Incarnation and the *Parousia,* between the first and second comings of Christ. Time appears entirely relative to the return of Christ who will surprise us "as a thief in the night." Since the day of Pentecost, we live in the latter days, and the *Parousia* that has begun strips the centuries of their apparent stability. For "those who love his appearing,"[1] the Christian city that the Empire of Constantine undertook to build is profoundly ambiguous, and this is why the monastic asceticism of virginity would like to hasten the end of the world by the extinction of the human species. If a couple began history, it is abstinence that will end it, Dositheus affirmed in the 3rd century. A little later, Basil of Ancyra wrote: "Now that the earth has been inseminated...virginity...will cause incorruption to flourish, beginning with the body."[2] The vow of celibacy, the *collective* rejection of procreation, expresses an extreme position with regard to history and the future of life on earth. The Gospel image of a sudden death accentuates the moribund state of the world, which bearing its own agony, advances from one survival to another, toward its

1 2 Tim 4:8. "Appearing" here has the meaning of the second coming of Christ.
2 *Sur la Virginité,* p. 55.

inevitable disappearance. Consequently the radical break of monasticism with society was required.

A very paradoxical reversal of the situation appears here. It is
no longer the pagan world that fights and eliminates the martyr.
It is the hermit who takes up the attack and eliminates the world
from his being. The desert Fathers brought back the struggle of
the first centuries, rediscovering the equivalent of the aggressive
forms of persecution. The arenas where wild beasts had torn the
martyrs apart were replaced by the immense desert where more
fearful beasts rise up, and where the demonic powers cast their
shadows. The "temptation of St. Anthony" or that of John of
Egypt offers the striking image of temptation by the evil one so
faithfully reproduced in the art of Hieronymous Bosch.

Burying themselves in vast solitudes, the anchorites sought to
penetrate the territory of the demons in order to fight them more
effectively at close range. They made a desert for themselves, a desert
of themselves, more agonizing than just an uninhabited place, a mere
retreat. It was this solitude willed by the human spirit that was visited
by both the noonday devil and that of nocturnal despair. Only a
powerful ascetic could size up the adversary and confront him "in a
most singular combat," according to St. Benedict.

The split from the world went further than mere flight from
human proximity. Those seeking unusual perfection placed themselves at the edge of the world, not to find a refuge, but to build a
new world, and to anticipate the heavenly city. The ascetics considered the desert to be an intermediary zone between the profane
world and the Kingdom. Exile became the pilgrimage of the *homo
viator,* man the traveler, seeking his heavenly origins. The hermits
were not exiles but "athletes of exile," fighters at the most advanced outposts. Above all, they were, in the magnificent words of
St. Macarius, "those intoxicated with God."[3] Monastic communities foreshadowed the future societies or republics of monks

3 "Homilies," *The Philokalia,* vol. III, 89, p. 324.

(Mount Athos) which were built not on the edge but right in this world, and which by their very nature are the radical negations of secular society. For the one who turns completely towards the East, towards Christ, conformity is unacceptable.

According to the firm belief of his disciples, St. Pachomius established his monastic community, which counted eight thousand members, on "the rule of the angel" who dictated it to him. The two letters that he left to his successors are written in an unknown language, called "the language of the angels." This symbolism is indicative of the transcendent origin of monastic society which contrasts sharply with bases of the city of man. An anchorite is God's rebel, and "the monastery is an earthly heaven," St. John of Climacus declares.[4] He proclaims the abolition of profane history and announces the coming of the new city inhabited by new beings. While every person is made "similar" to the image of God, the liturgical office of the holy monks calls them "very similar," and venerates them as "earthly angels and heavenly men."

Leaving a world entails entering another and implies a consistent strategy. A preliminary ascesis *undoes* the tainted heritage in order to *refashion* a purified human being. It experiments with the "anti-natural," anti-conformist conditions of life, as if the world of the living no longer existed or as if it presented only a deceptive and unreal aspect of being. In order to apply the ax of repentance to the roots of guilty conformity and behavior, the "dying to the world" practiced in the extreme forms of the asceticism of the desert is striking in its deliberate asymmetry, which at times attains an apparent ugliness, the exact opposite of the worldly ideal of ethics and aesthetics.

Thus "the grazers," descending to the level of the soil, feed on herbs and roots. They took the attitude of Adam hiding in the bush. They fled human society, making themselves akin to the animal world. St. Ephrem the Syrian, called "the lyre of the Holy

---

4 *The Ladder of Divine Ascent,* step 27, p. 264.

Spirit," wrote in his *Praise of the Solitaries:* "They went wandering in the deserts with the wild beasts as if they themselves were wild beasts." They lived as if they had cast off the burden of the flesh, and in their emaciation they retained no accumulated poisons. In appearance they imitated animal life, putting on a second nature just as those accomplished actors, "the fools for Christ," in order to create an atmosphere of contempt and abjection, and to become "the least" of this world in reaching the utmost limit of humility.

"The recluses" also led a strange life. Giving up light and language, they buried themselves in ancient tombs or in holes in the ground. We can see in this form the trials of abandonment, solitude and silence, this experience anticipating the conditions of death. "Pray often in the tombs and paint an indelible picture of them in your heart,"[5] St. John Climacus counseled everyone, in order to make death familiar, to live and meditate on its mystery before it comes. The recluses opposed the silence of the lips to the tumult of a soul on fire with passion. "Do not judge anyone and learn to be silent," said St. Macarius, for in the words of St. Isaac: "Silence will be the language of the future world."[6]

There were also "the dendrites" chained to a branch of a tree so that they would no longer touch the earth sullied by man. Like Noah in the ark, they relived the experience of humanity withdrawn by the grace of God from a contaminated world. By this withdrawal they measured the depth of man's fall and their penitent tears mingled the waters of the deluge with the waters of baptism. In tree branches, exposed to the winds, they led the life of birds intoxicated with the heavens and with God.

"The stationaries" remained motionless and petrified, with their arms in the form of a cross, in a state of perpetual prayer, a living symbol of the vertical vocation of man, of his spirit that stretches toward the Most High. "The stylites" continued this

5 *Ibid.,* step 18.

6 A. J. Wensinck, *Mystic Treatises of Isaac of Nineveh,* p. 115.

attitude. Perched on high columns, far above all agitation or tumult, they placed themselves between heaven and earth, though nearer heaven on the last rung of the "Ladder of Paradise."

All these forms of withdrawal represent a most puzzling phenomenon. The ascetics' rejection of the human city and of historical development brought about a return to the conditions of *prehistoric* life. The words, "become as little children," were taken literally, but this "spiritual childhood" hides an astonishing depth. We read in St. Isaac's works: "When you prostrate yourself before God in prayer, become in your own judgment like an ant, a worm, or a beetle. Do not speak before God as a man who knows anything, but stammer and approach him with a *childlike* spirit."[7]

Exteriorly this ascesis strikes us as an extravagance bordering on the inhuman, but within we discover a great sobriety and perfect moderation. Some of the words of the ascetics, such as those of Hesychius on the silence of the heart, a state of perfect recollection, reveal a profound knowledge of the human soul.

The extraordinary and the miraculous do not surprise us in the atmosphere of the desert. They become the norm for a nature that is inwardly on fire. Thus "the old man Joseph arose and lifted his hands toward heaven. His hands became as lighted candles. And he said to Abbot Lot: 'If you wish to be perfect, become all fire.'"[8] The ascesis of the desert entails the baptism of fire.

It is a great temptation for an historian to regard this ascesis as an aberration and to give "a comical description"[9] of it. A twenti-

---

7 Wensinck. *op. cit.,* p. 343.

8 *Apoph. patrum,* Joseph, 6.

9 The expression is that of Father Rousselot regarding the book by J. Lacarrière, *Men Intoxicated with God.* The author of this book presents a valuable collection of facts and texts, but he remains on the outside and does not touch upon any of the contemporary commentaries on this dramatic chapter of Christian spirituality. He in no way commits himself, remaining strictly objective, but such an attitude is ambiguous and implies a tacit judgment. In this perspective, it is instructive to study, following Aldous Huxley, the biochemical effects due to starvation, to exercises of the type "I kill my body because it is killing me," to high temperature, and

eth century university professor would automatically and illegiti-
mately reduce its secret depths to its surface appearance, and he
would do this less by what he says than by what he does not say
and by what he does not even suspect. When the desert Fathers
recognized the powerlessness of words, they counseled veneration
of the mystery by silence. This is just what the icon does. An icon
of a saint tells us nothing of his physical appearance and gives no
biographical, historical, or sociological detail. It shows the radi-
ance of the person beyond history. A saint bears history within,
but shows it in a different manner. By his transparence he reveals
a new dimension in which its meaning is made clear by its end.
The saint thus represents a meta-historical synthesis. We must
read the lives of the desert Fathers iconographically, just as we
might contemplate an icon.

To oppose culture to holiness[10] is like breaking down an open
door. A well-balanced tradition would affirm culture *and* holiness.
However, to make this balance and to establish it definitively, it
was necessary first to pass dialectically through the extreme polari-
zation of the terms. In effecting this passage, the asceticism of the
desert reveals its Gospel origin. The Holy Spirit led Jesus into the
desert to encounter the devil. The mysterious period of forty days
of silence inaugurated the mission of the Word. "He who truly
possesses the Word of Jesus can hear even his silence," declared St.
Ignatius of Antioch.[11] The tradition of the Church is precisely this
prayerful silence which surrounds the Word and from which both

> to darkness, or to compare Christian hesychasts to Indian yogi who experiment with
> breathing; in diminishing it, they lessen the wear on the heart. All these phenomena
> are encountered in the Himalayas as in the Thebaid, and spring from the same
> techniques, but they are insufficient as explanations. The biochemical processes are
> natural reactions of the organism. Used ascetically, they can at most facilitate the
> manifestations of the spirit. But every technical means that is used only leads to and
> stops at the threshold of the transcendent, as for example, the "Jesus Prayer." The
> critical mind can describe the threshold, but it can go no further, for beyond there it
> does not apply and does not explain anything.

10 Taken from the excellent work of Father Festugière.

11 Eph 15:2.

the liturgy and the icon emerge. Silence and the Word, holiness and culture, penetrate and complement each other.

It would be a flagrant error to see in the desert only the outcasts of monasticism, illiterates living in a degrading atmosphere. If we do not penetrate the deep motives of their souls, we ignore a unique fact that had incalculable consequences for the destiny of Christianity. The asceticism of the desert represents an inevitable moment in Christian spirituality. Certainly it belongs to a past age, and any return to the desert now would be an unacceptable break with tradition. Nevertheless, this asceticism keeps its unfailing significance for all ages and all times. It is the cornerstone of later monastic tradition.

It was not with the instruments of culture but with their bare hands that the ascetics maintained the Christian ideal at its transcendent height, and this is the miracle. They understood well the spirit of the Gospel. It is not the way that is impossible, it is the impossible that is the way, and they have traveled it.

Asceticism exerts, above all, a pedagogical influence. A worldly person, even the one most laden with cares, knew that somewhere, *in his place*, there were true human beings, who in the silence of their hearts were speaking with angels and were encroaching on the life of the future world. Crowds used to come to contemplate the stylites, and they had engraved on their hearts this image of "intoxication with God." Some of them, in order to have it always before their eyes, made a summary sketch of it and thus traced the prototype of the icon.

"By the virtue of the Spirit and spiritual regeneration, man is raised to the dignity of the first Adam," said St. Macarius.[12] Asceticism lessens the effects of the first sin and manifests the power of the spirit. The "bestiaries" of the desert recount an astonishing friendship, for the wild beasts recognized "the aroma of paradise" in the saints and ended by becoming more human,

12 "Homilies," *The Philokalia,* vol. III, 150, p. 353.

reflecting the human face with its gentle and intelligent eyes. The anchorites revived man's lost privilege, given to him by God, to rule the animals and to be king of the universe.[13]

The world finds its norm, its scale of comparison, in the extreme efforts of the ascetics, their "maximalism." It perceives also the insipid dullness of the spirit of self-sufficiency. In the face of the declaration of common sense, "God does not ask so much of us," the asceticism of the desert proclaims the terrible jealousy of God, who after giving all of himself, asks all from us. The desert Fathers have left us an icon of this total gift. Its excessive features command our attention and ask us what is the utmost each one of us can do. The Christian type would not be what it is were it not for this asceticism, which from remote times has unconsciously made its purifying influence felt.

We can go deeper still. The ascetics renounced culture in seeking the one thing needful. This desire had to become a passion for perfection: "Sell all that you have." Even more, "Sell all that you are." In the perfection of this attitude, all became a single act—the carrying of the cross. "Let him renounce himself and take up his cross." This is not the Liturgy, but is a preliminary to it, a rite of preparation, a compact and startling condensed version of immolation.

"Ground between the two millstones of humility," the ascetics sacrificed themselves in order that others would later profit from their "virginity of spirit," by inaugurating Christian culture. Asceticism in itself is not the ideal. It represents only the culminating point of the catharsis, or purification. Tertullian, as an already prejudiced and sectarian polemicist, asked: "What does Athens have in common with Jerusalem, and the Academy with the Church?"[14] He added: "All curiosity ceases after the Gospel." Now all curiosity really begins after the Gospel, but in a different manner than before.

13 They are a living commentary on Mark 1:13.
14 *De praescr. haer.*, 7.

There is a risk that peace will allow this curiosity to slacken. The asceticism of the desert, after having interiorized the persecutions, will later interiorize true peace in hesychasm, in the silent prayer of the heart, but this time with the contemplative knowledge of God and of the world in the light of Tabor.

Asceticism undoes the act by which Adam ceased to be fully himself, in wishing to belong only to himself and in refusing to go beyond himself in God. It takes up again the vocation of Adam and persues a conformity to the *obedient Christ.* The martyrs imitated Christ crucified. The ascetics "imitated," took literally the counsels of the Gospel: "If thy hand...thy foot...are an occasion of sin for thee, cut them off. If thy eye is an occasion of sin to thee, pluck it out...it is better for thee to enter the kingdom of God lame and with one eye than to be cast into the fire of hell...for everyone shall be salted with fire." In the heroic atmosphere of the desert this salt and fire were not mere metaphors. The moral binding of the instincts by the will was realized here by means of real, heavy chains. Their spiritual elevation caused the stylites to mount pillars. St. Anthony attained at the same time the summit of meditation and the peak of Qolzoum. The arid and burning desert flourished as "a spiritual meadow." Through the ascetics' thirst for the Kingdom, monasteries and deserts were transformed into microcosms of the heavenly city of the future.

The soul that has been drawn from nothingness desires to find its origins and asks to be recreated, to allow itself to be unmade and remade by having its elements purified one after another. The goal of the ascetics was a state anterior to fallen nature in its preconceptual, preaffective, prevoluntary center. They sought to reach the unsullied structure of the self made "in the image of God." In the extreme forms of asceticism, we perceive the attempt to change the human condition by the mutation of its psychosomatic elements. St. Macarius says this in his *Homilies*: "When the apostle urges the putting off of the old man, he means the entire man. He means: have other eyes than those the man has, another head than his, hands and feet that are no longer his." St. Symeon the New Theologian speaks as a mystic in his *Hymns*: "My hands are those of an unfortunate and my feet are those of Christ. I, unworthy, am the hand and the foot of Christ. I move my hand and my hand is all Christ, for the divinity of God is indivisibly united to me."

The "apostolic person" of the spiritual writers is not subject to the laws of this world but anticipates his eternal existence. The radical character of the change is emphasized by the fact that, though it is interior, it modifies, in certain cases, even outward appearance. This was the case of St. Alexis, the "man of God," who after his life in the desert was received as a beggar in his own home without being recognized. A woman named Athanasia joined her husband in the desert with the features of a man and was not recognized until the moment of her death. All ties, as well as sexual differentiation, became foreign to them and they to the world.

The ascetic technique "renders the earthly qualities of the body pure." An athlete exercises the body, an ascetic, the flesh. The icons show us those whose flesh has neither weight nor earthly heaviness, beings living in a new dimension. They have lost the material qualities that made them like things, but *not their reality.* More real than anyone else, they have gone beyond themselves.

The asceticism of solitude dims even the light and colors of the outer world in order to direct one's glance inward. The ascetics manifested a supreme indifference to social conventions. "Clothed with space," they often went naked, having found again a lost innocence. They did not wish to harm even the smallest insect, and they acted not from without and *on*, but from within with a boundless cosmic charity.

Their rejection of a contaminated world led to the abolition of all social traditions. The extreme forms of their asceticism effected a deliberate regression to the prenatal, mineral, animal stage, and a behavior against the grain of normal human condition and conformity. It led to an Adamic nakedness, to a physical and psychic indifference, a stripping of human attributes—upright posture, discursive reasoning, speech, rest. The ascetics ceased reacting *normally* to the needs of the flesh in order to purify at their roots all the essential elements of a human being, and to refashion a new man, spiritually as well as biologically. The Eastern Church conceives of salvation from a therapeutic point of view. She sees in it, before all else, a healing of death by eternal life. It avoids juridical terminology, and expresses redemption itself in biological terms. It is not so much a correction of sin as it is a *reparation of nature in Christ.*

Asceticism affirms that the encounter with God cannot be accomplished by starting from fallen nature. God remains exterior to the extent that the passions are interior and the "ego" is identified with "the dark spirits that nestle somewhere near the heart."[15] The ascent toward God begins with a descent into oneself—"Know thyself"—in order to force those passions which make us run from God, to alienate and exteriorize themselves. This first stage is called *praxis*, the practice of purifying and exteriorizing virtues. To be despised and rejected by all serves as a purging against concupiscence, explained St. John Climacus[16] in speaking of humility. Though the avoidance of all speculative thought may give the impression of "stultification," it is only a preliminary method in the search for "the place of the heart," for "the place of God." However, every seeking for what is natural "buries the heart under the haze of passions," arouses an immediate reaction from the dark "underground" from the obscure world of the subconscious.

With great psychotherapeutic insight, these spiritual masters, the desert Fathers, discovered the energies obscured below the threshold of consciousness.

15 Diadochus of Photike, "On Spiritual Knowledge and Discrimination: One Hundred Texts," in *The Philokalia*, vol. I, p. 263.

16 *P.G.*, 88, 717A-B.

The asceticism of the desert is a vast psychoanalysis followed by a psychosynthesis of the universal human soul. Origen, the brilliant commentator, compares the desert to Plato's cave. The desert with all its arsenal of phantasmagoria was a theater of shadows, a spectacle for men and angels. Only the shadows did not reflect the reality outside the cave. They were the projection of the world inside us.

For the authors of the New Testament, as for the Fathers of the desert, the world before the time of Christ was bewitched. The Gospel speaks of the possessed, of disruptive elements and of the perversity of the human heart. The abysses we discover are *haunted.* There are secret places where evil powers are crouching and they rule us if we are ignorant or unaware. Asceticism concentrates our attention and begins by an experimental phenomenology of our human interior. It was necessary to materialize and personalize the perverted elements of a being, the hateful ego with its self-love, the doubter and the demonic counterpart. Above all, it was necessary to completely eradicate them, to "vomit" them, and to objectify them, in order to look them in the face, detached and exteriorized. This "objectification" creates a distance, permits the projection of all interior elements as on a screen (Plato's cave of shadows), in the form of monsters, wild beasts and demons. This operation requires a very precise conviction of the reality of the enemy, in order to cut every bond and communion with him. Hieronymous Bosch gives an artistic interpretation in his striking imagery.

The Fathers of the desert have carried out this operation once for all and in place of all. "He who has seen himself such as he is and has seen his sin is greater than he who raises the dead."[17] They have stripped humanity of its masks, and they have put a face and a name to every obscure element of evil. The hidden play, both human and demonic, is demonstrated and brought to light. After this revelation, the one going to confession knows what must be

17 St. Isaac the Syrian, *Sayings,* 50.

done and what is going to happen. Each time he or she repeats the experience of the desert Fathers. One can look within oneself, but now without being troubled by the unknown. In order not to remain in a stifling tête-à-tête with our sins and with ourselves we can discern and exteriorize them through confession. Here only Christ, the absolutely innocent victim, can bring about the unique living transference, "having cancelled the bond which stood against us."[18]

When the asceticism left the caves of the desert and spread through the world, the veil and the shadows disappeared. All entered back into man but now in a *different* manner. The hierarchy of purified values, having been reestablished, allows one to see the evil before being tempted to commit it.

The metaphysical unity of the human race, the collective unconscious lying at the roots of consciousness, condition and explain the mystical fact: that humanity was different before the Incarnation from what it is now. One can say also that human consciousness was different before the asceticism of the desert from what it was after. Just like the event of Pentecost, this asceticism has modified the dominant energies of the psyche and renewed the human spirit.

The therapeutic effect of "the desert" in the depths of the human spirit is universal. It represents the collective vomiting, the objectification and the expulsion of the original and accumulated impurity. This is perhaps the meaning of the words of St. Paul, "to add to the suffering of Christ," something that the innocent Christ could not do in our place, because of our freedom and which only the sinner, the desert ascetic, could do in place of all and with a universal significance. From a positive point of view, it was *the formation of the ascetic human archetype.* It shaped "the violent" to fight evil and the Evil One inside and outside of man.

Human guilt does not do away with the reality of demons. That authorities of the stature of St. Athanasius, St. Cassian and St. Benedict speak of demons should give greater prudence to

18 Col 2:14.

every critical spirit who sees in them only obscurantism. The reality is more complex. The Gospel speaks of them, and the rite of exorcism bears witness to them.

The Gospel[19] speaks of the unclean spirit who, finding a human soul "swept and decorated," settles there again with seven other spirits. Asceticism has purified the soul. It also keeps its role of vigilant sentinel.

Certainly now a return to the conditions of the desert is no longer possible. We are in different times and have moved through different *spiritual ages*. Delays on one side and advances on the other do not allow exact dating, but it is clear that on the margin of chronology men such as Evagrius, the Macarius of the *Homilies*, and Diadochus, belong to another age than the ascetics of the desert. The collective projection is over, and every attempt to revive it would be a dangerous illusion. Excessive analysis and obsession with scruples are frowned upon as morbid. In placing themselves in antisocial conditions, the ascetics had prepared the return of the new man to history. The complete cycle had been achieved. Originally placed outside history, monasticism was to become a religious force that would most strongly influence history.

Tradition reestablished the balance in a masterly fashion. After the purification (*catharsis*) of the desert, the spiritual masters taught a new and definitive interiorization. "Enter your soul and there, find God, the angels and the kingdom."[20] "The purified heart becomes an interior heaven."[21] It is no longer by extraordinary conditions of life, but by true prayer that a monastic becomes *isangelos*, equal to the angels.[22] The rule of St. Benedict stresses this: "All that one formerly observed through terror and fear of hell, one now keeps through love of Christ."[23]

19 Mt 12:45.
20 St. Macarius, *P.G.*, 34, 776D.
21 Philotheus the Sinaite, "Chapter on Watchfulness," The Philokalia, vol. III, 1, 4, pp. 16-17.
22 Evagrius, "On Prayer," *The Philokalia*, vol. I, 113, p. 68.
23 *The Rule of St. Benedict*, Anthony C. Meisel and M. L. del Mastro, trans. (New York: Doubleday-Image, 1975), 9, p. 61.

Prayer participates in universal existence, and "the heart is aflame with love for every creature" (St. Macarius, St. Isaac),[24] the new consciousness blossomed into the cosmic charity of the saints.

One can look at random at some of the vigorous measures used to arrive at a more balanced asceticism. There was a tempering of excessive behavior and advice against following it, sometimes by the voice of the Councils. The Council of Ancyra threatened to condemn the intransigence of the ascetics who refused to eat vegetables cooked with meat. Cassian declared: "Excessive fasts do as much harm as gluttony."[25] The encratic and gnostic tendencies which despised the flesh and marriage were vigorously opposed.

When St. Simon the Stylite put a chain around his foot in order to reduce his movements to what was strictly necessary, Meletius, the Patriarch of Antioch, told him that one could attain immobility just by the will.

A text of the 6th century speaks of Theodulus the Stylite who lived forty-eight years on a pillar. To his naive question about the recompense due him, an angel told him it would be the same as that of the actor in Damascus who had given all his fortune to a woman in dire poverty. The *Historia Monachorum* recounts an episode in the life of Paphnutius, the great ascetic. He asked God to show him the perfect men whose equal he had proved himself to be. There followed a vision in which he saw three persons: a thief who had saved a woman lost in the desert, a village chief who was just and generous to all, a pearl merchant who distributed all his goods to the poor. *The Spiritual Meadow* of John Moschus describes a young monk who did not hesitate to frequent taverns but who kept his heart pure. He was the envy of an old monk who, after spending fifty years at Scete, had not acquired a like purity of heart.

24 Wensinck, *op. cit.,* p. 341. See also, *The Spiritual Fathers on Prayer and the Spiritual Life,* Sebastian Brock, trans. (Kalamazoo, MI: Cistercian Press, 1987), p. 251.
25 *Conferences,* II, 16.

Through the Church's teaching, the Gospel is recognized. Henceforth acts of charity surpass ascetic exploits and are placed at the very center. The *Apophthegmata*, or *Sayings*, tell of a hermit who after forty years in the desert, said to the abbot of a large monastery: "The sun has never seen me eat." The abbot replied: "As for me, it has never seen me in anger."

St. Basil made a long visit with the monks of Egypt and Syria, and later, with St. Gregory of Nazianzen, drew up his two *Monastic Rules* which later inspired St. Benedict. Profoundly impressed by the desert, he was nevertheless aware of his own times and wrote as a Father of the Church. In his vision of the future, he deliberately attributed less importance to the renunciation of the world and much more to love of neighbor and the service of mankind. Thus, if monasticism left the world, it was only to bless it from the vantage of retreat and to carry it in its incessant prayer. "The one who is perfect becomes the equal of the apostles...Such a one can return to others and tell what he has seen in God. He can and must, in fact, he cannot do otherwise."[26] St. Maximus the Confessor reacted violently against all pessimism of neo-Platonic origin, and the asceticism of St. Isaac the Syrian is striking in its extreme sensitivity to mankind and to God's creation.

The hesychast tradition, that of silent prayer in the heart, stresses the body's participation in the training of the spirit. Its asceticism does not seek suffering and affliction but endurance through abstention, resistance to distractions, and attention of the heart to the one thing needful. The great truth of the Gospel is clearly affirmed: the spiritual person is thus whole, both in soul and in body. For St. Gregory Palamas, this is our privilege and superiority over the angels.

In the 10th and 11th centuries, the great Lavra (monastery) of Athos began a very special experiment. Its eschatological context is expressed in the tradition of the Jesus Prayer and of the light of

26 L. Hausherr, "Saint Syméon le N.T.," in Orientalia Christiana. XII, p. xxx.

Tabor. The Gospel narrative of the Transfiguration reveals it as an anticipation of the *Parousia* and of the Kingdom, but after Pentecost, the light is interiorized. In rare cases it can manifest itself and be perceived by means of transfigured senses. The one who inwardly or outwardly contemplates it is transformed into light. This is because the light is not only the object but the means of the vision. Iconographically, as the nimbus of the saints shows, the corporeal luminosity of the saints is ontologically normal. This is the very being of a new creature.

With natural but transfigured eyes, the saint contemplates an immaterial light. But the saint's visions and knowledge are a gift, for in himself he never "possesses" the divine. God, in manifesting himself, safeguards his mystery and his total transcendence. If he accords us a participation in his life and his presence, he hides himself in his very manifestation. He hides his inaccessible Being. The hesychast tradition of prayer and silence is most firm on this point: the transcendence of God is not due to human weakness but to the nature of God. Unknowable by nature, God is more than God. Even in uniting himself to us, God remains transcendent. Participation in God is participation only in his energies, in his grace—the burning intimacy of his presence. According to St. Symeon: "God is the more invisible the more he radiates in man's spirit." This superessential principle of the divine essence conditions human love, its eternal epektasis, its attraction toward God, of which St. Gregory of Nyssa speaks.

The Tradition of the Church rapidly eliminated all imagination, all mystic intoxication with suffering, and imposed the greatest sobriety. Even ecstasy was held suspect. "When it seems to you that your spirit is drawn toward the heights by an invisible force, do not put any faith in it, but make yourself work." By work a monastic avoids all romantic abstraction and practices charity. "Very often one thinks that it is a spiritual joy that one is experiencing, and it is only sensuality aroused by the enemy; those who have had this experience can distinguish it," teaches Gregory the Sinaite.[27] Evagrius similarly said, "Do not desire to see either powers or angels lest you sink into madness."[28]

The Liturgy offers an efficacious means of filtering out every disordered emotion. That is why the life of a monastic is centered more and more on psalmody, prayer and prayerful meditation on the Scriptures. The soul listens to the Word and allows itself to be penetrated, filled. Biblical ontology forms the categories of emptiness and fullness, absence and communion. Every spiritual person aspires to the communion that fills him with God, as the Virgin or St. Stephen was filled with the Holy Spirit. From this biblical source comes the patristic definition of theology: *the experiential way of union with God.* "If you are a theologian, you will truly pray, and if you truly pray, you are a theologian."[29] This experience of "the sense of God" allows the transposing into eucharistic terms the nuptial or marital dwelling of God in us. We do not speculate but are changed. The clear realism of asceticism affirms for all times its essential principle. No asceticism deprived of love comes near to God. "We shall be judged for the evil we have done but especially for the good we have neglected and for the fact that we have not loved our neighbor."[30] *The Shepherd of Hermas* is likewise explicit in declaring that anyone who has failed to help someone in spiritual distress will be held responsible for his loss.[31] On Mount Athos today the old maxims have lost nothing of their value: "The true monk is the one who in the present life possesses nothing but Christ," and "the one who has in his heart even a trace of wickedness is unworthy of the charity of Christ."

Having arrived at the height of the greatest freedom, the hermit can find the world again since for such a one it is no longer bewitched. He can find people and their city again since he has

27 *De la vie contemplative*, 10.
28 "On Prayer," *The Philokalia*, vol. I, 114-116, p. 68.
29 *Ibid.,* 60, p. 62.
30 St. Maximus the Confessor, *P.G.,* 99, 932C.
31 *Simil.*, X, 3, 4.

acquired the love that urges him to leave his solitude. On this summit "one no longer condemns the Jews nor the Greeks nor sinners...the interiorized person looks at all men with a pure eye and rejoices then on account of the entire universe. He desires with his whole heart only to love and venerate each and every one," says St. Macarius.[32] As a messenger and a witness, he mingles with the crowd. As a charismatic, he opens the door of his cell and receives the world.

Contrary to the purely physical asceticism of mortification, the therapeutic art of Tradition rehabilitates the material world, and in letters of joy inscribes the Paschal message, the human destiny of eternal life, on all the tombs throughout the world. The eschatological tone of the asceticism of all ages remains.

The soul recognizes God in its avowal of its total powerlessness. It renounces itself and no longer belongs to itself. This oblation, this unconditional giving up of oneself, structures contemplative receptivity. It is humility that has become act. "The naked one follows the naked Christ." He keeps himself in expectation and in his soul he awaits the *Parousia*, the coming of Christ. But this soul bears the world of all people. Purified by asceticism, a spiritual person, according to the fine words of St. Gregory Nazianzen, is "the repository of the divine love for men."[33]

---

32 "Homilies," *The Philokalia*, vol. III, pp. 282-353.
33 *P.G.*, 35, 593C.

7

Interiorized Monasticism

1. The Transmission of the Witness

The universal crisis in monasticism suggests that an historic cycle is coming to a close. However, here as elsewhere, we must guard against simplification and distinguish between changeable forms and the permanent principle, between the transmission of the essential message of the Gospel and the appearance of new witnesses.

We can discover a similar transmission in the very origins of monasticism. Since the time of the first martyr and deacon, St. Stephen, the witness of blood has been the sign of the highest and most expressive fidelity. The ideal of the martyr, of that glorious company of "the wounded friends of the bridegroom," of those "violent ones who take heaven by storm" and in whom "Christ fights in person," makes the first centuries unique. On his way to his glorious death, St. Ignatius of Antioch confessed: "It is now that I begin to be a true disciple...do not hinder me from being born to life."[1] Likewise for St. Polycarp the martyrs are "the images of true charity...the captives laden with venerable chains, which are the jewels of the veritable elect of God."[2] This is why Origen made his somewhat harsh remark that a time of peace is propitious to Satan, who steals from Christ his martyrs, and from the Church her glory.

As a living image of Christ crucified, the martyr preaches him by being a "spectacle" to the world, to angels and to men. "Your

1 Rom 5:3-6.
2 Philipp. III.

bodies are pierced by the sword, but never can your spirit be cut off from divine love. Suffering with Christ, you are consumed by the burning coals of the Holy Spirit. Wounded by divine desire, your martyrs, Lord, rejoice in their wounds," sings the Church.[3]

"Can you drink the cup that I must drink?" our Lord asked the apostles. This formidable question equates martyrdom with the eucharistic chalice. The soul of the martyr bears the presence of Christ in a very special manner. According to an ancient tradition, every martyr at the moment of his death hears the words addressed to the wise thief—"This day you shall be with me in paradise"—and enters immediately into the Kingdom.

The peaceful existence of the Church, protected by law as of the fourth century, will never suffer any diminution with regard to the power of her message. The Holy Spirit immediately "invented" the "equivalent of martyrdom." In fact, the witness of the martyrs to "the one thing needful" is passed on to monasticism. "The baptism of blood" of the martyrs gave way to "the baptism of asceticism" of the monks. The celebrated *Life of St. Anthony,* written by St. Athanasius, describes this father of monasticism as the first who had attained holiness without tasting martyrdom.[4] When humanity had sunk below itself, monastic asceticism raised it above its own nature. Monasticism's *metanoia,* or transformation, deepened Baptism's second birth which brought to life already the "little resurrection." While the body awaits this glorification, the soul is already immortal.

The liturgical texts call the monks "earthly angels and heavenly men." Monastic holiness forms a type of man who is a "true

3 *Octoechos,* Greek.

4 See D. H. Leclercq, "Monachisme," in *D.A.L.,* XI, 1802. Mankind had fallen to a level below his nature; monastic asceticism elevated him to one above it. The *metanoia* or conversion deepened the second birth of baptism that brought about the "little resurrection." Even if the body had to await the "great resurrection," the soul was already immortal. See also *Athanasius: The Life of Anthony and the Letter to Marcellinus,* Robert C. Gregg, trans. (Ramsey, NJ: Paulist Press, 1980).

likeness," a living icon of God. One can say that at least here, confronted with the world's compromises, the *metanoia,* the complete reversal of all the economy of the human being, its perfect metamorphosis, had succeeded.

The dreadful Thebaid, cradle of so many spiritual giants, the arid and burning desert, was illuminated with their light. These astonishing masters taught the refined art of living the Gospel. In the silence of their cells and caves, in the school of these "theodidacts," those taught by God, the birth of the *new creature* was slowly effected.

2. The Universal Character of Monastic Spirituality

Father Georges Florovsky recalls that "too often one forgets the provisory character of monasticism. St. John Chrysostom declared that monasteries are necessary because the world is not Christian. Let it be converted, and the need for a monastic separation will disappear."[5] History has not vindicated St. John's hope. Monasticism will surely keep its unique testimony to the end of the world.

However, the baptized world is sufficiently Christian to hear the monastic message and to assimilate it in its own way. Here is the whole problem. As formerly, martyrdom was transmitted to the monastic institution, so today, it seems, monasticism evokes a certain receptivity in the universal priesthood of the laity. The testimony of the Christian faith in the framework of the modern world necessitates the universal vocation of *interiorized monasticism.*

Past history gives us two solutions. The first, that of monasticism, preaches a complete separation from a society which lives according to "the elements of this world," and from its economic,

5 "Le Corps du Christ vivant," in *la Sainte Église universelle: Confrontation Œcuménique,* Paris/Neuchâtel: Dalachaux et Niestlé, 1948, pp. 9-57. See "The Church: Her Nature and Task," in *Bible, Church, Tradition: An Eastern Orthodox View,* Collected Works, vol. I (Belmont, MA: Nordland, 1972) pp. 57-72.

political and sociological problems. This is "the flight to the desert" and the later autonomous existence of communities that care for all the needs of their members. The "monastic republic" of Mount Athos is a striking example of a social, self-governing life, separated from the world and even opposed to it. It is perfectly clear that since everybody cannot share this vocation, the monastic solution remains limited. It is not the solution for the world in its totality.

The second solution was the attempt to Christianize the world without leaving it in order to build the Christian City of God. The theocracies of the East as well as the West manifest this effort under the ambiguous forms of empires and Christian States. The resounding failure of this attempt proves that one can never impose the Gospel from above, nor prescribe grace as a law.

Is there a third solution? Without prejudging, one can at least say that this third ought to appropriate the two others in an interior way, that is, in applying their principles beyond their outward forms. "You are not of this world, you are in the world." These words of the Lord recommend a very special ministry, that of being a sign, a reference to "the wholly other." Formerly, it was realized differently. At present, it seems to show itself above the "desert" and the "city," for it is called to surpass every form in order to express itself everywhere and in all circumstances.

The Western Church has canonized monasticism and the lay state as two forms of life. One corresponds to the "counsels," the other, to the "precepts" of the Gospel. The unique absolute is then broken. On one side, the perfect advance, on the other, is the weaker position of living by half measures. Certain ascetics justified conjugal life only because it produces virgins and populates monasteries.

The essentially homogeneous character of Eastern Church spirituality ignores the difference between "the precepts" and "the evangelical counsels." It is in its total demand that the Gospel addresses itself to everyone, everywhere.

"When Christ," says St. John Chrysostom, "orders us to follow the narrow path, he addresses himself to all. The monastics and the lay person must attain the same heights."[6] We can see indeed that there exists only one spirituality for all without distinction in its demands, whether of the bishop, monk, or lay person, and this is the nature of monastic spirituality.[7] Now, this has been shaped by lay-monastics, which gives to the term "lay" the maximal spiritual and ecclesial meaning.

In fact, according to the great teachers, the monastics were only those who wished "to be saved," those who "led a life according to the Gospel," who "sought the one thing needful," and "did violence to themselves in all things."[8] It is quite evident that these words exactly define the state of every believing lay person. St. Nilus thought all monastic practices were required of people in the world.[9] As St. John Chrysostom said: "Those who live in the world, even though married, ought to resemble the monks in everything else. You are entirely mistaken if you think that there are some things required of ordinary people, and others of monks...they will have the same account to render."[10] Prayer, fasting, the reading of Scripture and ascetic discipline are imposed on all by the same prescription. St. Theodore of Studion in his letter to a Byzantine dignitary drew up the program of monastic life and specified: "Do not believe that this list is of value only for a monk and not *entirely and equally for a lay person.*"[11]

When the Fathers spoke, they addressed all the members of the Church, the mystical body, without any distinction between clergy and laity. They spoke to the universal priesthood. Our contemporary pluralism: different theologies for the episcopate, the clergy, monastics and the laity, unknown at the time of the Fathers, would

6 In *Epist. ad Haeb.*, 7, 4; 7, 41; *Adv. oppugn. vitae monast.*, 3, 14.
7 Cf. Pourrat, *La spiritualité chrétienne*, I, ix.
8 St. Nilus, *P.G.*, 79, 180D. See *The Philokalia*, vol. I, pp. 200-250.
9 *Epist.* I, 167, 169.
10 *Hom. in Epist. ad Haeb.*, 7, 41
11 *P.G.*, 99, 1388

be incomprehensible to them. The Gospel in its entirety is applicable to every particular problem in every environment.

On the other hand, certain great figures among the monastics show clearly that they went beyond their own state, as well as beyond every formula or definite form. We find an example of this in the luminous figure of St. Seraphim of Sarov. He did not attract disciples nor was he master of any school. Yet he is the master of all, for his witness in the Orthodox Church surpasses all that is a type, category, style, definition or limit. His Paschal joy did not come from his personality, but is the echo of Orthodoxy itself. In ordinary language he said extraordinary things which he had received from the Holy Spirit. After a terrible struggle, shadowed by a silence that hid a life no monk could endure, St. Seraphim left the extreme practices of the hermits and stylites and returned to the world. "An earthly angel and a heavenly man," he transcended even monasticism. He was no longer a monk retired from the world nor a man living among people. He was both, and in surpassing both, he was essentially a witness to the Holy Spirit. He said this in his famous conversation with Nicolas Motovilov: "It is not to you alone that it has been given to understand these things, but through you to the whole world, in order that you may be strengthened in the work of God and be useful for many others. *As to the fact that you are a lay person and that I am a monk, there is no need to think of that...*The Lord seeks hearts filled with love for God and their neighbor. This is the throne on which he loves to sit and on which he will appear in the fullness of his heavenly glory. 'My child, give me your heart, and all the rest I shall likewise give you', because it is in the heart of man that the Kingdom of God exists...The Lord hears the prayers of the monk as well as those of a simple lay person, provided that both have a faith without error, are truly believers and love God from the depths of their hearts, for even if their faith is only a grain of mustard seed, both of them will move mountains."[12]

12 *Little Russian Philokalia,* vol. I, St. Seraphim (Platina, CA: St. Herman Press, 1991), pp. 116-117.

Both, the monastic and the lay person, are a sign and a reference to "the wholly other." St. Tikhon of Zadonsk wrote in the same vein to ecclesiastical authorities: "Do not be in a hurry to multiply the monks. The black habit does not save. The one who wears a white habit and has the spirit of obedience, humility, and purity, he is a true monk of *interiorized monasticism.*[13]

The monasticism that was entirely centered on the last things formerly changed the face of the world. Today it makes an appeal to all, to the laity as well as to the monastics, and it points out a universal vocation. For each, it is a question of adaptation, of a personal equivalent of the monastic vows.

3. The Three Temptations, the Lord's Three Answers, and the Three Monastic Vows

The three monastic vows constitute a great charter of human liberty. *Poverty* frees from the ascendancy of the material. It is the baptismal transmutation into the new creature. *Chastity* frees from the ascendancy of the carnal. It is the nuptial mystery of the *agapé*, the marriage covenant in divine love. *Obedience* frees from the idolatry of the ego. It posits our relationship as children of the Father. All, whether monks or not, must ask God for these things in the tripartite structure of the Lord's Prayer: *obedience* to the will of the Father, the *poverty* of one who is hungry only for the substantial and eucharistic bread, and *chastity,* the purification from evil.

In Old Testament times, whenever the Israelites, as nomadic pilgrims, encountered the material civilization of "the settled countries," they discovered there three temptations: idols, opposed to *obedience,* prostitution, opposed to *chastity,* wealth, opposed to *poverty.* The prophets did not cease denouncing and fighting against the primacy of efficacy over truth, material success and its power as the standard of value, and justification of everything by

13 Anna Guippius; *Saint Tykhone de Zadonsk* (Paris), p. 15, in Russian edition. Saint Tikhon also referred to this as "untonsured monasticism"—ed. note.

force. Today's world has adopted these principles more than ever before. Formerly, against such principles were directed all the efforts of the prophets. They preached *worship* of the one God, the *purification* of the people, the practice of *charity* toward the poor.

The New Testament, in the account of the Lord's three temptations, takes up the same subject, but now under the form of a supreme and definitive revelation. The text stresses: "When the devil had tried every temptation, he departed from him."[14] The Servant of Yahweh, the *obedient* one, the *poor* one, who had "no place to lay his head," the *pure* one—"Behold, Satan has nothing in me"—went to the heart of the desert as the prototype of the monk, and proclaimed *urbi et orbi*, to the city and to the world, the triple synthesis of human existence.

Patristic thought attributes to this account a central place among the first events of the Gospel. Christ had come to fight against the evil, enslaving powers, and it is this liberating quality of his work that is in the forefront here. St. Justin[15] compared the temptations of the first and second Adam and showed in Christ the universal attitude of every son of God. Likewise, Origen saw here a decisive event that illuminates the ultimate struggle of all the faithful, for what is at stake is, neither more nor less, "*to make every man a martyr or an idolator.*"[16] He underscores the fact that the temptations were an effort to make of Christ a new source of sin, since its scope would put it on the level of original sin. For St. Irenaeus,[17] the temptation failed to make man definitively captive, and consequently the brilliant victory of Jesus orients the combat of the Church and frees the true follower from all satanic ascendancy. "I have given you authority to tread...over all the power of your enemy."[18]

14 Lk 4:13.
15 *Dialogue with Trypho,* 103, 6.
16 *Ad. Mart.,* 32.
17 *Adv. Haer.,* V, 20, 2.
18 Lk 10:19.

Thus, from the beginning the Fathers saw in the account of the temptations in the desert, the "ultimate words" (*ultima verba*) of the Gospel message. Indeed, against the archetype of man in divine Wisdom, the tempter set up his counterplan, the man of demonic wisdom. St. Paul even mentions a demonic Pentecost (2 Corinthians 11, 4). All human history unfolds in a striking summary where everything is unsettled in one way or another. Satan advances three infallible solutions for human destiny: the alchemist miracle of the philosopher's stone; the *mystery* of occult sciences and their boundless powers; and finally, one unifying *authority*.

To transform stones into bread[19] is to solve the *economic problem*, to suppress "the sweat of one's brow," to eliminate all ascetic efforts, and creation itself. To cast oneself down from the temple is to suppress the temple and even the need for prayer. It is to substitute magic power for God, to triumph over the principle of necessity, and to solve the *problem of knowledge*. Now knowledge without limits brings submission to cosmic and carnal elements, the immediate satisfaction of all covetousness, a duration made up of "little eternities of enjoyment," the destruction of chastity. Finally, to unite all nations by the power of a single weapon is to solve the *political problem*, suppress war and inaugurate the era of the peace of this world.

The first act took place between the God-Man and Satan. If Christ had prostrated himself before Satan, Satan would have retired from the world, because there would be nothing for him to do there. In ultimate captivity, humanity would live without knowing the freedom of choice, for it would never attain to good or evil.

Temptation would weigh once again and heavily in the prayer of our Lord: "Father, if it is possible, let this cup pass from me."[20] What the Father did not do, Satan could do, and he offered the

---

19 It is to make "bread without sweat."
20 Mt 26:39.

very real possibility of definitively withdrawing the cup and escaping the cross. The tragedy of God and of man would then have been resolved in a demonic "happy ending."

We must take an exact measure of the adversary and grasp the scope of the evil that forces God to leave "the summit of silence," and to utter the cry: "Why hast thou forsaken me?" It makes temptation very real, without doing anything fictitious or setting any stage. In leaving Lucifer the free will to pervert himself into the Evil One, God has posed to himself the question of being the *Unique* or not, at the risk of finding himself a Being alone, suffering and abandoned. To the God who entered time, Satan proposed an infallible messiahship that would have no risk of suffering, and that would be founded on a triple suppression of freedom, on a triple slavery of man: the violation of his freedom by miracle, mystery and power.[21]

The divine refusal changed nothing in the disposition of the tempter. His project continues to be offered to us, and it is this second act that conditions history.

The cruel times of the persecutions force one to salute the Christian empire. The paradoxical canonization of Constantine, declared "Saint," bears witness to the positive element of his gesture, justified dialectically by the principle of "economy." The Church was imposed on the pagan world. She obtained a wide hearing. Would the Church succeed? This is another question. In this confrontation, one party is going "to soil its hands," another will keep them clean from the compromise. Both are necessary and both complement each other. Moreover, it was not the official, functional Church that spoke the words of life. This task was given to the fathers of the Councils, and above all to those great spiritual masters, the monastics. The entire significance of monasticism is in the freedom of spirit that the exceptional culture of

21 This aspect of the three temptations is at the center of "The Legend of the Grand Inquisitor" of Dostoyevski.

charismatics would enjoy in the fringes of the world and of the established Church.

We must admit that the empire proclaimed Christian was built on the three solutions of Satan, certainly not entirely nor consciously, but in mingling light with darkness, God and Caesar, the suggestions of Satan and the refutations of Christ. It was an ambiguous empire, for it distorted the cross. No "Christian State" as a State has ever been a crucified State. It is about the Church that John of Saroug asks the question: "What bride has ever chosen a crucified one as a spouse?" On the contrary, misguided notions about the protective power of the cross delivers defenseless princes and politicians without defense to the three temptations. Constantine founded an empire whose greatness and prosperity were more dangerous than the cruelties of Nero.

It was at this moment that monasticism entered upon the stage of history. It is the most categorical *no* to all compromise, to all conformity, to all cooperation with the tempter, disguised now in imperial robes, now by the episcopal miter. It is the resounding *yes* to the Christ of the desert. One can never insist enough on the salvific character of monasticism. "Our Lord has left us as a heritage what he himself did when he was tempted by Satan," said Evagrius.[22] From its origin, Egyptian monasticism understood its spirituality as the continuation of the fight begun by the Lord in the desert.

While the empire found its secret temptation in the roots of Satan's three invitations, monasticism was openly built on Christ's three immortal answers. It is astonishing that no exegesis has ever recognized the triple word placed as a cornerstone in the very being of monasticism. *The three monastic vows reproduce exactly the three answers of Jesus.* As monk, Christ fulfilled them in accepting the cup and in ascending the cross "that he might destroy the works of the devil."[23] "Having cancelled the bond which stood

22 *Antirrhétique* (ed. Frankenberg), p. 472.

against us with its legal demands, this he set aside, nailing it to the cross."[24] Christ destroyed the satanic plan of triple slavery, and from the summit of the cross he announced the divine charter of triple freedom. St. Paul emphasizes this by his energetic warning in the passage that begins with "see that no one deceives you,"[25] or takes away that freedom of which the cross is the dazzling pledge. Every monastic is a *staurophore* (a cross-bearer), also a *pneumatophore* (Spirit-bearer), for the cross is the triumphant power of the Holy Spirit manifesting Christ crucified. "Give your blood and receive the Spirit," is an ancient saying which reveals that in every monastic, freedom takes flesh by the action of the Holy Spirit, each becomes an icon of freedom by that Spirit. Such were the first charismatics before democratization was necessitated by the increasing number of monastics, and before the need for organization led to the imposition of harsh monastic law. Those who knew how to make this law a source of grace responded to the authentic grandeur of monasticism. Above every organized institution, monasticism remained essentially an *event*.

Christ's three answers resounded in the silence of the desert. Therefore, it was here that the monks came in order to hear them again and to receive them as the rule of their monastic life, *in the form of the three vows.*

St. Gregory Palamas describes the type of holy monastics thus: "They have given up the enjoyment of material goods (poverty), human glory (obedience), and the evil pleasures of the body (chastity), and they have preferred an evangelical life; thus the perfect have arrived at maturity according to Christ."[26] In a letter to Paul Asen on the subject of clothes and exterior signs of the monastic degrees, St. Gregory counseled "to perfect the manner of life and not the changing of clothes." In the great figures of

23 1 Jn 3:8.
24 Col 2:14.
25 Col 2:8.
26 *P.G.,* 150, 1228.

monasticism we see how they went beyond every formal principle and every form; they passed from symbols to reality.

"I will lead her into the desert and speak to her heart."[27] This "advance of one alone toward the only One," shows the primacy of the anchorite and eremitical life over the cenobitic form. It points to an aristocracy of the spirit that frees itself from everything, even from a community and its rules. However, if one leaves society to find freedom, it is in order to find the human world again, and in a better way.

This level of freedom transcends institutional limits, and offers, as its universal significance, a solution to human destiny. The interiorized monasticism of the royal priesthood finds its own spirituality in taking to itself the equivalent of the monastic vows.

Formerly, fidelity implied the blood of martyrs or the exploits of the desert, spectacles striking in their visible grandeur. When the Constantinian epoch ended, the combat of the Christian king gave way to the martyrdom[28] and the heroism of the faithful in their daily life, which is not particularly spectacular.

4. The Vow of Poverty in the Interior Monasticism of the Laity

Our Lord's answer: "Not by bread alone does man live, but by every word that comes forth from the mouth of God," indicates the transition from the old curse, "In the sweat of your brow you shall eat bread," to the new hierarchy of values, to the primacy of spirit over matter, of grace over necessity. In the house of Martha and Mary, Jesus passed from the material meal and physical hunger to the spiritual banquet, to hunger for the one thing necessary. The version of the beatitudes in St. Luke's Gospel accentuates the reversal of situations: "Blessed are the poor...those

27 Hos 2:6.
28 Rev 20.

who hunger." Even physical poverty "in the sweat of your brow" is no longer a curse, but a sign of election placed on the humble, the last and the least, as opposed to the rich and powerful. The "poor of Israel" available for the Kingdom, and more generally "the poor in spirit," receive as a gift, freely given, "the food of angels," the Word of God in the eucharistic bread.

If the stones mentioned in the temptation had become bread, this miracle would have expelled "the poor man" above all, not the beggar who is the object of charity bazaars, but the poor One who shares his *being*, his eucharistic flesh and blood. Thus, every truly poor person, "in the sweat of his heart," shares his being. This form of poverty was preached by Fathers of the Church such as St. John Chrysostom. The Gospel requires what no political doctrine would demand from its adherents. Globally, only an economy based on need and not on profit has any chance of succeeding, but it entails sacrifices and renunciation. In an anarchy, one cannot enjoy material goods. True needs vary according to vocations, but the essential principle is found in independence of spirit regarding all possessions.

Absence of the *need to have* becomes a *need not to have*. The disinterested freedom of the spirit in regard to things restores its capacity for loving them as gifts from God. To live in what is "given in abundance" is to live between destitution and the superfluous. The monastic ideal does not preach formal poverty but a wise frugality of needs.

The measure of poverty, which is always very personal, requires a creative inventiveness and excludes every simplistic, sectarian mindset. The problem is not in the deprivation but in the use. It is the quality of gift that one puts in the proverbial glass of water that justifies one at the last judgment. This is why St. James makes clear the meaning of alms: "to visit orphans and widows in their affliction."[29] If there is nothing to be shared, there remains the

29 Jas 1:27.

example of the unjust steward of the Gospel parable who distrib-
utes the goods of his master (inexhaustible love) in order to win
"friendships in Christ."

He who possesses nothing becomes, like St. Symeon the New
Theologian, "the poor brother of everyone." Simeon, Anna, Joseph
and Mary were "the poor of Israel" looking for the consolation of
Israel, but they were already rich in God, for the Holy Spirit was upon
them.[30] Thus the Blessed Virgin kept all these things in her heart,
made them her very being, and the Holy Spirit made of her "the Gift
of Consolation" and "the Gate to the Kingdom."

5. The Vow of Chastity

"You shall not tempt the Lord your God." To tempt is to test. To
tempt God means to try the limits of his magnanimity. Has he not
created man "in his image," almost "a micro-god" (*microtheos*)?
"You are all gods, sons of the Most High." Conscious of his
greatness, this "little god" dares to claim the attributes of his high
dignity. To tempt the Lord in this case is to make use of God, of the
power equal to that of God, in order to satisfy one's every desire.

In the second temptation[31]—to cast himself down from the
top of the temple—it is not a question of the exploit of Icarus.
The latter only symbolized domination over the cosmic elements.
The temptation here is to covet the much vaster power to which
St. Luke refers when he writes: "I have given you authority to
tread upon serpents and scorpions, and over all the power of the
enemy; and nothing shall hurt you."[32] This power includes dominion over space. To throw oneself down from the roof of the
temple would be to overcome earth's gravity and to rule the heavens
and the spirits. "Do not rejoice in this, that the spirits are subject to
you (the submission of which Satan speaks); rejoice rather in this,

30 Lk 2:25.
31 Mt 4:6.
32 Lk 10:19-20.

that your names are written in heaven." The *name* designates the person. The text speaks of the joy of seeing oneself admitted into the spiritual heaven of the divine presence. We see here the message of the freedom of the children of God and of their heavenly power as opposed to all temptation by the power of earthly magic.

In the hands of "gurus," this magic power arouses the collective passions of crowds. It hypnotizes, charms and dominates. For everyone this magic means the power over space and all that it contains on the material plane. It violates the mystery of nature, profanes the sacredness of the cosmos, the creation of God.

We must remember the close relationship between woman and the cosmos. The whole gamut of pagan mysteries prefigured this even up to the cult of the Virgin Mary—"Blessed Land, Promised Land, Abundant Harvest." These liturgical names are the cosmic symbols of the new Eve—*Virgin and Mother.* This mysterious linkage explains the command not to tempt God, not to sully and profane *chastity.* This virtue goes beyond the physiological and expresses the entire and chaste structure of the human spirit. It constitutes the charism of the sacrament of marriage. In a wider sense, it inspires the meaning of the sacredness of every particle of God's creation, inviolable in its expectation of salvation that is to come from one who is chaste.[33] The power of chastity is the opposite of the power of magic and signifies the return to the true "supernaturally natural power" of paradise.[34] "Thou shalt not tempt thy God" means then that you shall not make of your conformity to God the accomplice of your passions, the opposite of chastity.

Origen speaks of the "chastity of the soul"[35] which the Fathers of the desert called "the purification of the heart." Even those

33 See Rom 8:21.
34 According to St. Clement of Alexandria, the sacrament of marriage brings "an edenic grace." *P.G.,* 8, 1096.
35 *P.G.,* 12, 728C.

monastics who were once married attained this spiritual progress. There was already a transcendence of the physiological state itself.

Chaste love is attracted by the heart that remains virginal beyond every physical consideration. According to the Bible, there is a total "knowledge" of two beings, a conversation of spirit with spirit in which the body strikingly appears as the vehicle of the spiritual. This is why St. Paul says that man should learn "to take a wife for himself in holiness and honor."[36] As pure material, suitable for liturgical use, the chaste man is entirely, body and soul, the matter of the *sacrament* of marriage, with the sanctification of his love. The charism of the sacrament effects the transcendence of the self. This is the transparent presence of one for the other, of one toward the other, so that both can offer themselves together as a single being to God.

Chastity—*sophrosyne*—integrates all the elements of the human being into a whole that is virginal and interior to the spirit. That is why St. Paul speaks of the salvation of every mother by means of chastity.[37] The Pauline dialectic of the circumcision of the flesh interiorizes it even to "the circumcised...heart."[38] The same dialectic interiorizes chastity: "He who is not spiritual in his flesh becomes carnal even in his spirit," and again, "the virginity of the flesh belongs to a small number, the virginity of the heart should belong to all."[39]

Love penetrates to the very root of instinct and "changes even the substance of things," says St. John Chrysostom.[40] It raises the empirical aims to the ends created by the spirit, and makes of them a pure source of immaterial joy.

Familiarity with icons purifies the imagination, teaches "the fasting of the eyes" in order to contemplate beauty chastely. In the beauty of the body, the soul is its form, and in the beauty of the soul, the image of God delights us. Islamic wisdom has under-

36 I Thess 4:4.
37 I Tim 2:15.
38 Rom 2:26-29.
39 St. Augustine, *Enarr. in Ps.* 147.
40 *P.G.,* 61, 273.

stood this, as can be seen in the saying: "The paradise of the faithful gnostic is his own body, and the hell of the man without faith or gnosis is equally his own body."[41]

Bishop Nonnus of Edessa, in contemplating the beauty of a dancer (the future St. Pelagia), "took it as a subject for glorifying the sovereign beauty, of which her beauty was only the reflection, and feeling himself transported by the fire of divine love, shed tears of joy...He was raised," continues St. John Climacus, "to a wholly incorruptible state before the universal resurrection."[42]

An erotic imagination decomposes the spirit by an inextinguishable thirst for hell. On the contrary, the sign of chastity, according to Clement of Rome, is when a Christian, looking at a woman, has no carnal thought in his mind. "O singular woman, you are the entire species for me," says the poet of the "one" in singing of chaste conjugal love.

The story of Tobias admirably describes the victory over concupiscence. The angel's name, Raphael, signifies "the remedy of God." It is the chastity that is present in every *great love* when it is kindled by the "blazing fire of the Eternal One."[43]

Berdyaev clearly describes this inward chastity: "Love is called upon to conquer the 'old' and to discover a new flesh in which the union of two is not a loss but an accomplishment of virginity, that is, of its entirely new completeness. In this incandescent point the transfiguration of the world can uniquely begin."[44]

"To throw himself from the pinnacle of the temple"[45] means to alienate himself and to render himself useless. To this tempta-

41 See H. Corbin, *Terre céleste et corps de résurrection,* p. 161.

42 *P.G.,* 88, 893.

43 cf. Song of Songs, 8:6.

44 *Destin de l'homme* (Paris), p. 260, in Russian edition. [*The Destiny of Man,* (NY, Harper and Row, 1935).]

45 The treatise *Beracot* of Talmud of Babylon (fol. 55) contains the following passage: "The one who climbs in a dream onto a roof will climb to greatness; the one who comes down from a roof will come down from greatness." Satan's secret desire is to make the Son come down from the summit of divine greatness.

tion and to the *concupiscence* that inclines a man to seize the power that Christ possesses, even over the angels, the response is *chastity*. "To cast himself down" designates the movement from the high to the low, from heaven to hell. This was Lucifer's exact itinerary and that of the fall of man which brought about concupiscence. Chastity is an ascension. It is the Savior's itinerary, from hell to the Father's Kingdom. It is also an inward ascension toward the burning presence of God. It is in the spirit that one casts oneself into the presence of God, and chastity is only one of the names of the nuptial mystery of the Lamb.

6. The Vow of Obedience

"You shall love the Lord your God and him only shall you worship." The liturgical definition of man, the being who sings "Holy, holy, holy," the *Trisagion* and the *Sanctus,* excludes all passivity. True obedience to God implies the supreme freedom that is always creative. Christ shows this in his manner of fulfilling the whole of the Law. He fulfills and raises the Law to his own mysterious truth. He makes the Law grace. Likewise the negative and restrictive form of the Decalogue—"You shall not"—is fulfilled in giving way to the Beatitudes, to the positive and limitless creation of holiness.

Obedience in the Gospel is receptive to truth, and this above all sets one free. This is why God does not issue orders, but he makes appeals and invitations: "Hear, O Israel." "If anyone wills..." "If you wish to be perfect..." It is an invitation to find freedom again: "If anyone wishes to come to me and does not hate his..."—the possessive adjective here indicates a captive state, and "hate" means to free oneself from it in order to find the true nonpossessive charity.

It is an enlightened teaching that comes from the school of "spiritual fathers." They warn of the great danger inherent in searching for a helper. The greater the authority of a father, the

greater should be his self-effacement. A disciple can indeed formulate the true and only aim of his request: "Father, tell me what
the Holy Spirit suggests to you to heal my soul."[46] Abba Poemen
defines the art of a *staretz* (elder): "Never command, but be for all
an example, never a lawgiver."[47] A young man once went to an old
ascetic to be instructed in the way of perfection, but the old man
did not say a word. He asked the elder the reason for his silence.
"Am I then a superior to command you?" he answered. "I shall say
nothing. Do, *if you want*, what you see me do." From then on the
young man imitated the old ascetic in everything and learned the
meaning of silence and of free obedience.[48]

A spiritual father is never "a director of conscience." He is before
all else a charismatic. He does not engender his spiritual son, he
engenders a son of God. Both *mutually* place themselves in the school
of truth. The disciple receives the gift of spiritual attention, the father
receives that of being the organ of the Holy Spirit. St. Basil advises us
to find "a friend of God," who gives the assurance that God speaks
through him. "Call no one father" means that all fatherhood shares in
the unique fatherhood of God, that all obedience is obedience to the
Father's will in sharing in the acts of the obedient Christ.

John of Lycopolis counsels: "Discern your thoughts according
to God. If you cannot, ask one who is capable of discerning
them."[49] The aim is to destroy the wall raised by desires between
the soul and God. To those who have practiced the art of humility,
Theognostus says: "The one who has practiced submission and
spiritual obedience and has made his body subject to his spirit, has
no need of any submission to a man. He is subject to the Word of
God and to his law, and is truly obedient."[50] And again: "He who
wishes to dwell in the desert should not need to be taught. He

46 *Apophthegmata Patrum.*
47 *P.G.*, 65, 363, 65, 564.
48 *P.G.*, 65, 224.
49 See *Recherches de science religieuse*, 41 (1953), p. 526.
50 *The Philokalia*, vol. II, p. 361.

ought to be himself a teacher, otherwise he will suffer..."[51] However, this is for the strong. The advice explains the essential—no
obedience to human elements, no idolatry of a spiritual father,
even if he is a saint. Every counsel of a *staretz* leads one to a state
of freedom before the face of God.

Obedience crucifies our own will in order to arouse the final
freedom—the spirit listening to the Holy Spirit.

7. Christian Unity and Monastic Freedom

When there have been historical distortions, they have betrayed
the magnificent type of monastic, one absolutely free in the
service of his King.[52] They have made him a being broken by
submission to harsh laws.

While we may notice, from the time of the Middle Ages, a
divorce between mystical spirituality and theology, *the world of
today has need of saints of genius,* in order to find again the unity of
prayer and dogma. For the Fathers of the Church: "A theologian
is one who knows how to pray." "For those who are not capable of
receiving the burning rays of Christ, the saints are there to furnish
them with a light. This illumination is inferior, but since they are
scarcely capable of receiving it, it is sufficient to fill them."[53]

Whoever builds his life on the three monastic vows does so
also on the three replies of Christ. By these three vows a Christian
is not bound but is free. The Christian can then turn to the world
and tell what he has seen in God. If the Christian has learned how
to grow to the stature of "the new man," of maturity in Christ, the
world will listen to him.

The one who *knows* because his faith sees the invisible. The
one who can raise the dead, if God wishes it, because he already

51 *Vitae Patrum,* VII, 19, 6.
52 Mark the Ascetic declares: "After baptism, the exploit of every Christian is solely the
affair of his faith and of his freedom" (*P.G.,* 65, 985).
53 Origen, *In Joann.,* I, I, 25.

lives "the little resurrection," the one who can glimpse *meaning* because he can put the true name to everything, having the name of Jesus "attached" as it were to his every breath—this one can inaugurate the last times and announce the *Parousia.*

The division of Christianity is not at all an obstacle, but a lack of true freedom, rooted in complete Truth. More than anyone else, monastics can bring about this unity because they would do it *liturgically.* Their "orthodoxy" does not harden anything into rules. It opens all the pathways. In their adoration and songs of praise, they exclude no one. They invite each and every one to "adulthood" in Christ. Such maturity places one beyond distorted situations in the body of Christ, at the level of the One and Only.

According to the beautiful sayings of St. Symeon the New Theologian, the Holy Spirit fears no one and despises no one. As an image of the Holy Spirit, monasticism is a living ecumenical *epiklesis*, a coming down of the Holy Spirit. Unity can be found only in this dimension of universal monasticism, if it makes itself as free as the breath of the great liberator, the Holy Spirit.

8

The Human Being

The Bible knows nothing of the Greek dualism of mind and body in conflict, of the body as the prison of the soul. It knows only the moral struggle between the desire of the Creator and the desires of the creature, between what is normal—holiness—and sin-perversion, but in this conflict the entire person is engaged. Thus, the opposition between *man as animal and as spiritual* concerns the totality of the human being. According to St. Augustine, we are carnal even in our spirit or spiritual even in our flesh.

The soul vivifies the body and makes it living flesh. The spirit spiritualizes and makes of both a spiritual being. The spirit does not place the soul and body side by side, but manifests itself through the psychic and the corporeal, qualifying them by its energies. In accordance with this structure of the human being, asceticism constitutes a very exact science and a vast culture that renders the body and the soul transparent and submissive to the spiritual. On the other hand, we can "extinguish the spirit,"[1] cause the source of our life to dry up, have carnal thoughts and reduce ourselves to animal flesh, the prey of death and hell.

The biblical vision thus allows us to take an exact measure of evil and to discover its secret origins. Sin never comes from below, from the flesh, but from above, from the spirit. The first fall occurred in the world of angels, pure spirits.

Carnal perversion manifests and condemns the *sin of the spirit against the flesh.* That is why chastity transcends physiology alone

1 1 Thess 5:19.

and depends upon the entire structure of the spirit. The emptiness of a roaming, uncentered spirit causes dispersion of its energies. Conversely, spiritual masters teach the silence of the heart, "the language of the future world," and the recollection that is opposed to all dissipation of thought. They seek inwardly saying: "Do not seek anything outside, but enter within yourself, into your heart, and there find God, the angels, and the Kingdom."

The *heart* of which the Bible speaks does not coincide, however, with the emotional center of which the psychologists speak. The Jews thought with their hearts. As a metaphysical center, it integrates all the faculties of the human being. Reason, intuition and will are never strangers to the choices and sympathies of the heart. Radiating and penetrating everywhere, it is nevertheless hidden in its own mysterious depths. "Know thyself" is addressed above all to this secret heart.

"Who can understand the heart," Jeremiah asks, and he immediately answers, "I, the Lord, alone probe the mind and test the heart."[2] This means God alone can penetrate to the hidden sphere of the unconscious and subconscious. St. Peter also speaks of "the inner life of the heart."[3] It is at this unfathomable depth that the human ego resides. St. Gregory of Nyssa clearly indicated this depth, showing it to be in the image of God: "Man, in his *unknowability* of himself, manifests the imprint of the ineffable."[4]

"Where thy treasure is, there also will thy heart be."[5] We are worth the desires of our hearts and the objects of our love. "The prayer of Jesus," called "the prayer of the heart," makes the heart the place of his presence, "for God has put into the human heart the desire for him."[6] To find in God that which is absolutely desirable and to place one's heart there reveals an astonishing

2 Jer 17:9-10.
3 1 Pet 3:4.
4 *P.G.*, 44, 155.
5 Mt 6:21.
6 St. Gregory of Nyssa, *P.G.*, 44, 801A.

intimacy with God. Indeed, the Gospel places above the morality of slaves and mercenaries that of *the friends of God.* "No longer do I call you servants...but I have called you friends,"[7] Christ said. God does even more in asking us to accomplish his will as if it were our own will. In saying "Thy will be done," we say, "I desire it, it is my will that thine be done." Such a harmony between the two *fiats,* the yes of the one and the other, raises the human person to the level of the heart of God.

The Latin word *persona,* as well as the Greek *prosopon,* signifies "mask," and contains a profound philosophy of the human person. To exist is to participate in being or in nothingness. I can make of myself "an icon of God" or acquire a demonic face, a horrible distortion of God. "He who is near me is near the fire," declares an ancient *agraphon* (unwritten tradition).[8] The one who understands it "does not cease adding fire to fire."[9] One can revive either the flame of love or the fire of Gehenna. We can convert our *yes* into an infinity of unions. We can also, by our *no,* fragment our being into infernal separations and solitudes.

Created in the image and likeness of God, we possess an essential orientation that determines us. The resemblance proferred is in the personal realization of the objective image. It releases the *epektasis,* the tension of striving toward the Most High. As every copy is attracted to its original, man as an image aspires to go beyond himself in order to cast himself into God and to find there the appeasement of his longing. Holiness is nothing else but an unquenchable thirst, the intensity of desire for God. By its light the asceticism of spiritual attention learns the inestimable art of seeing everything as an image of God. "A perfect monk," says St. Nilus of Sinai, "will esteem after God all others as God himself."[10] This iconographic manner of looking at every person

7 Jn 15:15.
8 A. Resch. *Agrapha,* 150.
9 St. John Climacus, *The Ladder of Divine Ascent, P.G.,* 88, 644A.
10 See Evagrius, *De Oratione,* 123.

explains the astonishing optimism of the great ascetics, the striking tone of their joy, their authentically evangelical appreciation
of man. They always show an infinite respect for man as "the place
of God."

St. Seraphim addressed everyone he met as "My joy." He saw
in each person God himself coming to meet him. He read his love
on every face, and joyously saluted his presence.[11]

As created incarnate spirits, we are placed between the spirituality of the angels and the carnal corporeality of this world. St.
Gregory of Palamas saw in this situation our primacy over the
angels. The angels are "the second lights," reflecting the light of
God. Man is *transmuted* into light and illumines the world. "You
are the light of the world." In the icons, the nimbus of the saints
shows this. The cosmic nature of the world as well as his own
body is the biosphere of the human spirit. As artists and creators,
we are called upon to create the values of the Kingdom, and this
is why the angels serve us.

11 See our study, "St. Seraphim of Sarov," in *The Ecumenical Review* (April, 1963), also
reprinted as *St. Seraphim, Icon of Orthodox Spirituality,* (Minneapolis: Light & Life).

9

The Asceticism of the Spiritual Life

"Put on the whole armor of God, that you may be able to stand against the wiles of the devil."[1] St. Paul exhorts all the faithful to train themselves in the combats of the faith using metaphors from military life and from sports—the soldier and the athlete.

The word "asceticism" comes from the Greek *askesis* and means exercise, effort, exploit. One can speak of athletic asceticism when it seeks to render the body supple, obedient, resistant to every obstacle. The asceticism of scientists and doctors shows the magnificent abnegation that sometimes costs them their lives.

Monastic tradition has given to this term a very precise meaning. It designates the interior combat necessary for the spiritual person to acquire a mastery over the material world.

Among the first monks, there were some called Messalians, who hoped to form an aristocracy of super-Christians. Tradition, especially in St. Basil, has always rejected this false conception. In his works, St. Basil hesitated to use the word "monk" on account of these messalianic pretensions. He insisted in his *Rules* on the fact that the monk is anyone of the faithful who wishes to be thoroughly Christian to the very end. He did not wish to hear monasticism spoken of as a state above another. A saying of Macarius specifies that "a monk is called a monk because he converses day and night with God."[2] This is a grace given to all Christians.

1 Eph 6:11.
2 Paul Evergetinos, *Synagoge Rematon,* Const. 1861, I, p.75, c. 2.

In this wide sense Christian asceticism protects the spirit from being held captive by the world. It recommends overcoming evil by the creation of the good. Thus asceticism is never anything but a means, a strategy. Evagrius gave the counsel never to make a passion out of the ascetic means against the passions. "Do not turn into a passion the antidote of the passions,"[3] he said. He thus foresaw the ascetic obscurantism that would consider itself an end. This comes from an excessive concentration on sin and from a mortification in which the ends and the means are identical. "Because many who used to weep over their sins have forgotten the aim of tears, they have been seized with madness and have been led astray."[4] We can create a morbid and fantastic atmosphere where we see only evil and sin, where we live in the company of demons and in the fear of hell. We must admit that some ascetic literature fosters such a state of mind, but there is an abyss between the Gospel and such literature. In the Gospel it is God who speaks. In mediocre texts it is a misguided human voice which discourses without ever having assimilated the spirit of the Gospel. Christ was a perfect ascetic, but he lived among us and descended into our hell in order to bring his light there. Then the good thief, in a moment of repentance, sees opening before him the door to the Kingdom, and tax-collectors and sinners may perhaps advance beyond "the righteous ascetics" on the path of salvation.

The Gospel is messianic and explosive. Its rejection of the world is unique, for it is never ascetic but eschatological. It sets before us the exigency of the end, the balance sheet, the passage to fullness (the pleroma). During the liturgy, before the anaphora, there is a command to close the doors of the church. In fact one closes the doors of time and opens the one giving access to eternity. All of history enters and finds itself "in the marriage chamber of Christ."[5]

3 De Oratione, 7. See The Philokalia, vol. I, Palmer, Sherrard, Ware, trans. (London and Boston: Faber and Faber, 1979), p.58.

4 Ibid, p. 58.

5 Maximus Confessor: Selected Writings, George C. Berthold, trans. (Mahwah, NJ: Paulist Press, 1985), "The Church's Mystagogy," p. 201.

The Gospel ascetic is a witness and an apostle. That is why the monastic tradition, which came later than that of the desert, dwelt upon the letters of St. John and insisted on love of one's neighbor and the asceticism of the heart. It is striking in its excess, not of fear, but of overflowing love and of cosmic tenderness "for every creature, even for reptiles and demons."[6]

The "individual salvationist" who is concerned only with the salvation of his own soul manifests a dangerous distortion. We can never stand alone before God; we are only saved together, "collegially," as Soloviev said: *he will be saved who saves others.* St. Dorotheus[7] gives a beautiful and clear picture of salvation by the image of a circle. Its center is God, and all people are on the circumference. In directing oneself toward God, each follows a radius of the circle, and the more one approaches the center, the nearer the paths are to one another. Thus the shortest distance between God and each person is through one's neighbor. Those exclusively devoted to action should understand that the hermits, by their incessant prayer, intervened actively in history. The efficacy of all human action is dependent on the intercession of their faith, on the fervor of the prayer that they send into the heart of the world. They know that one cannot respond to all the cries of this earth, and that is why they become hermits. St. Isaac the Syrian (in his *Sayings*) said so to his disciple: "Here, my brother, is a commandment that I give you—let mercy shift the balance of your scales until the moment you feel in yourself the mercy that God feels toward the world." At this moment of maturity the recluse can return to the world.

This asceticism requires a great lucidity in order to see oneself as one really is. The balance that is sought is accompanied by a clear vision of one's own reality, but it advises against too much

6 St. Isaac, Wensinck, *op. cit.,* p. 341.
7 *Philocalie* (in Russian), II, 617.
   See *Dorotheus of Gaza: Discourses and Sayings,* Eric P. Wheeler, trans. (Kalamazoo, MI: Cistercian Publications, 1977).

self-analysis. To look perpetually at oneself as in a mirror can cause a morbid state of excessive scruples. More than anywhere else perfect moderation is necessary here, as well as an experienced guide and the beneficial atmosphere of a living community.

Self-love and its tyrannical wishes build a wall between the soul and God; the art of obedience destroys it.

Origen admirably explains the ministry of the elders: "In every place where masters are found, Jesus Christ is in the midst of them, on condition, however, that the masters keep themselves in the temple and never leave it."[8] "The temple" for Origen meant an uninterrupted contemplation of Jesus.

8 *Hom. in Luc.*, 20.

10

The Ascetic Effort

Spiritual masters always return to a concrete level of realistic efforts in order to open the soul and make it receptive and active. They are not concerned with doctrinal abstractions, with a search for merits or with prescriptions of grace and freedom. They left this preoccupation to the theologians and expressed themselves only in terms of experience. "God *does everything* in us...What is ours is the good disposition of our will."[1] If they spoke of "labor and sweat," they meant the human action within the divine action. We formulate it in this manner: God "works," and we "sweat."

Asceticism has nothing to do with moralism. The opposite of sin is not virtue but the faith of the saints. Moralism exerts natural forces, and its fundamental voluntarism submits human behavior to moral imperatives. We know how fragile and ineffective every autonomous and immanent ethical system is, for it is not a source of life. We can respect a law, but we can never love it as we love a person—Jesus Christ, for example. Christ is not the principle of good but good incarnate. That is why in the tragic conflicts of existence, in the depths of some overwhelming sorrow or loneliness, moral and sociological principles are powerless. They do not have the power to say to a paralytic: "Get up and walk!" They cannot pardon or absolve, wipe out a fault or raise the dead. Built into a system, such principles' rigid, impersonal and general appearance hides the pharisaism of "the pride of the humble." This is pride's most dangerous form, for once "pride is taken for humility, the illness is without remedy."[2]

1 St. Maximus the Confessor, Ad. *Thal.,* q. 54, *P.G.,* 90 512D. See *The Philokalia,* vol. II (London and Boston: Faber and Faber, 1981), pp. 114-163.
2 Ignatius Brianchaninov, *Oeuvres* (in Russian), Vol. I, p. 619.

163

On the other hand, the "virtue" of the ascetics has an entirely different resonance and designates human dynamism set in motion by the presence of God. There is no question here of any "meritorious" work. "God is our creator and savior. He is not the one who measures and weighs the price of our works."

No juridical idea of recompense is applicable here. "My child, give me your heart." These words of the Old Testament already announce the Gospel. "Seek the Kingdom of God and all these things shall be given you besides."[3] In seeking the one thing needful, we put ourselves in harmony with it, and give our heart as an offering. What comes from God is the Kingdom, and this is a free gift. "If God regarded merits, then no one would enter the Kingdom of God."

The spiritual masters, in their search for salvation, are not concerned with the mercantile calculations of those who are too interested in their own lot. Humility forbids our feeling "saved," but it makes us think ceaselessly of the salvation of others. The soul is occupied above all with God's destiny in the world, and with the response that God expects from us. In the vision of mystics, God sometimes appears as abandoned and suffering in his wounded love. If it is necessary to save anything in this world, it is not human action before all else, but the love of God, for he has first loved us and his power bears and sustains the expected response. In the interaction of grace and sin formulated by the theologians, the spiritual masters contemplate the interaction of the *two fiats*, the encounter of the descending love of God and the ascending love of man.

If "man is condemned and saved at the same time,"[4] and if "the Church is the salvation of those who are perishing,"[5] this can be a question only of the full expression of our faith. It is the free

3 Lk 12:31.
4 St. Ambrose, *P.L.* 15, 1502.
5 St. Ephrem the Syrian, quoted by Father Georges Florovsky, *Les Pères du IVe siècle* (Paris, 1931), p. 232, in Russian edition.

choice not of "works" but of the irresistible desire to be a child of God. It is for me to open the door of my soul so that he can enter. I can only prostrate myself and hide my face as did the disciples on Tabor, blinded by the splendor of his presence. The violence of which the Gospel speaks refers to the human heart. That is why "God will judge the *hidden* secrets of men."[6] He will judge them because we are masters of our hearts.

6 Rom 2:16.

11

The Progression of the Spiritual Life

Seen from below, the spiritual life seems to be an incessant combat, an "invisible struggle," where every pause becomes a regression. Seen from above, it is the acquisition of the gifts of the Holy Spirit. This double movement stands out clearly in the prayer addressed to the Holy Spirit: "Cleanse us from every impurity," but also "Come and *abide* in us."

This purification begins with a most realistic vision of one's state. "Know thyself " was the ascetic teaching of Socrates. "No one can know God unless he first knows himself."[1] "The one who has seen his sin is greater than he who raises the dead." "He who has seen himself is greater than he who has seen the angels."[2] Our vigorous penetration into the darkness of our heart of hearts, though it is a formidable undertaking, gives us the power to judge ourselves. We must make the descent supplied with an ascetic diving suit, the spirit of discernment, in order to explore its caverns populated by phantoms, and to seize our perverted will, and our anticipated death, in short, our irremediable natural deficiency. This is the triple barrier of nature, sin and death that the Lord has passed through for us all. The vision must be brief, instantaneous, in order to avoid all pleasure in sorrow or despair. Sin is never a subject of contemplation. We must set our eyes on what obliterates it—grace. The soul can now truly utter the cry: "From the abyss of my iniquity I invoke the abyss of your mercy."

1 *Philocalie* (in Russian), Vol. V, p. 159.
2 St. Isaac, *Sayings*.

The ascent is gradual. Thus the *Ladder of Divine Ascent* of St. John Climacus describes the upward progress as following the rungs or steps in the order that he has studied perfectly. Charity, for example, is placed at the end, crowning the ascent and situated at the top of the ladder. An insightful teacher, St. John warns against any activity of emotional love, for here it is a question of crucified love. The great spiritual masters left their solitude and returned to the world at the moment of their perfect maturity. The wisdom of Climacus shows souls how to avoid many failures and disappointments, for some are too impatient, forgetting the Gospel's words, "Physician, cure thyself."[3]

Mindful of the *metanoia* or conversion, the spiritual life takes its point of departure in *humility.* A spiritual person is a saint who confesses himself a sinner. "Anthony said in groaning: Who will then escape? And a voice answered him: Humility."[4] Abba Sisoes at the moment of his death, being already fully enlightened, said humbly: "I have not even begun to repent."[5] These words mean that repentance is the ever more acute awareness of the love of God and of our inadequate response. It is not an act that can be finished, but a constant state of the soul which deepens the nearer it approaches the end.

For the ascetics, humility signifies the art of finding one's own place. "He who knows his exact measure possesses perfect humility."[6] While we of the world covet what is inordinate and excessive and desire to be the master and the bridegroom, the Gospel gives us a luminous picture of humility. St. John the Baptist finds all his joy in being only the friend of the bridegroom, and the Blessed Virgin finds her joy in being the handmaid of the Lord. They decrease in order that the other, the true Bridegroom and Master,

3 Lk 4:23.
4 *P.G.,* 65, 77B.
5 *P.G.,* 65, 396.
6 Callistus and Ignatius, *Philocalie* (in Russian), Vol. V, p. 330.

may increase. The one is the function of the other. God does not take his rightful place among us except when he finds perfect conformity. He came "unto his own," and he was received by his friend and his handmaid. Their humility is an exact replica of the divine humility, of the *kenosis,* the self-emptying of the servant of Yahweh, of "the Man of sorrows." It reflects and follows the Kingdom's "reversal of values." The Pantocrator, the Lord of all, becomes the lover of mankind, and the King, the crucified servant.

"Among those born of women no one has arisen greater than John the Baptist."[7] These words are antithetical for they abolish the limits of the covenants. To the "greater" corresponds the enigmatic:"the least in the Kingdom of heaven is greater than he." St. John is at the same time the greatest and the least, and he is the greatest *because he is the least.* Hearing the voice of the Bridegroom, his friend says: "This my joy, therefore, has been fulfilled."[8] The joyous self-effacement is so deep that at this level the Bridegroom and his friend converge in the ineffable grandeur that unites them. God had become man and man had become God to the point that people asked themselves whether John was not the Christ.[9] Now for all of us God manifestly places St. John and the Virgin at the summit of the universal priesthood, as a "guiding image" in the service of his Church. This is clearly shown in the composition of the *Deisis,* the icon that represents the Lord in royal garments with his mother on his right hand and his friend on his left.[10]

Nietzsche committed a flagrant error in declaring that Christianity is the religion of rebelling slaves. Over against all populist and vindictive resentment of offenses, the Christian confesses his guilt, and this is the attitude of nobility. No confusion is possible

7 Mt 11:11.

8 Jn 3:29-30.

9 Lk 3:15.

10 See our work *Woman and the Salvation of the World,* Anthony P. Gythiel, trans. (Crestwood, NY: SVS Press, 1994), pp. 227-248.

between humility and humiliation, weakness or spineless resignation. Humility is the greatest power, for it radically suppresses all
resentment, and it alone can overcome pride. The best definition
of it would be to say that it *places the axis of a human being in God.*

From the psychiatric point of view, self-centeredness is indicative of every hysteric neurosis. It makes the universe revolve
around the human ego: "I, and no one else." The desire of
equality caused the fall of Lucifer, notes St. Gregory Nazianzen.
According to St. Gregory of Nyssa, Satan was offended at learning
of the creation of man in the image of God. Likewise Islam shows
him in revolt, refusing to bow down before Adam. The anti-
Christ in Soloviev's *Legend*[11] becomes conscious of his demonic
nature at the moment he feels the impossibility of prostrating and
adoring anything but his ego. We go back here to the source of the
sin that explains the aim of asceticism: to break pride and to make
humility the unshakable foundation of the human spirit: "To
allow oneself to be ground between the grindstones of humility in
order to become a sweet and agreeable bread for our Lord."[12]

The Golden Legend tells us the story of a humble man who
had "two right hands." He had the habit of putting into his right
hand all the joys received each day and all his sorrows into his left
hand. It was his left hand that was always full. Then, through a
spirit of humility, all that fell into his left hand, he put into his
right hand, and his life became all light and joy.

11 *Les trois entretiens.*
12 An ascetic adage that goes back to St. Ignatius of Antioch, *Rom* 4, 1.

12

The Passions and the
Technique of Temptation

The biblical account of the "forbidden fruit" stresses the power of suggestion. It arouses desires by its sensual and aesthetic appeal. "The tree was good for food, pleasing to the eyes, and desirable." The arrow of temptation that wounded human freedom and perverted its choice went beyond formal disobedience. We can see the essence of the fall: the desirable fruit, sensually coveted, immerses us in the life of senses chosen in preference to a spiritual deepening of our communion with God. We appear guilty not so much negatively by disobedience, but positively by not enriching ourselves by nearness to God. "If he had attached himself to God from the very first movement of his being, he would have immediately attained his perfection," says St. Gregory of Nyssa.[1]

In its attractive appearance, the fruit symbolizes a secret covetousness of the attributes of God. The love of the human heart, originally directed toward the being of God, is no longer centered on its object, but deviating; it has oriented itself only toward his attributes, the source of enjoyment. The grace of "resemblance" gives way to the magic of equality. "You will be as God."

The mystical image of *consumed fruit* is not a coincidence. It is clearly of a eucharistic nature. Evil, a principle initially foreign to innocent mankind, is introduced into him by this consumption. Evil thus comes to be within us. On the other hand, it is God who has become exterior. The order is perverted. The biological animal

1 *P.G.,* 46, 373.

seems foreign to the true nature of man, for the animal was assumed *before* its spiritualization, before man had arrived at the mastery of the spiritual over the material. Communion with nature, good in itself, proved to be bad since it was *premature*. The error came from a premature identification. Clement of Alexandria sees original sin in the fact that "our ancestors gave themselves to procreation *before* the appointed time."[2]

Good in itself, animal nature, on account of the perversion of the hierarchy of values, now poses a permanent threat of causing the downfall of man. It was the faculty of ethical appreciation, the spirit of discernment, that was wounded. "Outside God, reason became like the beasts and the demons, and estranged from its nature, it desires what is foreign to it."[3] Illegitimate concupiscence is *against* nature. The human being is then dominated by passions, by the life of the senses. That is why asceticism, before all else, neutralizes the passions in order to objectify and exteriorize these deifugal tendencies.

We can see this remedy at work in studying the sacrament of confession. "A hidden thought destroys the heart," notes St. John Cassian.[4] The action of evil can be traced to the redoubtable *philautia,* the self-love that encloses us within ourselves. On the contrary, the opening up of the soul hinders the formation of complexes, denounces them and cures morbid scruples.[5] This is why confession entails the admission of guilt, followed by absolution. For Clement of Alexandria, the confessor is like "an angel of penance," capable of penetrating and opening the souls of sinners; he is a "physician of God." "You have come to the doctor, do not leave without being cured," says the prayer before confession. Likewise the Council of Trullo (692) defines that "those who have received from God the power of binding and loosing behave as

2 *Strom.* III, 18.
3 St. Gregory of Palamas, *Homilia,* 51.
4 *P.L.,* 49, 162.
5 Dorotheus, *P.G.,* 88, 1640C.

physicians attentive to finding the particular remedy that is required by each penitent and each fault of the penitent."[6]

An age-old experience clearly shows the danger of repressions and the liberating power of confession. "Many passions are hidden in our soul, but they escape our attention," says Evagrius.[7] This is because the fault is rooted in the soul and poisons our inner world. It calls for a surgical procedure that will cut the roots and exteriorize the fault. This necessitates the presence of a witness who will listen, and by thus destroying the solitude, will bring the penitent into the communion of the Body of Christ. Psychoanalysis has rediscovered the value of confession. It tries in its own way to lead the patient to accept a dialogue, to go beyond his very ineptitude to dialogue and the anguish that hinders him from going toward others.

Sozomen (fifth century) forcefully declares: "To ask forgiveness one must necessarily confess one's sins."[8] The soul is unburdened of the sin, but how can this be made non-existent? A bad conscience comes not only from remorse for the fault committed but also from a nostalgia for lost innocence. We seek forgiveness, but in the utmost depths of our hearts we crave the annihilation of evil. For this desired abolition, sacramental absolution is required. The fault has been exteriorized, even recounted and thus made objective, projected, so to speak, to the outside. Yet it can plague us from the outside. Sacramental absolution alone can destroy it and bring a total cure. Psychiatrists who are believers know the liberation effected by the action of the sacrament, and they often complete their treatment by sending their patients to the "ecclesial clinic." The immense importance of confession is in this final liberation. To become free again, one must know how to utilize one's past, even if it has been guilty, to create a present that

6 Canon 102.
7 *Centuries.* VI. 52.
8 *P.G.,* 67, 1460.

is again innocent. The soul's passivity and behavior, subject to instincts, must be transcended. Then we can progress in the creativity of spirit, cleansed by absolution. To escape these instincts is to become master of one's destiny, open to the liberating action of divine power.

The act of forgiveness places us in the heart of the relationship between God who is holy and man who is the sinner, and we must grasp the infinite gravity of this act. It is not a question of the almighty power of God to wipe out sin and to make it non-existent. It is rather Christ who, according to St. Paul, canceled "the decree against us...nailing it to the cross."[9] If "the Lamb is immolated from the foundation of the world," this means that the creation of the world was already rooted in the immolation of the Creator. The power to forgive comes from the price of the blood shed by the crucified Lamb. Christ takes *on himself* all the sins and transgressions of the world, and for this remains in agony until its end. Because he thus responds to the love of his Father by his ineffable love *in our stead,* he has the moral power to blot out and pardon, making us innocent children of the Father. The Lord's Prayer, "Forgive us our trespasses as we forgive," makes our "imitation" of God the condition of our pardon. We are invited to descend, in Christ's footsteps, to the hell of universal guilt where all are culpable. Every faithful member of the Orthodox Church confesses before communion: "I believe, O Lord, and I confess that You art truly the Christ, the Son of the Living God, who came into the world to save sinners of whom I am first."

The prayer before confession, accompanied by the reading of Psalm 50 is of immense significance. It testifies to the reattachment, the first reunion of the sinner—with the Church. Through the prayers of the priest, the penitent is taken in charge, as it were, by the Church. It is by her that he is then brought and presented before the face of God. It is in finding ourselves in the maternal

9 Col 2:14.

bosom of the Church that we can truly confess our sins and be healed, for every sin places us outside the body of Christ. Reintegrated into the Church, we can weep tears of repentance. These tears, says Symeon the New Theologian, "purify and confer the second baptism of which the Lord speaks, the rebirth in water and in the Spirit; the baptism of tears is no longer a figure of the truth, it is truth itself."[10] There cannot be an "automatic" effect of the sacrament. Rebirth by the Spirit requires full consciousness on the part of the one who, in "fear and trembling," crosses the abyss.

The asceticism of the spiritual life follows the path of repentance and penance. It aspires above all to free us from the ascendancy of our passions. To attain this, it fosters spiritual attention, a guard over the heart. "I sleep but my heart watches." Even in a state of sleep the spirit keeps watch. Vigilance thus practiced allows us to recognize evil before being tempted to commit it.

The ascetics give a minute description of the progression of evil, laying bare the rather simplistic technique or mechanism of temptation.

The first movement of "contamination" comes from a representation, image, idea, desire crossing our mind. Something very fleeting arises abruptly and solicits our attention. From the subconscious the appeal rises to consciousness and makes an effort to be kept there. This is not yet sin, far from it, but it is the presence of a suggestion. It is in this first moment that the immediate reaction of one's attention is decisive. The temptation is going to leave or remain. The spiritual masters make use of an image that was familiar in the desert: "Strike the serpent on the head" before he enters the cell. If the serpent enters, the struggle will be much more laborious.

If our attention does not react, the following phase is indulgence. A willing attentiveness to the tempting solicitation causes a

10 *Chapitres théologiques, gnostiques et pratiques,* J. Darrouzès, L. Neyrond, eds., Sources Chrétiennes, vol. 51 (Paris: Cerf, 1980).

certain pleasure, becoming an equivocal attitude that is already cooperating. St. Ephrem speaks of the "pleasant conversation" of the soul with a persistent suggestion.

An enjoyment by anticipation, imaginary at the moment, marks the third stage. A tacit agreement, an unavowed consent, orients one toward an accomplishment deemed possible, for it is passionately desirable. Theoretically, the decision has indeed been made. In coveting the object, the sin has been mentally committed. This is the judgment of the Gospel on the impure gaze in which adultery has already been pre-consummated.

The fourth stage effectively consummates the act. It forms the beginning of a passion, of a thirst henceforth unquenchable. When it has become a habit, the passion neutralizes every resistance. The person disintegrates in powerlessness. Bewitched, he leans toward his implacable end: despair, fearful *accedia,* disgust or anxiety, madness or suicide, in all cases, spiritual death.

III

The Charisms of Spiritual Life
and the Mystical Ascent

1

The Evolution of the Spiritual Life
in the East and in the West

In the West, after the contributions of the Irish missionaries, who introduced a most austere rule—St. Columban's *maxima pars regulare monachorum mortificatio est*, "The principal part of the monastic life and rule is mortification: death of self."—St. Benedict's spirituality dominated. It followed the ancient tradition of St. Basil, above all, and of St. John Cassian. A well-balanced asceticism regulated and divided the monk's time among the *lectio divina* (spiritual reading), chanting of the office, fasting and manual labor. However, this balance did not last long. The Cluny Benedictines made the offices more solemn, prolonged them too, in order to lessen the manual work that was not very attractive to the monks. Citeaux was established in reaction to Cluny. The Cistercians returned to the greatest severity in the rule, and were striking in the sobriety and bareness of their style of life, and by the deliberate poverty of their abbeys: *cum Christe paupere paupers* (to be poor with Christ, the poor one).

The Camaldolese of St. Romuald and the Carthusians of St. Bruno cultivated the eremitical life alongside life in community. From the beginning of the Middle Ages, penance was introduced among the austere hermits with extreme means of discipline, flagellation and the hairshirt. It was a potentially dangerous throw-back to the asceticism of the desert, to which was added a completely new element—mortification practiced in view of an expiation for sins committed and also in view of a reparation for the sins of the world. It is sufficient here to mention Peter Damian.

The eleventh century saw the growth of pilgrimages to sanctuaries—Jerusalem, St. James of Compostella, Rome. A mass of pilgrims took to the road as beggars. The Crusades led the Westerners to Palestine. This discovery was decisive for Western mysticism: it made a strong impression on the imagination of the West and aroused an ardent imitation, a conformity to the humanity of the historic Christ of the Gospel. The twelfth century turned its asceticism and spirituality towards the image of Jesus, poor, humiliated and crucified. St. Francis espoused Lady Poverty and received the stigmata. Later Henry Suso gave himself to extreme mortification in imitation of Jesus scourged.

In the thirteenth century the Dominicans emphasized study to the point of making an asceticism of it. On the other hand, St. Bernard and St. Bonaventure accentuated the monastic vows and again took up the classical stages of the spirituality of Dionysius: purgation, illumination, perfection (*purgatio, illuminatio, perfectio*).

The end of the Middle Ages was marked by a certain lack of spirit and an impoverishment of the spiritual life. Scholastic studies were directed to the intellect and replaced spiritual reading (*lectio divina*) and prayerful contemplation; prayer itself became formalistic. What is called *devotio moderna* widened the gap between spirituality and an increasingly speculative theology. The Dutch school of Gerard de Groote inspired Thomas à Kempis, whose *Imitation of Christ* summarizes the tendencies of the recent past and makes concrete this unfortunate divorce. Union with God also meant anti-intellectualism, a reaction against scholastic theology and knowledge. In its effort to escape the dryness and rigidity of formal rules, fifteenth-century piety threw itself into the emotionalism of sorrow and suffering. Intense devotion to the suffering humanity of Christ developed into a cult of sorrow with disturbing forms of mortification.

The Renaissance humanized asceticism, aligning it with its integral but still devout humanism. Spirituality fragmented into a multitude of devotional practices. In the sixteenth century, the spirituality of Ignatius of Loyola made asceticism a method and a technique of conversion, and St. Francis de Sales formed, in the beginning of the following century, a psychological asceticism of the interior states. They both went beyond the monastic environment and initiated a secular asceticism.

Asceticism became more psychological, attentive to states of consciousness. St. Thomas had already analyzed the ecstasy of St. Paul and had shown a lively interest in the relation between soul and body and the modes of knowledge. Likewise, with St. Teresa and St. John of the Cross, Spanish mysticism analyzed the interior and psychological aspect of the mystical ascent.

The asceticism of St. Cyran, Port Royal and Jansenism mistrusted human nature. Its soteriological and pastoral preoccupation accentuated the rigorist austerity of the penitential practices imposed upon the faithful. Besides its moral relaxation, the eighteenth century, in which the austerity of the seventeenth was in a sense prolonged, manifested a spirituality that appears intellectually impoverished and somewhat static, without the spontaneity and warmth of former times.

A special reaction manifested itself in quietism, but it was with St. Margaret Mary Alacoque that the entirely new devotion to the Sacred Heart showed *reparational asceticism.* Mortification in order to satisfy divine justice and on behalf of all sinners took the place of the effort for personal perfection.

The shock of the French Revolution accentuated the practices of reparational penance and expiatory asceticism. The psychologism and rationalism of the nineteenth century even more completely separated spirituality from dogma and theology. At present we are witnessing a vigorous return to the sources of the patristic past and original monasticism.

If we turn toward the East, we shall see that it has remained faithful to the spirituality of former times that had been common to both East and West. Eastern monasticism had already reached a peak of development in the fifth and sixth centuries. Under Justinian it was proclaimed "a sacred thing" and "mystery", because it expresses in a compact and exemplary form the universal vocation of the priesthood of the faithful, because each and every one is called to interiorize and adapt it. The priesthood does not come into play here except as sacramental ministry. It does not constitute an essential element of monastic vocation.

As an organic part of the Church, monastic spirituality synthesizes the ideal life offered, in its general outlines, to all. The dogmatic definitions on hesychasm in the fourteenth century only stated precisely what had existed from the beginning and showed the homogeneous character of Eastern spirituality. It is inseparable from "mystical theology," a theology of mystery that came to full expression during the golden age of the Fathers.

At the present time, the two spiritualities—Eastern and Western—complement each other; we can apply the saying of Evagrius: "The *gnosticos* (knower) and the *practicos* (doer) have met, and in the midst of them is the Lord."[1] They meet in search of the essence of the experience of the past in order to establish a balanced spirituality, freed from the extreme forms that were stressed too much in the asceticism of a past age. This is a spirituality rooted in eschatology, in the Kingdom, fully conscious of the present state of the world, and preoccupied, above all, with its destiny.

---

1 *Aux moines qui habitent dans les coenobia*, 121. See Evagrius Ponticus: *The Praktikos; Chapters on Prayer*, J. E. Bamberger, trans., Spencer, MA: Cistercian Publications, 1970).

2

The Passage from the Old Testament to the New

In the days of the old covenant, spiritual life was manifested in three forms—almsgiving, prayer and fasting. It received its completion in the Sermon on the Mount that placed it in the service of evangelical love. The post-apostolic age added to it martyrdom and celibacy without making them a novelty. Indeed in late Judaism, believers sealed the confession of their faith with their blood. Furthermore, St. John the Baptist reflected the spirituality of the Essenes, and the Lord and the apostles scandalized no one by their celibacy. On the whole, this spirituality responded to the call of the one thing needful and sought freedom from the bonds of this world in order to go more joyfully to meet the One who was coming.

The great joy and optimism of the first spiritual teachers came from their unshakable trust in the image of God. Christ shows this conformity of the divine and the human, already full of grace by its nature and makes it efficacious for all. In its dynamic function, it is "a guiding image" toward the fullness of healing. The Bible stresses the therapeutic understanding of salvation, and thus shapes Christian spirituality at its very source.

In the light of revelation, salvation has nothing juridical about it. It is not the sentence of a tribunal. The verb *yéchà* in Hebrew means "to be without restraint," at ease. In a wider sense, it means to deliver, to save from a danger, from an illness, from death. This makes clear the very particular meaning of reestablishing a vital

balance, of *healing.* The substantive *yéchà,* salvation, signifies total
deliverance with peace—*shalom*—at the end. In the New Testament *soteria* in Greek comes from the verb *sozo.* The adjective *sos*
corresponds to the Latin *sanus* and means to restore health to one
who has lost it, to save from death, the natural end of every illness.
That is why the expression "Thy faith has *saved* thee" includes the
version "thy faith has *healed* thee," the two terms referring to the
same act of divine pardon that touches soul and body in their very
unity. In accordance with this idea, the sacrament of penance is
thought of as a "medical clinic," and St. Ignatius of Antioch calls
the Eucharist *pharmakon,* a remedy of immortality.

Jesus the Savior thus appears as the divine Healer, saying:
"Those who are well have no need of a physician, but those who
are sick...I came not to call the righteous, but sinners."[1] Sinners
are the sick who are threatened with spiritual death, more fearful
than that of the body. We can then specify the therapeutic meaning of salvation: it is the healing of a being and the elimination of
the seed of mortality. This is why the Savior called himself the
Life, and the saved receive eternal life. The end joins the beginning when we, having received the breath of life, live by participation in the Holy Spirit, creator of life. Asceticism seeks to
rediscover that deep and adequate conformity of man to his own
truth, his norm, and of woman to the fertility of the earth and to
beauty. Asceticism is practiced in order to return us to God's idea
of us, to make us "very similar" to him. In this perspective, "the
works of faith" are neither means nor "merits," but symptoms of
health-salvation.

The extent of evil can be measured by the power of its antidote. The sick are healed by a treatment that befits the stature of
God. The physician, instead of the patient, passes through death
and inaugurates his universal healing: "Unless the grain of wheat
falls into the earth and dies, it remains alone. But if it dies, it bears

1 Mt. 9:2-13.

much fruit."[2] The cross is planted at the threshold of the new life—*vita nova*—and the water of baptism receives the sacramental value of the blood of Christ. From then on, asceticism teaches participation in the "health" of the Savior, but this entails a victory over death and therefore a preliminary purification. Only the trial of suffering can so deepen and purify life as to lead to conscious and true joy. The Church announces that "by the cross joy has come to all the world," and this message delineates for us an unchanging and perfect itinerary. If every destiny is thus placed under the sign of "the bearing of the cross," "the cross is life-giving" and its joy transcends every attachment to sorrow and agonizing sensitivity. Asceticism leads beyond psychic techniques, and spiritual mastery fosters extreme sobriety of feeling.

The Old Testament expectation of the messianic age had already formed a pilgrim type. The New Testament fulfillment only accentuated this state of *homo viator*. It entrusted us with a precise and human task.

According to the Gospel, time is short. This world as we see it is passing away. Now that the Bridegroom has been taken away, we can no longer enjoy the world and live in the penultimate values of existence. Since Pentecost, we qualitatively live in the last times. This situation suggests a great liberation from the cares of the world in order to make our waiting active. Such an ascetic "activism" corresponds to the tastes of our age, which in its spirit of invention and its social preoccupations is opposed to quietism. If we see that spiritual masters constantly insist on manual work, this is not simply to occupy their leisure time, because ascetics earn their living in order to practice charity.[3] The true "impassibility," or freedom from passion, according to Evagrius, "is accompanied by an immense love of God and a boundless fervor for the works of charity."[4] An angel revealed to Pachomius that "the will of God is that we should put ourselves in

2 Jn 12:24.
3 See St. Basil, *Greater Rule, 37.*
4 *Pract.* II, 57.

the service of others." Pachomius later said that "the love of God consists in our taking trouble one for another."[5] Thus ascetics were true to this task, discovering in it the dimension of the Kingdom. They saw perfection in the fear "of wounding love, however slightly."[6]

The Fathers were very much conscious of changing ascetical forms. The *Apothegms* recount this incident. "The holy fathers were prophesying on the last days. 'What have we ourselves done?' they wondered. One of them, the great Abba Ischyrion, answered: 'We have observed the commandments of God.' 'And those who will follow us,' continued the others, 'what will they do?' Ischyrion replied: 'Those will succeed in doing only half of what we have done.' The fathers still insisted. 'How will it be with those who come after them?' 'The men of that age,' the Abba answered, 'will not be rich in works. The time of the great temptation will arise against them. Those then who are good will be greater than we are and than our fathers were.'"[7]

Today the spectacular practices of former times are interiorized. Exploits of the spirit are hidden under the mantle of daily life. The ascetical superman has become more human, taking better account of the modern world, its needs and its mentality. Spirituality, without compromising anything, seeks to adapt itself to the evolution of the human psyche. Thus asceticism in its beginnings manifested a biological exuberance. Now anxiety, stress and our lack of resistance advise rather the avoidance of ascetical violence. Medicine, where it can, relieves suffering and thus makes us more vulnerable, more sensitive to physical pain by the fact that pain has become more rare.

Asceticism now places its emphasis elsewhere, and very fortunately it shares the major preoccupations of all free philosophical

5 *Vie copte de saint Pacôme.*
6 Cassian, Conf. IX.
7 *Apophthegmata Patrum*, P.G., 65, 241. See Dom Stolz. L'Ascèse chrétienne, p. 8.

reflections. After Jung, psychologists know well that a little freedom causes anxiety, but much freedom heals it. This is exactly the aim of asceticism: to transcend every limit, to expand souls by the audacity of love, and to develop the person by means of gifts and charisms.

3

The Charisms of the Spiritual Life

1. The spirit of discernment, impassibility, silence, vigilance, repentance and humility

St. John Climacus describes the spiritual life under the reassuring figure of a heavenly ladder (*scala paradisi*). The heavenly powers, the angels, assist our efforts. They go up and down "Jacob's ladder" accompanying us on this journey in which we are gifted with grace, with charisms. St. Cyril of Jerusalem enumerates some of them: "For one, the Spirit strengthens his temperance, to another he teaches mercy, to still another how to fast, and in short, to practice the spiritual life."[1]

The spiritual life is entirely and at once charismatic. Above all, *the spirit of discernment* shows how not to confuse the end with the means. Evagrius insightfully notes that the worst error would be to make a passion out of the struggle against passion. "Prayer, fasting, vigils, and every other practice...are only indispensable means to attain the acquisition of the Holy Spirit," teaches St. Seraphim.[2] Here the end is stated most precisely. St. Isaac adds that the simplicity of God unites but the complexity of evil disperses.[3]

The Sixth Ecumenical Council noted this dispersion and affirmed that "sin is the sickness of the soul," directing its attention to a therapeutic asceticism.

1 *Cath. myst.*, 16, 12.
2 *Little Russian Philokalia,* vol. I, St. Seraphim (New Valaam Monastery: St. Herman Press, 1991), p. 86.
3 Wensinck, *op. cit.*, p. 202.

That is why St. Paul,[4] in praying very particularly for the spirit
of discernment, had in mind spiritual appreciation that makes us
capable of distinguishing and of making decisive choices. Here an
obstacle arises: every conscious command elicits a secret resistance
from the subconscious which paralyzes the will. St. Paul notes:
"For I do not understand my own actions...For I do not do what
I want, but the very thing I hate." He discovered the interior law
that fights against the law of understanding, and thus he formulated the law of irrational resistance that comes from the subconscious.[5]

The Bible knows well our impenetrable subterranean depths.
"The heart is deceitful above all things and desperately corrupt,
who can understand it? I, the Lord, alone search the mind and try
the heart,"[6] which means the human ego and the obscure sphere
that surrounds it. The Gospel judges a person by the content of
his heart, by the object of his desires, by his Eros. "It is from the
heart that man draws good things and bad." The possibilities are
in one direction or the other.

The great masters of asceticism were perfectly clear on the role
of the subconscious. Evagrius teaches: "Many passions are hidden
in our soul, but escape our attention. It is sudden temptation
which reveals them."[7]

"Depth psychology" fortunately comes to give scientific substance to the art of asceticism and to help us understand ourselves.
It analyzes the dynamism of affectivity, the obscurity of the unconscious, the irrational root of the soul where the instinct of "the
will to live" is active. Jarred by the real, subject to social censure,
this interior world is remodeled. Part of its vitality is repressed.

4 Phil 1:10.
5 Rom 7:15-23.
6 Jer 17:9-10.
7 *Centuries*, VI, 52. See Jung, *Types psychologiques*, p. 111. Jung quotes Cynesius,
  Bishop of Ptolemais, for whom the imagination is the middle sphere between the
  eternal and the temporal; it is through it that we live more fully.

Reflexes of inhibition and compensation are elaborated. A mysterious and hidden life flows on beneath the threshold of consciousness, ceaselessly exercising its pressure. One's health depends on the balance between the conscious and the subconscious, on the mind's capacity to project its light there, on integration with its "shadow."

Dark and malevolent powers make use of our psychic elements. In this sense Jung mentions a resemblance between complexes and demons. Ascetical teachers counsel us to be attentive and discerning in the soul's interior chaos. Diverse elements may be at work—animal, rational, or affective. Likewise they advise distinguishing between an interior or exterior cause, whether it is simply biological or more complex and moral. Thus Evagrius (in his *Antirrheticos*) specifies the somatic cause of gluttony and of lust, representing as they do perversion of the instincts to live and to survive. For St. Gregory Palamas, the passions coming from nature are less severe, and express only the pressure of our material being and our failure to spiritualize it. In the fourteenth century, long before Freud, he spoke of sexual manifestations among very small children as *natural manifestations*. Sin and passions that are dangerous come from the mind.

The perverted will turns away from the original direction of the heart in order to seek the absolute in idols (the principal vices or passions). It throws itself into the cult of the ego with its self-love and its desire for power, making of it an infernal self-idol. The transvaluation of values (*Umwertung*), the method practiced by the Viennese school, is used to unmask these idols in order to make the true absolute evident.

Psychology is in harmony with asceticism. It observes that too detailed memories of the past, too long a time of thinking about them, risks doing more harm than good. The Freudian method of introspection and of reducing the present to the past alienates us. It has been completed and surpassed by the Jungian method of prospection that leads to the construction of the future. Jung teaches the forging ahead that is formulated in the words of St. Paul: "Forgetting what lies behind and straining forward to what lies ahead, I press on toward the goal."[8]

Important here are the inclinations that allow us to gain knowledge of the actual measure of ourselves. Mental vigilance, a guard over the heart, the invocation of the name of Jesus—these are the charisms that restrain and stop all problematic interior colloquies before there is consent, or a passion that makes the soul captive. We must descend to the irrational roots of the soul, toward the clear or muddled source in the imagination, to grasp its exact nature.

Psychoanalysis and asceticism have indeed understood this, and search into the soul's contortions in order to shed the light of the mind upon them. One cannot act on the subconscious by commands, for it is opposed to every direct order. One enters there most efficaciously by the imagination. Then one discovers the great power of images.[9]

Indeed, in the face of the natural powerlessness of man to fulfill the Old Testament Law and to submit to the prohibitions of the Decalogue, the New Testament offers the grace of the Beatitudes. Furthermore, in order to arouse and sustain our action, grace operates by positive suggestions, in the form of invitations and appeals. These suggestions are reinforced by "beautiful images," by the "absolute desirability" of the New Jerusalem that unfolds before our eyes in the magnificent description in the Apocalypse.

Grace aims above all at the reconstruction in us of the image of God (*imago Dei*), of our initial form, tending toward God, as a copy of the Original. We can see the importance of the biblical notion of "image." By being an image, this structural form can

8 Phil. 3:13-14.

9 Asceticism purifies the imagination and then directs it toward what is beyond the image. Such is the ultimate meaning of the Orthodox icon; it raises our spiritual gaze toward its own apophatic, negative limit.

only be seized by the imagination, and consequently, only the imagination can penetrate the subconscious and structure it in "the image of God."

The imagination always tends toward the incarnation of its images. To the suggestive power of art can be added the living language of symbols of sacred art. According to Jung: "Only the religious symbol sublimates totally." We say, "the symbol of faith," since the *Credo*, said liturgically, leads us beyond images and even symbols. The Creed brings us into the presence of the persons invoked, there where the relations between the human *I* and the divine *Thou* are made concrete. While Kant's categorical imperative is powerless, since it is abstract and impersonal, the Gospel instead reveals the living person of Christ, the source of charismatic imperatives.

Origen commented on the words of St. Paul, "until Christ is formed in you,"[10] seeing in them the act of "imagining" Christ in the hearts of his disciples. The German word *ein-bilden* is most expressive here and designates the essence of the activity. Once his image is formed in the soul, the person of Christ in turn forms the soul and transforms it into His own type: "It is no longer I that live, but Christ who lives in me." In the end the soul appears truly Christified.

Asceticism thus constitutes an immense project of sublimation.[11] However, we must understand this in the sense of a tension toward *sublimissimum,* toward the Most High. It refines the imagination through the fasting of the eyes and spiritual hearing. We ceaselessly collect innumerable images that surround and invade us. We constantly experience suggestions from speeches, scientific formulas, political slogans, artistic forms,[12] human faces and cosmic landscapes. If everything in existence concurs in *suggesting,* in exerting pressure on the soul, in impressing it, the

10 Gal 4:19.
11 See Kristian Schielderup, *Die Askese* (Berlin, 1928).
12 See Baudouin, *Psychanalyse de l'Art.*

"theodidacts,"[13] those "taught by God," receive the strongest suggestion, for it is God who suggests by the creative images of his
wisdom. Here the attention of the mind is required; Abbot
Philemon tells us: "By your imagination look within your heart,"
for "the pure heart sees God as in a mirror."[14]

The purification of the heart comes above all from the liturgy,
where rite, dogma and art are closely bound together. The images of
the Liturgy are symbols that lift our gaze to the level of the invisible
presence of God. According to St. John of Damascus, the icon is not
a representation of the visible, but an apocalypse, a revelation of the
hidden. Its power is maximal by reason of its opening upon the
transcendent that has no image. The gaze thus purified and made
attentive can descend, scrutinize and reveal the interior of the soul.
"He who manifests his thoughts is soon healed; he who hides them
makes himself sick." "It is an evident sign that a thought is from the
demon when we blush to disclose it to our brother."[15]

John of Lycopolis expresses the tradition in ceaselessly returning to the need for watchful attention. "Judge your thoughts
piously before God; if you cannot do this, ask one who is capable
of discerning them."[16]

Such openness of soul and charismatic attention to what takes
place within hinder the formation of complexes. Wounds that are
detected or declared do not grow worse.

Exterior behavior is always symptomatic of the inward state,
and their intimate correspondence conditions and justifies corpo-
ral asceticism. Yet this relationship limits ascetic restraint to what
is strictly necessary: to ward off debilitating comfort and the
tyranny of habits. The ideal state has the most paradoxical name
of *apatheia* which means "impassible passion," and designates a

13 St. Macarius, *Hom. XV, 20.*
14 *Philocalie* (in Russian), vol. III, p. 372.
15 Cassian, *P.L.* 49, 161-162.
16 See *Revue des Sciences religieuses,* 41 (1953), p. 526.

most *impassioned* state, for it is a question of awakening the spirit from its sluggishness and making one wide awake, *neptikos*. It takes a whole life to live what faith affirms once for all, and it is for this reason that the spirit is watchful. St. Teresa of Avila asserted that we should "neither creep, nor advance like a frog, nor walk with chicken steps." "What must one be? One must be a fire," notes St. Exupéry.[17]

Ascetic impassibility then is not insensitivity. Neither does it seek to resemble those whom Bernanos called "the stoics with dry eyes," nor to cultivate delight in bloody mortifications and in the groanings of the flesh. By lack or by excess, the two destroy the balance, and manifest an asceticism that is illusory and "without fruit."[18] For ascetics, the capacity to become impassioned indicates their inward dynamism, which must be oriented, not suppressed. It receives its value from the goal to be attained, and this suppresses art for art, science for science, and above all, asceticism for asceticism. "The perfect soul is one whose passions are turned toward God," whose energies are directed toward divine love of mankind. This is why Diadochus says: "Woe to the knowledge that does not turn to loving." The state of the passions is centered on the one passion *par excellence,* evangelical love, "ontological tenderness" toward every creature of God. This is the fundamental charism. "What is a heart full of love?" asks St. Isaac the Syrian. "It is a heart aflame with love for the entire creation, for people, birds, beasts, evil spirits, all creatures...moved by an infinite pity that is awakened in the hearts of those who resemble God."[19] Such a passionate lover "condemns neither sinners nor the children of this age...Such a one desires to love and venerate all without any distinction," for "after God he esteems all as God himself."[20] St. Symeon, following St. Paul, certainly speaks of

17 *Pilote de Guerre* (Ed. Pléiade), p. 366.
18 St. Macarius, *P.G.,* 34, 761; St. Dorotheus, *P.G.,* 88, 1780.
19 Wensinck, *op. cit.,* p. 341.
20 St. Nilus, *P.G.,* 79, 1192C.

himself when he confesses: "I know a man who would desire the salvation of his brothers with such ardor . . . that he would not even wish to enter the kingdom of heaven if in so doing he would have to separate himself from them."[21]

Oral prayer gives way to contemplative prayer, in which the heart opens itself *in silence* before God. "When the Spirit comes, we must cease praying," St. Seraphim teaches. It is "the silence of the spirit" (hesychasm). The more alert the soul, the more *peaceful* it is. In the counsel given by St. Seraphim to seek above all interior peace, the latter designates the silence or hesychasm in which a person becomes the *place* of God. If "the Word came forth from the Father in silence,"[22] among us, silence teaches us to give up our thoughtless chatter, and then the silent one becomes "a source of grace to the one who listens to him."[23]

The current opposition between adhering to the world and leaving it is spatial. The basis of the problem is in the vertical dimension. "When you pray, enter into thy chamber and close the door." It is not a question of the place, but of a closed door. In this way El Greco used to seek colors in the depths of his soul, and looking for inspiration, he used to draw all the curtains of his studio and of his soul. We must know how to make a place for silence, for recollection. Without these moments, charged with interior dynamism, the spiritual life risks being dissolved in sterile agitation. When we attain to a certain maturity, the prayer of Jesus teaches us to have these moments, even in public places, and to be present and attentive to others by our silence.

In these moments of recollection, the masters of the spiritual life warn us against the ecstasy that belongs only to inexperienced beginners. In our progress, we should aspire to constant awareness of the invisible presence of God and to turn aside relentlessly from

21 *P.G.*, 120, 423.
22 St. Ignatius of Antioch, *Rom.* 2, 1, *Magn. 8, 2.*
23 St. Basil, *Lesser Rule,* CCVlll.

all visual or sensory phenomena, all curiosity, all seeking for "the mysterious." Evagrius insists on this: "Do not strive during prayer to discern any image or figure...otherwise you risk falling into madness."[24] Gregory the Sinaite (fifteenth century) advises: "Be watchful, friend of God. If you see a light, or some image, or an angel, refuse to accept it...When it seems to your spirit that you are drawn to the heights by an invisible force, do not allow this and force yourself to work."[25] As long as one can resist or oppose an apparition, it is a sign that the phenomenon does not come from God. What comes from God comes irresistibly. All the teachers strongly insist on the extreme sobriety of what is spiritual and its lack of any materialization.

"If you see a young novice mounting by his own will to heaven, seize him by the feet and throw him to the ground, because his action would be of no value to him."[26] Satan disguised as an angel of light came one day to a hermit to assure him of his spiritual progress. The hermit contented himself with saying, not without humor: "You must be making a mistake, it is to another that you have been sent. I have not made any spiritual progress."[27]

Unusual phenomena may disturb novices, but have no connection with the spiritual life, which is always oriented toward the interior. "If you are pure, heaven is within you, and it is within you that you will see light, the angels and the Lord of the angels."[28]

This entrance of the soul into itself is opposed, however, to any passive quietism. St. John Climacus insists on the dynamism of the spirit: "The one who keeps his fervor to the end does not cease to add, even to the end of his life, fire to fire, ardor to ardor, zeal to zeal, desire to desire."[29] "The Lord is always victorious, when

24 "On Prayer," 114-116, in *The Philokalia*, vol. I, p. 68.
25 *De la vie contemplative*, 10.
26 *Vitae Patrum; P.L.*, 73, 932B-C.
27 *P.L.*, 73, 965C.
28 St. Macarius, *P.G.*, 34, 776.
29 *P.G.*, 88, 634c.

he struggles along with Christian athletes. But if these are overcome, it is clear that they have deprived themselves of God by
their irrational will."[30] The dynamism of the will is indeed required, for "God does nothing by himself alone," St. Macarius
insists.[31] To a monk who had asked Anthony to pray for him, the
abba answered: "Neither shall I have pity on you, nor will God, if
you do not set yourself seriously and particularly to prayer."[32]

The spiritual life then has nothing unconscious or passive
about it. Our attention develops sensitivity to signs and warnings.
A sluggish spirit lets these constant appeals pass by. Vigilance, on
the contrary, fosters *repentance* which is an active manner of
listening ceaselessly to the words: "Be perfect as your heavenly
Father is perfect."

The giving up of repentance marks the cessation of the spiritual life and is accompanied by the fearful state called "the insen-
sibility of a petrified heart." We must distinguish this from the
"withdrawal of God" or "desolation," which the divine Teacher
uses to teach the soul to be more humble. This dereliction is for
healing, notes Origen, and St. Macarius says: "Grace is taken away
in order that we may seek it all the more."[33] Is not the sphere of
the trial the very field of freedom? Once when St. Anthony had
overcome his distress, he asked: "Where were You, Lord, during
this time?" He received the answer: "Nearer than ever to thee."[34]

"We shall not be accused," says St. John Climacus, "of not having
performed miracles...but we shall surely have to answer to God for
not having wept ceaselessly for our sins."[35] Repentance meditates
constantly on our rejection of the one who is crucified Love. It is a
question here of tears, not of the soul, but of the spirit. These are

30 St. Isaac, Wensinck, *op. cit.*, p. 340, p. 187.
31 *P.G.*, 34, 757A.
32 *P.G.*, 65, 80C.
33 *Hom. 27; P.G.*, 34, 701D
34 *Apophthegmata Patrum.*
35 *The Ladder*, 7th step, p. 145. *P.G.*, 88, 816D.

considered a charismatic gift. They mingle with the tears of joy and continue the purifying waters of baptism. "Blessed are they who weep for they will be comforted." Such repentance, according to St. John of Damascus, is "the return to God from captivity, the healing trembling of the soul before the gate of the Kingdom."[36]

Repentance is clearly a form of humility. The two are not "virtues" but a permanent state of the soul. Only their power can heal egocentric idolatry, self-love, pretensions, or inferiority complexes. Humility teaches "to be as if one were not," and "not to know what one is." "To bow down before the divine majesty is the highest victory," as St. Bernard profoundly notes.[37] The love of God excludes all self-complacency. When St. Anthony asked to be shown a model of piety, an angel led him to a very humble man. In his prayer, this man used to present before God all people, thinking that there existed no one who was as great a sinner as himself. Abba Sisoes on his death-bed, already fully enlightened and surrounded by angels, sighed: "I have not even begun to repent."[38] "Perfection," declares St. Isaac, "is the depth of humility."[39]

In his *Letters to the Ashram*, Gandhi correctly opposes humility to inertia: "True humility requires...the most arduous and constant effort."[40] Humility, for Baudoin, the psychologist, has a biological role and a function of adaptation; it puts us in our place.[41]

In humility lives "the communion of sinners," this other aspect inseparable from "the communion of saints." While he was dying, a fool for Christ said: "May all be saved, may the whole world be saved." Another, at the end of a life of scorn and persecution, affirmed that he had not met a truly bad man.

36 *P. G.* 94, 976A; St. Isaac, Wensinck, *op. cit.,* p. 310.
37 *Lettre,* 185.
38 *P.G.,* 65, 396.
39 *Homélie* 78.
40 *Études Carm.* (1947), p. 183.
41 Quoted by O. Clément, *L'Église Orthodoxe* (Paris, 1961), p. 122.

Today, in countries where, because of persecution, life is placed under the sign of the cross and silence, humility becomes the spirituality of martyrs. Its grandeur shines forth in its astonishing hymns of praise. It gives thanks to God for suffering and persecution, even placing the demons in the hands of God. Having reached the end of what is bearable, one can only say: "Glory be to God," and redouble prayer for the living and the dead, for the victims and the executioners. It is then that one takes on the heart of God and understands the ineffable.

Christ has come to "awaken the living and change death into a sleep of expectation," into vigils of the spirit. The living are on the other side of death and the dead are the living; such is the joyous revelation of Christian faith, its royal charism.

2. The charism of "joyful dying"

If it is true, as Plato says, that "of death there is no knowledge," if it is probable that the future holds for us both sadness and joy, unforeseen and problematic events, the only absolutely certain thing that awaits us is death. This fact is universal and indisputable.

Heidegger had the courage to place it at the center of his philosophy. It alone radically limits human freedom. Therefore, it is against this background that we must understand ourselves.

Modern education is most revealing of its own mentality in that it never speaks of death. It seems to be directed at "immortal" children. It is afraid to touch upon the mystery of death except with distractions and lies.

Forgetfulness of death is characteristic of our world. With great artistry everything is shaped by this, as if modern man could not bear the idea of it so brutally imposed, as if behind the statement that "all are mortal," there were hidden an unavowed and senseless thought, an obscure desire that there may be some exceptions, that this end did not immediately concern me. In any event, there is never an opportune moment to think of it. We bury the dead with uneasiness, almost in secret, rapidly, discreetly. The dead are spoilsports. They disturb the rest of us who are enjoying life. Certain cemeteries in their almost hideous monotony give the horrible idea of a death that has become industrialized as it were, and of forgetfulness in the anonymity of a common fate. For those who do remember, their memories refer to what no longer exists. The poetry of their sadness comes from a dead past. On the contrary, memory itself depends on life, and it keeps the past completely present. Each one of the dead is a singular and irreplaceable being, living eternally in the memory of God. The Church in her prayers for the dead asks this of God ("memory eternal"), as she asks also for the grace of the *constant remembrance* of death. St. Benedict's Rule prescribes contemplating it every day.

In existentialism, death conditions the famous "transcendence," but the latter is proved to be powerless since it does not transcend death. It is the living being who is transcendent toward death (*Sein zum Tode*). Certainly, such a dialectic vigorously presents the problem, but at the same time it shows its insufficiency. The end and nothingness are granted, but no light is shed here on the meaning of death. A cessation or lessening of reflection such as this leads one at the most to say: the one who wishes nothingness will have it. Simone de Beauvoir fails when she tries "to conjure up death with words."[42] True transcendence ought to affirm the contrary: it is not life that is a phenomenon of death, but it is death that is an episodic and passing phenomenon of life. Only in this perspective does death receive a particularly luminous significance.

The profound pessimism of Freud and Heidegger appears to have been formed naturally, as soon as we reflect on life in relation to its end. To recognize and to accept this end is already a deep and true philosophic attitude, for as Julian Green notes: "No one speaks so well of life as death does." Indeed an infinite duration in the conditions of this earthly life, time being cut off from its

42 *La Force de l'âge*, p. 617.

ending, would deprive existence of all meaning. In *Tous les hommes sont mortels* Simone de Beauvoir agrees with Berdyaev and shares a correct intuition: the indefinite duration of biological existence would culminate in infinite boredom. We can add that the horror of a fate in hell comes exactly from such a boredom being made eternal. For the Fathers of the Church, life without end in earthly conditions could only be a demonic nightmare. The love of God for his creatures hinders the immortalization of such a state of life that would be only death suspended.

The meaning of history, even its possibility, is a direct function of its end, its balance sheet, its transcendence, more inevitable than death itself toward "the wholly other." "The last enemy to be destroyed is death,"[43] St. Paul emphatically declares. The final evil is pregnant with the ultimate solution of the human condition. Death, "the king of terrors," according to Job, causes legitimate anguish, puts a stop to what is habitually profaned by forgetfulness, and in its depth is striking in the greatness of its mystery. At the beginning of his life, St. Augustine wept for the death of a friend, confessing: "Having become an enigma to myself, I questioned my soul."[44]

The valour of a human being is measured by his attitude toward death. Plato taught that philosophy was the art of dying well, but philosophy does not know of the victory over death. It can postulate it, but it cannot teach *how* one must die in the resurrection. It only affirms, and in this is its greatness, that time cannot contain eternity, that time without its end would be more absurd than death, and that this world which kills Socrates the righteous is not the true world. Furthermore, its crimes testify to another world where justice reigns, and where Socrates lives forever young and beautiful. For Justin Martyr, the fate of Socrates prefigured the destiny of Christ who died and rose, and in whom Socrates was born again for eternity.

43 1 Cor 15:26.
44 *Conf.*, 4, 4.

Death is not just momentary. It coexists and accompanies us all along the path of our lives. It is present in all things as their obvious limit. Time and space, moments that vanish and distances that separate, are so many ruptures or partial deaths. Every good-bye, change, forgetfulness, the fact that nothing can ever be reproduced exactly—all bring the breath of death even to the heart of life and fill us with anguish. Every departure of a loved one, the end of every passion, the traces of time on a human face, the last look at a city or a landscape that we shall never see again, or simply a faded flower—all arouse a profound melancholy, an immediate experience of our anticipated death.

Nature does not know any personal immortality. It only knows the survival of the species. Atheists can dream only of survival in their works or in the memory of the generations to come. It is a dreary dictionary-immortality at best.

The virulence of death can be neutralized only by its own negation. That is why the cross is raised in the center of the world, and life freely accepts passing death in order to shatter it and bring it to nothingness. "By death, you have conquered death," sings the Church on the night of Pascha, Easter. Origen reports a tradition according to which the body of Adam was buried where Christ was crucified.[45] Another tradition has it that the wood of the cross had its origin in a tree in Eden. The Bible knows nothing of natural immortality and reveals the resurrection as coming from beyond—from the death and resurrection of the God-Man. Thus Christianity *alone* accepts the tragedy of death, and looks at it face to face, for God has passed along that road and all follow him.

While philosophy brings knowledge of death, Christian asceticism offers the art of going beyond it and thus anticipating the resurrection. Indeed, death is entirely in time. For those around a

45 *P.G.*, 13, 1777. The icon of the crucifixion shows Adam's skull at the foot of the cross. The chapel of Adam in the Church of the Holy Sepulcher in Jerusalem bears the inscription: "The place of the skull has become paradise."

dying person, his death is dated, but for the one who has just died, it has no date, for he already finds himself in another dimension. Just as the end of the world will have no earthly tomorrow, death is not a day on the calendar for anyone. This is why the death of each one, like the end of the world, is *for today*. Just as it is not tomorrow but on the very day of the eucharistic feast that one enters the Kingdom.

For one whose spirit has been rendered immortal, the nonexistence of death is evident, because it is on this side, while he is on the other. As an element of time, *death is behind us*. Before us is found what has already been experienced in baptism: the "little resurrection," and in the Eucharist: life eternal. The one who follows Christ "does not come to judgment, but has passed from death to life." "The one who eats my flesh and drinks my blood has eternal life." The final reality of ourselves lives on the threshold of this paschal passage. The act of faith discovers it and sees things "that are not seen," according to St. Paul.

"If anyone comes to me and does not hate...even his own life, he cannot be my disciple."[46] Thus, to hate means to oppose an obstacle, an excessive attachment to life here below or a fear of death—all of which make the spirit captive. To a thoughtful person, death deprived of anguish manifests one's own grandeur and nobility. It purifies and takes from the dead what is merely accessory, inclines us to keep "a good memory" of them, to appreciate them in a disinterested way, to rectify the scale of values beyond time and in the face of eternity. The face of a dead person has for some moments a peaceful and majestic spiritual beauty: "that impenetrable smile of the dead which is in such harmony with their marvelous silence."[47] The presence of death has something august about it. It ennobles our feelings, and in a brief instant makes each one truer and greater. The death of another is a trial,

46 Lk 14:26.
47 Bernanos, *Journal d'un curé de campagne* (Ed. Pléiade), p. 1167.

and the one who experiences this receives the dignity of surviving and of preparing himself for the mystery of his own accounting.

Normally death is the time of harvest for a life "laden with days," and ripe for eternity. According to the beautiful words of ancient martyrologies, it is the *dies natalis,* the heavenly birthday, and only God knows the day and the hour. The words of Pascal, "One dies alone,"[48] and those of Kierkegaard, "That I die is not a generality for me,"[49] mean that each one of us totally assumes his death. We are the priests of our death. We are what we make of our death. The last anointing admirably introduces us into this priesthood, offering "an oil of gladness" and an exaltation of the heart beyond the agony of the body.

Diadochus[50] notes that grave illnesses take the place of martyrdom. Even more, to *each one* is given the grace, the charism of martyrdom, when, in the face of death that replaces the executioner, we can still call it "our Sister Death," and confess the *Credo,* evidence that we have already passed from death to life (cf. Col. 2:12; John 5:24). Great spiritual teachers have often slept in their own coffins as if they were in the marriage bed, manifesting a brotherly familiarity, an intimacy with death, that is only a passage and a definitive point of departure. Erasmus observed this intimacy in the saints and thought it constituted a second nature that had dislodged the first.

St. Seraphim of Sarov used to teach "joyful dying." "For us, to die will be a joy," he was accustomed to say to his disciples. That is why he addressed each person he met with the paschal salutation: "My joy, Christ is risen." Death no longer exists and life reigns.

In his letter to the Corinthians, St. Paul presents an astounding vision: "All things are yours...life or death...all are yours,"[51] both gifts of God, charisms.

48 British Edition, p. 211.
49 *Concluding Unscientific Postscript,* vol. I, Howard V. and Edna H. Hong, trans. (Princeton: Princeton University Press, 1992).
50 Chap. 94, *The Philokalia,* vol. I, pp. 291-292.
51 1 Cor 3:22-21.

3. Prayer

The State of Prayer

"Pray without ceasing,"[52] insists St. Paul, for prayer is at the same time the source and the most intimate form of our life. "But when you pray, go into your room, shut the door and pray to your Father in secret."[53] This means to enter into yourself and make a sanctuary there. The secret place is the human heart. The life of prayer, its intensity, its depth, its rhythm are a measure of our spiritual health and reveal us to ourselves.

"And in the morning, a great while before day, he went out to a lonely place, and there he prayed."[54] With the ascetics, "the desert" is interiorized and signifies the concentration of a recollected and silent spirit. At this level, where we know how to be silent, true prayer is found. Here we are mysteriously visited. Paul Claudel notes that the Word is the adopted son of silence, for St. Joseph passes through the pages of the Gospel without uttering a single word. To hear the voice of the Word, we must know how to listen to his silence, and above all, to learn it ourselves. Speaking from experience, the spiritual masters are categorical. If one does not know how to give a place in his life to recollection and silence, it is impossible for him to arrive at a higher level and to be able to pray in public places. This level of prayer makes us aware that part of us, immersed in what is immediate, is always worried and distracted, and that the other part observes this with astonishment and compassion. A man too busy with many things would make the angels laugh, if they could do so, Shakespeare remarks.[55]

The water that quenches thirst is distilled in the silence that offers us the indispensable retreat. Only then can we view ourselves in the right perspective.

52 1 Thess 5:17.
53 Mt 6:6.
54 Mk 1:35.
55 *Measure for Measure,* Act II, scene 2.

Recollection opens our soul to heaven, but also to the other. St. Seraphim states admirably: the contemplative life *or* the active life—this is artificial and not the real problem which is that of the heart's dimension. Is this vast treasure chest, of which Origen speaks, capable of containing God and all people? If so, St. Seraphim says: "acquire interior peace, and many around you will find their salvation."[56]

There are evident realities in the world, the Kingdom, for example, and there are symbols also. "The Kingdom of heaven is like...," and then comes the idea, the theory, which is an impoverishment. That is why poetry, and even more so, prayer, is nearer truth than is prose. Lao-tse used to say that if he had absolute power, before all else he would reestablish the original poetic meaning of words. In this time of verbal inflation that aggravates loneliness, only the person of prayerful peace can still speak to others, and show them the word that has become a face and the gaze that has become a presence. Such a one's silence will speak where no preaching can reach. His mystery will make others attentive to a revelation that has now become close and accessible to them. Even when the one who knows silence speaks, he easily finds the unsullied freshness of every word. His answer to questions of life and death comes as the *amen* to his perpetual prayer.

St. Thérèse used to say: "To pray means to treat God like a friend." The "friend of the Bridegroom...stands and hears him."[57] The essence of the state of prayer is to "stand and hear" the voice of another, that of Christ, but likewise that of the person I meet, in whom Christ addresses me. His voice comes to me in every human voice. His face is that of many: it is that of one traveling to Emmaus, of Mary Magdalen's gardener, of my next-door neighbor. God became incarnate so that man may contemplate his face through every face. Perfect prayer seeks the presence of Christ and recognizes it in every human

56 *Little Russian Philokalia,* vol. I, St. Seraphim, pp. 71 ff.
57 Jn 3:29.

being. The unique image of Christ is the icon, but they are innumerable, and this means that every human face is also the icon of Christ. The attitude of prayer reveals this.

The Degrees of Prayer

In the beginning, prayer is agitated and silence is inwardly talkative. In the words of Péguy, we should not pray like geese waiting for their food! Being emotional, we pour out all the content of our minds. Before we feel weariness from this mono-logue, the spiritual writers advise occupying our time of prayer with reciting the psalms and in reading. St. John Climacus con-demns prolixity: "Let ther be no affectation in the words of your prayer. How many times do the simple and monotonous stam-merings of children move a father. Do not throw yourself into long speeches so as not to dissipate your mind in a search for words. A single word of the publican touched the mercy of God. A single word, full of faith, saved the good thief. Longwindedness and talkativeness in prayer fill the mind with images and distract it, while often a single word has the effect of recollecting it."[58] "It is not necessary to use many words. It is sufficient to keep one's hands raised," says St. Macarius.[59] In Chapter XX of his *Rule,* St. Benedict declares: "It is not in the abundance of words that we shall be heard, but by the compunction of our tears."

The Lord's Prayer is quite brief. A hermit on Mount Athos used to begin this prayer at sunset and end it saying *Amen* to the rays of the rising sun. Talking is not the question. It is a question of fully living the realities created by each word of our prayer. The great spiritual masters are satisfied with pronouncing the name of Jesus, but in this name they contemplate the Kingdom.

If we understand this lesson, we will rectify our attitude, making it agree with the liturgical aspiration: "Make of my prayer

58 *The Ladder of Divine Ascent,* step 28, p. 275.
59 *P.G.,* 34, 249.

a sacrament of your presence." Man should lend an ear to the voice of God. St. Seraphim counsels: "We ought to pray until the Holy Spirit descends upon us...When he has come to visit us, we cease praying."

With us, in our time, the difficulty comes from the separation of the intellect from the heart, of knowledge from value judgments. Ancient tradition suggests: "In the morning place your intellect in your heart and remain all day in the company of God." In other words, bring together the fragmented elements of your being, and thus regain integrity of spirit. An ancient prayer asks: "By your love, bind my soul," that from its many moods, a single soul may spring forth.

It is a serious distortion to make prayer the mechanical repetition of formulas and texts that have been learned. True prayer changes into a constant attitude, into a state of mind that structures and molds our whole being liturgically. Here is seen the great truth that to *have* is still a symbol, the reality is to *be*. According to spiritual teachers, it is not enough to *have* prayers, rules, habits; one must *be* prayer incarnate.[60] It is in his very structure that man sees himself as a liturgical being, as the man of the *Sanctus,* the one who by his whole life and his whole being prostrates and adores, one who can say: "I sing praise to my God while I live."[61] To make of one's life a liturgy, a prayer, a doxology, is to make of it a sacrament of perpetual communion. "God descends to the soul in prayer and the spirit rises to God."[62]

Our rising corresponds to God's lowering of himself to us. Leon Bloy tells of an old man who constantly walked bareheaded, for he always felt himself in the presence of God. A very expressive image of a prayerful attitude has become one's very life. St. Paul relates it to the act of faith. "Examine yourselves, to see whether

60 Origen, *P.G.*, 11, 452C-D; St. Basil, *P.G.*, 31, 244A.
61 Ps. 104:33.
62 St. John of Damascus, *P.G.*, 94. 1089.

you are holding to your faith. Test yourselves. Do you not realize that Christ Jesus is in you."[63]

Though it is an act, faith rejects all formalism which soon creeps into exterior prayers, into routine duties in which our attention is absent, likewise into all tacit complacency in mystical experiences where we are all too present. "Prayer is not perfect if man is conscious of himself and perceives that he is praying."[64]

Faith invites us to follow Christ naked even in his priestly prayer which is the liturgy of universal intercession.

The Forms of Prayer

The Lord taught authentic prayer in the Sermon on the Mount. The disciples asked him: "Teach us to pray," and Christ gave the gift of the *Our Father.*

All prayer comes from three forms—request, offering, praise. We find all three in the Lord's Prayer: "Give us this day our daily bread," "forgive us our trespasses," "deliver us from evil"; then, "thy will be done on earth as it is in heaven," "kingdom come." which means "Accept the offering of our lives for this end; accept our pardon of others and make us thy servants and thy witnesses." Finally, "hallowed be thy name," "for thine is the Kingdom, the power and the glory."

St. Basil in his *Monastic Constitutions* advises: "Begin to say humbly: 'I am a sinner; I give you thanks, Lord, for having patiently borne with me...' Then ask for the Reign of God and then for respectable things, and do not cease until you have obtained them."

We can recognize these three forms in the responses to liturgical litanies. In the story of a tanner who learned humility from St. Anthony, in the description of his prayer, we see he followed them exactly and thus showed how these forms become a state of prayer

63 2 Cor 3:5.
64 Cassian, *Confer.,* IX, 31.

sanctifying all moments, even for those who do not have any particular time for prayer at their disposal. In the morning this craftsman presented all the inhabitants of Alexandria to God, saying "Have pity on us sinners." During the day, his soul did not cease to think of his work as an offering: "To thee, Lord." In the evening, being very happy that he had been kept in life, he could say only: "Glory to thee."

For the faithful Jews, the Law was engraved on their hearts, always present before their eyes, written on their hands. Their entire being was thus structured by the Law. They recognized the Law in the life of the world, the creation of divine wisdom. Finally the Law was accomplished by their hands, by their everyday acts.

Prayer follows the same universal pattern. Everything is sanctified and blessed by it. Everything becomes a form of prayer. This is the prayerful conception of life where the most humble labor of a worker and the creation of a genius are equally entitled to be an offering before the face of God, and are received as a task given by the Father.

For the spiritual life it is also a decisive passage from "Jesus before the eyes" to "Jesus in the heart" according to the hesychast tradition of the Jesus prayer.

The Jesus Prayer[65]

The Jesus prayer, or "prayer of the heart," was developed on Mount Athos. Associated with the names of St. Macarius, Diadochus of Photike, St. John Climacus, St. Symeon and all the great spiritual masters, it originated in the biblical conception of the Name.

According to the Bible, the name of God is one of his attributes where he is present and where he shows himself, a theophany. In a special manner, the invocation of the name of Jesus makes the grace of his Incarnation universal, allowing each of us our per-

65 See *The Jesus Prayer,* by a monk of the Eastern Church (Fr. Lev Gillet; Crestwood, NY: SVS Press, 1987). Also *The Way of a Pilgrim and The Pilgrim Continues His Way,* Helen Bacovcin, trans. (New York: Doubleday, 1992).

sonal share and disposing our hearts to receive the Lord. The strength of the divine presence in his name proves its greatness. "Behold, I send an angel before you, to guard you on the way...give heed to him...for my name is in him."[66]

"My name is in him" and consequently the angel is the bearer of his formidable presence. When the divine Name is pronounced over a country or a person, these enter into an intimate relationship with God. The invocation of the Name of God is accompanied by its immediate manifestation, for the name is a form of his presence. This is why his name could only be pronounced by the high priest on the day of Yom-Kippur, in "the holy of holies" of the temple in Jerusalem. The Incarnation makes each of us a high priest, but at every moment we are the bearers of the name. The name of Jesus—*Jeshua*—means Savior. *Nomen est Omen*. It contains the power of salvation. "The name of the Son of God sustains the entire world," says Hermas,[67] for he is present there and we adore him in his name.

The "prayer of the heart" frees and enlarges it, and attracts Jesus to it by the incessant invocation: "Lord Jesus Christ, Son of God, have mercy on me, a sinner!"

In this prayer, which is that of the publican in the Gospel, the whole Bible with its entire message is reduced to its essential simplicity: confession of the Lordship of Jesus, of his divine sonship, therefore, of the Trinity and then the fall that called for the abyss of divine mercy. The beginning and the end are gathered here in a single word charged with the sacramental presence of Christ in his Name. This prayer ceaselessly resounds in the depths of our souls, even outside our will and consciousness. Finally, the Name of Jesus resounds of itself, taking on the rhythm of our breathing, in some way "attached," even during sleep: "I slept, but my heart was awake."[68]

66 Ex 23:20.
67 *Pastor.* III, 14.
68 Song of Songs 5:2.

When Jesus is drawn into the heart, the liturgy becomes interior and the Kingdom is in the peaceful soul. The Name dwells in us as its temple, and there the divine presence transmutes and Christifies us. This was the experience of St. Paul, whom we can better understand in the light of this prayer: "It is no longer I that live, but Christ lives in me."

At present, many believers of all confessions find an enormous help in this essentially biblical practice of prayer, a privileged ecumenical place of unity and of encountering the Name of Jesus.

"There are powerful beings like St. Michael, but for us, the weak, there remains nothing but it: take refuge in the Name of Jesus," confesses St. Barsanuphius.[69] St. John Climacus adds: "Strike your adversary with the Name of Jesus; there is no more powerful weapon on the earth or in heaven."[70]

The invocation of the Name of Jesus is within the reach of all in all the circumstances of our lives. It places the Name as a divine seal on everything, and makes the world its dwelling place. By this prayer we adapt the most precious tradition of hesychasm, of silent prayer. Within us, then, lives the thousand-year experience of the greatest masters, making us vigilant witnesses united to all, giving them comfort and refreshment like a tree or a spring of water.

"Pray for those who do not know how to pray, who do not wish to do so, and especially for those who have never prayed," said the Patriarch Justinian in Romania in 1953. His exhortation is closely connected to the Jesus prayer.

Liturgical Prayer

The distinction between mental and vocal prayer is highly theoretical. For the ancients, psalmody was the natural expression of interior prayer, "the psalmody of the soul."

69 Correspondence of Barsanuphius and John. See *The Jesus Prayer*, p. 37-38.
70 *The Ladder of Divine Ascent*, step 27, p. 270.

The prayer of the Church was formed in monastic communities and provided the wonderful rhythm for their days and nights. The people did not participate in it except on Sundays and feast days. This imposed on the laity an effort to interiorize it in order that they might find themselves in the same prayerful rhythm through their hours of work and difficulty in the world.

In the beginning, the Eucharist was celebrated only on Sunday, the day of the Lord. The weekdays brought matins, vespers and the other hours, following the prayer of the synagogue. It was a prayer of praise extended throughout the week, and a thanksgiving inspired by the *mirabilia Dei*, the wonderful works of God.

The blessing of the day means that each day we restore to all things their biblical meaning: to be creatures of God, destined to praise him. "Do not return evil for evil...but on the contrary, bless, for to this you have been called."[71]

In the evening, the blessing of the night expresses our astonishment that, in spite of our failures, we are still living and can thank God for having helped us. The day just spent is thus presented as a particle of sacred history, of the divine economy of salvation in which we have accomplished the task entrusted to us by God. It receives an accent of eternity, and as the ear of wheat, it carries the sun in each of its grains and bends under the weight of its own fullness.

Terce, Sext, None, marking the third, sixth and ninth hours of the day (9:00 am, Noon, 3:00 pm), effect a triple return to God in the midst of work, a pause that opens time to its liturgical and heavenly dimension. The offices of *Prime* and *Compline*, which begin and end the day, have their last chord in the middle of the night with Nocturn, which is the vigil of the spirit, the watchful waiting of the wise virgins in order not to forget themselves and not to forget the Bridegroom who is already coming and is now at the door.

St. John Chrysostom speaks profoundly of the Christian house as a place of prayer that makes it a "house church," an *ecclesia*

71 1 Pet 3:9.

domestica. "Let your house be a church; rise in the middle of the night. During the night, the soul is purer, lighter. Worship your Master. If you have children, wake them and let them unite with you in a common prayer."[72] Even those who waste time or kill it are included in the vigils of those who pray in this way. They present to God people's cares and their thoughtlessness, their suffering, their sorrows and their joys. Every instant of our time is rejuvenated and refreshed by this contact with the fire of those praying. Time is directed toward its accomplishment. Each of its rhythmic moments appears full of meaning and creativity. It preaches and sings the Kingdom.

Liturgical Prayer, the Rule of All Prayer

The prayer of the Church reverberates with biblical revelation. It comes from the totality of truth and has its culmination there. That is why every rule of prayer begins with an invocation of the Trinity and includes the confession of the Creed.

While the needs of the moment naturally inspire individual prayer, liturgical prayer loses this note of the particular and introduces us at once into a collegial consciousness—according to the word, *liturgy,* which means common work. It teaches the true relationship between myself and others, and helps me understand the words: "Love thy neighbor as thyself." It helps us to be detached from ourselves and to make the prayer of humanity our own. Liturgical prayer makes the destiny of every person present to us.

The liturgical litanies lead the individual beyond himself, toward the assembly, toward those who are absent, those who suffer, and finally those who are in their agony. Liturgical prayer embraces the city, nations, humanity, and asks for peace and unity of all. Every isolation or individualistic separation sounds as a false note in this perfect harmony. Formed liturgically, every soul knows by experience that one cannot stand alone before God and

72 *Hom. on Acts,* 26, 3-4.

that, liturgically, one saves oneself with others. The pronoun in the liturgy is never in the singular.

The liturgy filters out all subjective, emotional and fleeting tendencies. Full of a healthy emotion and powerful affective life, it offers us its finished form, made perfect by long centuries and by all the generations that have prayed in the same way. As the walls of the church bear the imprint of all the prayers, offerings and intercessions, the liturgical prayers across hundreds of years are the breath of innumerable human lives. I hear the voice of St. John Chrysostom, St. Basil, St. Symeon, and so many others who have prayed the same prayers and have left in them their spirit of adoration. They help me to find their ardor and to associate myself with their prayers.

However, if the liturgy gives the measure and the rule of all prayer, it also calls for spontaneous and personal prayer in which the soul sings and speaks freely to the Lord. The liturgy teaches it, in calling each one by name as if he were the only one, and each one is called upon to profess the Creed, *I* believe. Even in the framework of the liturgy, this profession puts stress on the most personal act possible. No one can do it in my place. The liturgical texts are attuned to the soul and impel it to a direct and intimate conversation that keeps all of its own value.

Difficulties and Obstacles

The most frequent difficulty, the one that everybody knows by experience, is to harmonize our psychic realm—its changing content, agitated and burdened with the cares of the present—with the content of liturgical prayer or with our personal rule of prayer. Behind the very real tension of seeking harmony, there is often hidden a secret resistance, a very refined form of temptation. It usually is advanced by the argument of sincerity: We do not find ourselves just now in the state of prayer. In forcing ourselves we risk profaning what is sacred, for in every way we would remain distracted, exterior, and in the end, boredom, and sluggishness would triumph. In this case, should we wait for the moment of inspiration, with the risk that we shall never find it?

To suppress this form of temptation at the very outset, and to avoid all misunderstanding, it is important to realize that prayer requires a preliminary state, an ascetic *effort*.

Here is the experience of a hermit: "I believe there is nothing so painful as prayer. When a man begins to pray, then his enemies, the demons, try to hinder him from it...Prayer requires that we fight to our last breath."[73]

There is also the natural resistance that comes from laziness and heaviness of spirit. We can better understand this dark side of human nature in the words of Origen: "A single saint by his prayer is stronger in his struggle than a crowd of sinners."[74] Elsewhere this author notes the fact that climbing up a high mountain is exhausting.[75] So too with prayer.

Prayer thus possesses its own struggle. It is no stranger to that "violence" that carries away the Kingdom, violence to those whom it casts to the ground in adoration, violence to God in making him incline toward earth and toward the man in prayer.[76]

"By his death, he has conquered death." Likewise every prayer entails its own cross, and by its effort it conquers effort so that finally it springs forth freely and joyfully. The body conditions the effort. Fasting, genuflections, prostrations help the spirit to concentrate, tune it like a musical instrument.

The masters tell us that we must go beyond the first difficult moment by attentively reading the psalms. We must act "as if" inspiration were not lacking, and then the miracle of grace will take over. St. Ambrose of Optino, a *staretz*, has said: "Read a

73 *Apophthegmata.* See Stolz, *L'Ascèse chrétienne,* p. 159.

74 *Hom. in Num.,* 25, 2.

75 *P.G.,* 12, 743B.

76 "The Master inclined toward earth and found his image" (N. Cabasilas, *The Life in Christ,* p. 50).

chapter of the Gospel every day and when anxiety seizes you, read
again until it passes away. If it returns, read the Gospel once
more."[77]

The Fathers teach that the Holy Spirit is a gift, the only one
which, once requested, is never without an immediate answer. It
is the *epiklesis* of prayer, the invocation of the Spirit that reaches
the very nature of the One who is giving himself and impels him
to manifest himself.

Why pray? Does not God know what we need? This objection
is aimed at the prayer of petition and intercession. The Gospel
makes no distinction between the forms of prayer and states
clearly: "If two of you agree on earth about anything they ask, it
will be done for them by my Father."[78]

One cannot be united except in a third party, in the will of
God who desires unity, and then, according to the Gospel, such
unity moves the will of the Father. God listens to our prayer, he
rectifies it and makes it an element added to his decision. The
violent insistence of the widow of the Gospel exacted a response
that makes the power of faith stand out clearly. St. Paul begged the
Lord three times to remove the thorn from his flesh. The life of St.
Seraphim gives an account of the prayer of a saint for the soul of
a condemned sinner. Day and night the saint was in prayer. He
struggled with divine justice, and though struck by lightning, his
ardent prayer in its very boldness caused the mercy of God to
triumph, and the sinner was pardoned. Perhaps hell depends also
on the violence of the charity of saints, and God may expect that
our prayers may bring about the *apocatastasis* (universal salvation).

Have we enough time to pray? Certainly, and much more than
we think. "How many moments of torpor, of inattention, could
become instants of prayer, so that we might become vigilant,
attentive to persons and things—even worry, if it is expressed in

77 P. Tchetverikov, *Optino* (Paris, 1926), in Russian.
78 Jn 15:16; Mt. 18:19.

dialogue with God, in questioning, in abandonment. We can even offer the exhaustion that hinders prayer and even our powerlessness to pray."[79]

In these frequent states of loneliness and weariness, the name of Jesus can become an interior appeal during a conversation, the light that illumines monotonous work, the sound of reality that dispels daydreaming, in short, a simple blessing on persons and things.[80] "The remembrance of God, without formulating a single word, is already a prayer and a help,"[81] says St. Barsanuphius.

However, "in the hours when the mind wanders, it is better to attach oneself to reading rather than to prayer," until the moment when "the Spirit himself will teach the heart."[82] That is why, St. Isaac explains: "Prayer is the key that opens the understanding to the Scriptures." [83]

79 O. Clément, "Témoignage de la foi," in *Contacts* (1961), nos. 35-36, p. 246.
80 *Ibid.*
81 *Philocalie* (in Russian), vol. II, 584.
82 *St. Isaac,* Wensinck, *op. cit.*, p. 299, 62.
83 *Ibid.*, p. 220.

4

Lectio Divina: Reading the Bible

"May the rising sun find you with a Bible in your hand."[1] This exclamation of Evagrius expresses well the patristic tradition. Canon 19 of the Council in Trullo enjoined priests to initiate the faithful into the greatest intimacy with the Bible. St. John Chrysostom vigorously insists: "I am not a monk, some of you say...But your mistake is in believing that the reading of the Scriptures concerns only monks, because *for you it is even more necessary* since you are in the midst of the world. There is something worse than not reading the Scriptures, and that is to believe that this reading is useless...a satanic practice."[2]

"Having returned from church, the husband should repeat what has been read. Thus one will set a spiritual table, as well as a material one."[3] The saint counsels studying at home the passage that is to be read in church so that the children will be accustomed to a daily and attentive reading of Holy Scripture.[4]

For Origen,[5] such reading is not simply an exercise added to one's daily life, it is an organic part of one's spiritual life, transforming the day into a living reading of the Word, where the Word himself speaks unceasingly. It directs the struggle and the progress of the soul. By this reading one becomes truly an ecclesial soul, *anima ecclesiastica*, and according to Clement of Alexandria,[6] we are "taught by God" (*theodidacti*).

1 *P.G.*, 40, 1283A.
2 *Hom. on Matt.*, 2, 5.
3 *In Gen. Serm.*, 6, 2.
4 *In Ephes.*, 21, 2-3.
5 *P.G.*, 13,166.
6 *Strom.*, 1, 20.

In the Rule of St. Pachomius, Scripture is to nourish the mind
of the monks all day long. During the hours of work, they sing and
recite the sacred writings, and in the evening all are together in
order to listen to the commentaries. The recitation of the Scriptures
by heart was a common practice. For St. Nilus, hunger for the
Scriptures was the measure of our spiritual being.[7] For St. Isaac:
"The constant meditation on the Word is the light of the soul."[8]

All spiritual writers sound a warning—never profane the Word
by making it an object of speculation or of knowledge for the sake
of knowledge, for "to understand what we read is a grace from
God."[9] Hermas teaches that asceticism and prayer are like a
question to which the Lord answers by a revelation of the meaning of the Scriptures.[10] Likewise a *troparion* (hymn) of the Ninth
hour says: "In the midst of two thieves, your cross was revealed as
the balance-beam of righteousness, for while the one was led
down to hell by the burden of his blasphemy, the other was
lightened of his sins to the knowledge of things divine."

Reading presupposes then "the state of prayer" that brings
words to maturity. "Prayer causes God to illumine man's mind in
order that it can grasp what he reads." God became man "in order
to be closer to us than our own soul," and to give us "the same
mind which was in Christ Jesus."[11] That is why for Nicholas
Cabasilas, "the Gospel *represents* Christ,"[12] which means that it
lets Christ speak by himself, inviting us to fill our eyes and hearts with
"the one who attracts to himself alone and unites to himself alone."[13]
For St. Justin, the Scriptures effect a decisive encounter,[14] and every
martyr by his death testifies that he has read them correctly.

7 *P.G.,* 79, 213C.
8 Wensinck, *op. cit.,* p. 61.
9 St. Symeon, *Discourse on the Scriptures, P.G.,* 120, 385.
10 *Vision* 11, 1-4.
11 Phil. 2:5.
12 *A Commentary on the Divine Liturgy,* J. M. Hussey and P. A. McNulty, trans.
    (Crestwood, NY: SVS Press, 1983), p. 61.
13 *The Life in Christ,* (*P.G.* 150, 501A).
14 Dialogue, 91, 94.

The essential method of reading the Scriptures, according to Nicodemus the Hagiorite, is to go "from the written word to the substantial Word," and it is in this passage, decisive for the spiritual life, that the patristic commentaries are sure guides.

The Fathers of the Church lived the Bible. They thought and spoke by the Bible, with that admirable penetration which extended to the identification of even their being with the biblical substance itself. If one tries to learn from them one understands that the word read and heard leads always to the living person of the Word. St. John Chrysostom prayed before the Holy Book: "Lord Jesus Christ, open the eyes of my heart so that I may understand and fulfill thy will...illumine my eyes by thy light." Likewise St. Ephrem advised: "Before every reading, pray and supplicate God that *he may reveal himself to you.*" St. Athanasius declared: "In the words of Scripture the Lord is found, whose presence the demons cannot stand."[15]

We can say that for the Fathers, the Bible *is Christ*, for each of its words puts us in his presence: "Him whom I seek in books," confessed St. Augustine.[16]

Clement of Alexandria shows that we must nourish ourselves on the seeds of life contained in the Bible as we do on the Eucharist.[17] It is Origen who fixed the meaning of the "eating" of the Scriptures,[18] and tradition has followed him. We consume "eucharistically" the "Word mysteriously broken."[19] St. Jerome says: "We eat his flesh and drink his blood in the divine Eucharist, but also in the reading of Scripture."[20] St. Gregory of Nazianzen compares the reading of the Bible to the consumption of the paschal lamb.

15 *P.G.*, 27, 45.
16 *Confes.* II, 2.
17 *Strom.*, 1, 1.
18 *P.G.*, 13, 130-134.
19 Origen, *P.G.*, 13, 1734; see also St. John Chrysostom, *In Gen. Serm.*, 6, 2; St. Gregory Nazianzen, *Oratio*, 45, 16.
20 *In Eccles.*, 3, 13.

This eucharistic manner of consuming the Word presupposes the *epiklesis*, the coming down of the Spirit, in every reading. The Word is living by the Spirit that rests on him, as he placed himself over the Son at the Epiphany, when he was baptized in the Jordan. We must read then in the dimension of the Paraclete, which is that of the Body of Christ, of the Church and of Tradition in which the Word speaks. God willed that Christ form the Body where his words resound as words of life. It is then in Christ, within him, in the Church that we must read and listen. The Church alone keeps the Word for, as Origen teaches,[21] she possesses the Spirit that has dictated it.

In the liturgy, the people are gathered first to hear and then to consume the Word. This hearing builds up the People of God, forms the eucharistic syntax, the preparation for consuming the Word incarnate, and for entering into substantial communion with the Word.

St. Luke's Gospel tells us[22] that Christ opened the minds of his disciples. He showed them how one must read the Bible in order to discover there all that was written concerning him. Beginning with Moses and all the prophets, he explained to them what was written of him in all the Scriptures. It was thus that the Lord "opened the meaning of the Scriptures" and revealed that the entire Bible is *the verbal icon of Christ.*

In reading the Scriptures we can discern the prefigurative and the typological meaning, and the accomplishment of the prophecies in the messianic period of the coming of Christ. We can grasp also the historical and eschatological meaning and the accomplishment of history in leading to the Kingdom. However, it is the liturgy that offers the method of ecclesial meditation in which the Word is proclaimed, sung, prayed and experienced. The liturgy is prolonged in the life of the faithful and is found again in the daily

21 *In Matt.,* 14.
22 Lk 24:45.

lectio divina, which continues to be a form of prayer and of communion. Here God speaks, intervenes in the life of every person, and invites each to be on the way in company of the angels and saints. Such reading is at the source of its being and is its end. According to St. John Chrysostom, the reading of Scripture is the priesthood of the laity that leads them to sanctity.

That is why in every reading and meditation we must avoid the fearful dryness of reasoning and suppress also emotional dreaming. We can easily make a dead letter out of a text. We cannot give it life, for this comes from the presence of God.

We can read the Bible in a continuous manner, extended over a year. We can choose one book or follow a theme through all the books. We can meditate on a verse or a single word. Each method is good, if it nourishes our spiritual life. Contemplation is added to the understanding. A description evokes historical realities, contemplation grasps their silent depths. Starting from history, every true reading contemplates the icon of the Kingdom.

Thus, reading opens the way to God,[23] but it imposes also the duty of communicating to others the revealed message.[24] The *lectio divina* leads to mission, for "the Word," according to St. Paul, consists "in the demonstration of the Spirit and of power."[25]

---

23 Hermas, *Simil.* VIII, 6, 7.
24 *Ibid.,* X, 4.
25 1Cor 2:4.

5

The Universal Priesthood of the Laity in the Eastern Church Tradition

The Greek translation of the Hebrew text of the Old Testament (such as the Aquila version) applies the word *laikos*—profane or lay—not to men but to things, for example, a "profane land," a "profane journey." The "profane" or "common bread"[1] (*bebelos* in the Septuagint, *laices panes* in the Vulgate) are "profane things" that are not destined for the service of the temple.[2]

The first Christian document that mentions the word "lay" is the letter to the Corinthians, said to be by St. Clement of Rome (ca. 95 A.D.). It speaks of the conduct of men according to "lay rules." From the third century, with Tertullian and St. Cyprian in North Africa, the term "lay" takes its place beside that of "cleric." Here there is already a juridical interpretation that opposes "lay" to "cleric." Finally we find with St. Jerome (the beginning of the fifth century) not a definition but a clearly pejorative statement. Opposite the clergy, those set aside for the things of God, are the lay people, those who look after the things of this world, who marry, carry on business, cultivate the land, testify in court.

In the Bible the word "lay" is rare and somewhat vague, yet it contains a very rich and clear notion of the *laos,* the People of God. Alongside a functional priesthood (the levitical, priestly caste), Scripture speaks of the universal priesthood of the People of God in its totality. Since the giving of the Torah to Moses, the

1 1 Sam 21:4 (1 Kgs 21:4).

2 1 Sam 21:5-6 (1 Kgs 21:5-6); Ezek 48:15.

Lord declares: "You shall be to me a kingdom of priests (*mamleket kohanim*) and a holy nation."[3] The Greek text translates it as *basileion hierateuma,* a royal priesthood, a "people of priests" in the service of the heavenly King. In the New Testament, St. Peter takes up the expression, "You are a chosen race, a royal priesthood."[4] The People of God, set apart and formerly linked with the temple of Jerusalem, is now associated with the *acts and passion of Christ in the flesh.* From the prophetic anticipation, the people now constituted as the Church pass to the revealed reality. Henceforth they are united in Christ and share in the unique priesthood and royalty of Jesus. Christ has made of all Christians "a kingdom of priests, and they shall reign over the earth."[5]

The idea of a profane or lay people has no place in the Bible. It would be absolutely unimaginable. The Scriptures teach in a most firm and consistent manner the sacred and priestly character of each member of the people.

The first disquieting signs appeared as early as the end of the fourth century—a premature result of the age of Constantine. It was the lay people themselves who relinquished their dignity as a universal priesthood, and then inevitably the bishops became more and more the point of focus of the sacred, the priestly, "the consecrated." A distance was created by the indigence, the progressive impoverishment of the laity, by the regrettable rejection of the gifts of the Holy Spirit. This was the great "betrayal of the laity," a relinquishing of their priestly character. Of the two poles of the *laos,* the People of God, one was that of the Christian king who protected the Church and was called "the secular bishop" and "ecumenical deacon" (title of the Byzantine emperors), and the other was that of the monastic, who lived among the things of God. These two poles safeguarded the charismatic dignity of the laity. But the remainder between these two poles, fell into a

3 Ex 19:6.
4 1 Pet 2:9.
5 Rev 5:10.

vacuum now really *profane*. The majority of people, though baptized, was identified with the things of this world, and took on the Old Testament meaning of the word "lay" that had been applied to things. They thus became themselves part of the profane things of this world. It is in this state of rapid decadence that the pejorative terms of *biotikoi* and of *anieroi* are applicable—those who live in the world and are strangers to sacred and holy things. Since then the definition of the laity has been negative. A lay person is a passive article of pure receptivity. He (or she) has nothing to do *in* the Church (except contribute financially), for he has no ecclesiastical function, no ministry or charism.

Now the *Epistle to Diogenetus* (beginning of the third century) affirms: "Each one dwells in his country as a resident foreigner. Every foreign land is to him a fatherland, and every fatherland, a foreign country. He lives on earth, but he is a citizen of heaven." This text only accentuates the teaching of St. Paul: the faithful, the laity, are the chosen of God and fellow citizens of the saints. They have here below no lasting city. From this state of dignity of the "saints" (those called to holiness) we see a dizzying descent to the profane state of those occupied solely with the things of this world. This is a radical profanation of the sacred.

In the face of this decadence, the true tradition has nevertheless survived unchanged. We find it in the dogmas, in the sacramental and liturgical consciousness, in the rich and explicit teaching of the Fathers of the Church.

Universal priesthood implies no opposition to the functional priesthood of the clergy. Neither is the latter an emanation of the laity, a delegation of the congregationalist type. The Church has received a hierarchical structure from the institution of the college of the Twelve Apostles in conformity with the divine plan. The People of God is differentiated by God in its "priestly principle," by means of charismatic ministries. The episcopate is chosen from among the people. It is of its priestly flesh and blood. The episcopate does not form a structure above, for it is an organic part of the Body, of the ontological unity of all its members. Its origin is divine and it is exercised by virtue of apostolic succession. Every candidate is put forth by God: "I have chosen you, and have appointed you."[6] The sacramental power of celebrating the mysteries, and above all, of being an apostolic witness to the Eucharist, and the power of promulgating doctrinal definitions, the charism of the certainty of the truth—*charisma veritatis certum*—belong to the episcopate by virtue of the apostolicity of the Church. There is also the pastoral charism of leading the Body, the royal priesthood, toward the glorious *Parousia*. As a living image of Christ, the bishop has only one true power, that of love, and only one true force of persuasion, and that is his martyrdom, his witness. As these beautiful words declare magnificently: "We are not the masters of your faith, but the servants of your joy."

We can clearly see here the essence of the Eastern Church tradition. There is neither an anti-clerical egalitarianism nor a division by the clergy of the one Body into two parts, but the sacerdotal participation of all in the one divine Priest, Christ, by means of two priesthoods. Each one is established by God, and it is this divine origin that raises them from this world and from every profane perspective.

What is gathered in the One and only Christ, the unique priest, is spread throughout the whole Body. This High Priest moves toward the Kingdom and the universal priesthood. Pascha (the Passover) and the *Parousia* (Second Coming) are not yet fully realized. From this comes the coexistence of the two priesthoods, without confusion or separation, and beyond any impossible opposition. It is in the differentiation of charisms and ministries that the one Christ is realized.

Thus, far from leading to confusion, the tradition decisively affirms the equality of nature. Before everything else, all are equal

6 Jn 15:16.

members of the People of God. By baptism, "the second birth," all are already priests, and it is in the heart of this priestly equality that the functional differentiation of charisma is produced. It is not a new "consecration" of a bishop or a priest, but an ordination for a new ministry of one who was already consecrated, already changed in his nature once for all, having already received his priestly character.

The sacrament of the *anointing by chrism* (confirmation in the West) establishes all the baptized in the same hieratic, priestly order. From this equality, some are chosen, set apart and established by a divine act, as bishops and presbyters.[7] A *functional difference* of ministries suppresses all ontological difference of nature and makes all separation between clerics and laymen impossible. Balsamon, a canonist of the twelfth century, offers the opinion that episcopal ordination brings with it a plenary absolution from sins, which would make of it a "second baptism" and would thereby change its nature. Such a doctrine has never been accepted by tradition, for it would institute a difference in nature between bishops and the faithful. The possibility of reducing a priest to the lay state with the authorization of conjugal life demonstrates just the contrary. In this case, the cleric sets aside the functional ministry and remains a priest of the universal priesthood. He does not undergo, either before or after, any ontological change. This affirmation stands out more sharply in the presence of two traditions which express, each in its own order, the principle of "divine paternity." One goes back to St. Ignatius of Antioch,[8] for whom every bishop is a "father" by reason of his liturgical function. By water and the Spirit he generates divine sonship.[9] Another tradition goes back to the "desert fathers." They were great

---

7 The New Testament uses the term *presbyteros* to designate the particular ministry (the clergy) and keeps the term *iereus* for the priesthood of the laity. This Greek word designated the Jewish priesthood. Christ abolished the *hiereus* as a distinct caste. All Christians have become *hiereis*, priests of the royal and universal priesthood.

8 *Magn.* 3, 1.

9 *The Apostolic Constitutions*, II, 26, 4.

spiritual laymen whose charisms were not institutional and functional, but personal. A spiritual father, *pneumatikos pater*, was a
"theodidact," taught by God and guided by the Spirit. Though
simple monks, they were the "spiritual fathers" of everyone.

Thus, if the bishop participates in the priesthood of Christ by
his sacred function, every lay person does so by his very being.
The lay person participates in the unique priesthood of Christ by
his *sanctified being*, by his *sacerdotal nature*. In view of this dignity,
of being a priest in his very nature, every baptized person is sealed
with the gifts, anointed with the Holy Spirit in his very essence.
Every lay person is the priest of his or her existence; offering in
sacrifice his entire life and existence.

A close correspondence between the "initiation" of the faithful
(baptism and anointing) and the ordination of priests confirms
this. In fact, the prayer for the eighth day after baptism mentions
"the imposition of the hand of God" that establishes the baptized
in "the dignity of his sublime and heavenly vocation." The white
color of the baptismal robe is the color of the priesthood in the
two covenants. We can understand that for practical reasons only
the clergy have kept it. The rite of tonsure signifies the total
consecration to ecclesial service. Therefore, all, clerics and laity,
are set apart for the things of God. All are consecrated. For a male
child, an ancient tradition prescribed a procession around the
table of the altar, corresponding to the dignity of a priest of the
universal priesthood. According to Hippolytus of Rome,[10] the
baptized received the kiss of peace (just like a bishop), as one who
is worthy of his new state—*dignus effectus est*. With regard to "the
white stone" on which is inscribed the new name,[11] Hippolytus
specifies that this name was pronounced during the Eucharist. It
symbolized admission to the Kingdom, it was the name of a new
creature, a member of the royal priesthood. The astonishing

10 *Trad. Apost.*
11 Rev 2:7.

liturgical symmetry of these rites with the ordination of the clergy underscores the sacerdotal dignity of every baptized person.

The initiation (the three great sacraments of the faithful) introduces every Christian into the order or sacred hierarchy of the People of God, differentiated solely by functional ministries.

This perfect equality of nature in all the members of the Church corresponds to the fundamentally homogeneous character of Orthodox spirituality. Likewise there exists no separation between the teaching Church and the Church taught. It is the whole Church that teaches the Church, just as it is in the whole of its teaching that the Gospel is addressed to each and very one. Prayer, fasting, the reading of the Scriptures and ascetic discipline are imposed on all for the same reason. That is precisely why the laity develops the state of *interiorized monasticism.* Its wisdom consists essentially in assuming, while living in the world and precisely because of this vocation, the eschatological maximalism of the monastics, their joyous and impatient expectation of the coming of Christ, the *Parousia.*

As an example of interiorized monasticism, common to all, we might mention the ancient tradition that looked upon the period of betrothal as a monastic novitiate in order to prepare for "the conjugal priesthood." Thus the crowns of the betrothed, at the time of the Eastern Church rite of Coronation (the sacrament of marriage), were kept for seven days, and it was then that the priest gave the blessing to put an end to this time of abstinence for the spouses. Likewise in former Russia, after the ceremony of marriage in the church, the spouses left directly for a monastery. They were initiated for a time into the monastic life in order to be better initiated into their new conjugal vocation, their *conjugal priesthood.*

Nicholas Cabasilas, a great liturgist and layman of the fourteenth century, entitled his treatise on the sacraments, *The Life in Christ.* St. John of Kronstadt, a holy priest from the end of the nineteenth century, described his eucharistic experiences in *My Life in Christ*. All this shows that the true fatherland of Orthodox souls is the Church of the liturgical mysteries. Nicholas Cabasilas even paraphrased the text of the Acts, saying: "It is by the sacraments that we live, that we move and have our being."[12]

The sacrament of anointing by chrism is the sacrament of universal priesthood. The Holy Spirit descends on the one newly born in baptism, to pour out the gift of Christian action. The anointing is the sacrament of strength which arms us as "soldiers and athletes of Christ," in order "to render testimony without fear or weakness," thus to accomplish the ministry of charismatic love. St. Cyril of Jerusalem said to the catechumens: "The Holy Spirit arms you for combat...He watches over you as over his own soldier...You will stand firm against any opposing power."[13] Every lay person is before all else a combatant.

The sign of the cross made with chrism on all parts of the body (in the Eastern tradition) symbolizes the tongues of fire of Pentecost. It is accompanied by the sacred formula: "The seal of the gift of the Holy Spirit." It is therefore in one's entire being that every lay person is sealed with the gifts. Each baptized Christian is an entirely *charismatic* being.

The prayer at the heart of the sacrament specifies the aim of these gifts: "That it may please him/her to serve you in every act and every word." This is the consecration of one's whole life to the ministry of the laity, a ministry that is essentially ecclesial, of the Church.

The total and absolute character of the consecration stands out clearly in the rite of tonsure, identical with that performed for one entering monastic life. The prayer asks: "Bless your servant who has come to offer you as first gifts the tonsure of the hair of his/her

12 N. Cabasilas, *The Life in Christ*, p. 49.
13 *P.G.*, 33, 996, 1009.

head." Its symbolic meaning is unmistakable—it is the total offering of one's life.

The eschatological emphaisis of the prayer reinforces this meaning: "May he/she give glory and have all the days of his/her life the vision of the joys of Jerusalem." Thus every instant of time is directed to its eschatological dimension. Every act and word is in the service of the King. In undergoing the rite of tonsure, every lay person is a monk of *interiorized monasticism,* subject to all the requirements of the Gospel.

To the *epiklesis* of the sacrament, the request for the Holy Spirit, the heavenly Father answers by sending him who clothes the baptized person with Christ, "Christifies" him. In the prayer over the holy chrism, the bishop asks: "O God, mark them (those who are to be confirmed, anointed, made "Christs") with the seal of the immaculate chrism. They will bear Christ in their heart in order to be a *dwelling-place of the Trinity*." We can note here how the Orthodox Church centers all in the Trinity. The trinitarian balance is stressed here. One is sealed with the Holy Spirit, becomes a Christ-bearer, in order to be the dwelling-place of the Holy Trinity.

For a liturgical service, the choice of a reading is a commentary in itself. During the sacrament of anointing, the last verses of St. Matthew's Gospel are read: "Go therefore and make disciples of all nations." By this reading the Lord's great commission is addressed to every chrismated Christian, to every member of the laity. To accomplish this the sacrament offers its grace. "One must preach to others what he has received in baptism." Besides the accredited missionaries, every baptized and confirmed person is "an apostolic being," each in his or her own way. It is by my whole being and life, that I am called to give constant testimony.

The idea of a passive people is in flagrant contradiction to patristic ecclesiology. The universal priesthood of the faithful shares in the three powers—government, teaching and sanctification.

The first Council of Jerusalem in the time of the apostles[14] united all the elements of the Church—apostles, elders and brethren. The words, "It has seemed good to the Holy Spirit and to us," became the sacred formula of the Ecumenical Councils, and this "we" is the collegial we of the Body in its totality. The bishops constitute the Council, but they bear within them the whole Body, and their supreme power is exercised only in the mystery of the consensus of all. The bishops act out of the consensus of the Church (*ex consensu ecclesiae*). As the encyclical of the Eastern patriarchs in 1848 states so well: "With us, innovations cannot be introduced either by the patriarchs or by the Councils; for with us, the safeguarding[15] of religion dwells in the whole body of the Church, that is, in the people themselves who wish to preserve their faith intact."[16] Lay persons are not *judges* (*kriteis*) of the faith. The promulgation of doctrinal definitions is the charism proper to the episcopate. On the other hand, laymen are the *defenders* of the faith. The "shield" is the Church in its entirety, and that is why the ability to distinguish truth from error, "to verify and to testify,"[17] is given to all. This defense is the very sacred obligation of each lay person. We know that the laity played this role at the time of the Arian crisis in the fourth century, and later in the fifteenth century, but above all, in the sixteenth and eighteenth centuries, in the southwestern part of Russia, when the Orthodox brotherhoods saved the purity of the faith and constituted the real ramparts of truth in the face of a faltering episcopate. The *consensus* of the universal priesthood appeals, in the case of a weak episcopate, to the episcopate enlightened by the Holy Spirit.

In the rites of episcopal ordination, the *axios* ("Worthy!"), or the *final amen* in other services, is the sacred signature of the body

14 Acts 15.

15 The act of *protecting* and *defending;* the Greek word used here implies the idea of someone who bears a shield.

16 *Mansi,* 40, 407, 408.

17 1 Thess. 5:19-21.

in its totality to every act of the Church. During the liturgy, every one of the faithful is co-celebrant with the bishop. The people participate actively in the eucharistic anaphora, and in the *epiklesis* where the plural is always employed. The priest says in the name of all: "*We* pray thee," and then he is the apostolic witness of the miracle accomplished. The communion of spirit between the celebrant and the assembly is total, corresponding to the word *liturgy,* which means action in common.

In teaching, and this is a fact peculiar to Orthodoxy, the professors of theology are very often from the laity. The ministry of the Word is linked with the charism of holy orders, but the bishops delegate to chosen ones among the laity the power of teaching and of preaching in virtue of their universal priesthood. In the theocratic society of Byzantium, the emperor had the power of calling Councils, and imperial preaching had a normal place. We know also the beautiful homilies of Nicholas Cabasilas, a layman and great liturgist. We can mention, too, the name of Cyril of Philea, an ardent hesychast, who was married and the father of a family. In the 1950s-60s, in Greece, laymen were authorized by the Synod of bishops for ministry, to teach and preach in the churches. Here they exercised their priestly charism.

In a diocese, the councils and consistories administer temporal matters. The bishop is a spiritual father, pastor and liturgical celebrant. When it happens, as for example in Greece today, that the State exercises supremacy in the material organization of the Church, it is because the State theoretically represents the Christian people.

On the level of sanctification, the monastic state is entirely independent from ordination.[18] The spiritual direction of the *staretz* is not linked to the priesthood. The "pneumatics," the "spiritual masters," whether monastics or lay people living in the

18 The episcopate according to canon law is incompatible with the monastic degree of the "great schema or habit," (*mégaloschème*).

world, and whom the people call "the men of God" or "the fools for Christ," enjoy a very great spiritual authority. The people recognize them as spiritual fathers. Often it is simple monks who are the spiritual fathers of bishops and patriarchs. This purely charismatic ministry will never cease to exist in the Church alongside the ministry of the clergy.

The laity forms an ecclesial dimension that is, at one and the same time, of the world and of the Church. Lay people do not have access to the power of administering the means of grace (the sacramental power of the clergy) but, on the other hand, their sphere is "the life of grace" and "the state of grace." By the simple presence in the world of "sanctified beings," of "priests" in their very substance, of "trinitarian dwellings," the universal priesthood of the laity bears the power of the sacred in the world, celebrating the liturgy of the entire cosmos therein. Beyond the church walls, lay people continue the liturgy of the Church. By their active presence, they introduce into society and relationships the truth of the dogmas they live, thus dislodging the evil and profane elements of the world.

In addition to an active participation in the powers of the Church, the Fathers emphasize the triple dignity of the laity. St. Macarius of Egypt says: "Christianity is not at all something mediocre. It is a great mystery. Meditate on your own nobility...By the anointing, all have become *kings, priests* and *prophets* of the heavenly mysteries."[19]

The *royal dignity* is of an ascetic nature; it is the mastery of the spiritual over the material, over the instincts and impulses of the flesh, the freedom from all determination coming from the world. St. Ecumenius expresses it as "kings, by the ascendancy over our passions."[20] St. Gregory of Nyssa says likewise: "The soul shows

19 *P.G.,* 34, 624B-C.
20 *P.G.,* 118, 932.

its royalty in the free disposing of its desires. This is inherent only in a king. Dominion over all is characteristic of a royal nature."

The royal dignity is thus the "how" of existence, the royal quality of dominating, of being one's master and lord. Its "what," its content, is in the *priestly dignity.* St. Paul exhorts us to offer our bodies as a living sacrifice, a "spiritual service,"[21] to make of our being and its existence worship, a liturgy, a doxology. Origen expresses this admirably: "All those who have received the anointing have become priests...If I love my brothers even to give my life for them, and I fight for truth even to death...if the world is crucified to me and I to the world, I have offered a sacrifice and I become the priest of my existence."[22] With the same meaning, St. Gregory of Nazianzen sums up: "We are priests by the offering of ourselves as a spiritual sacrifice."[23]

In order to define the *prophetic dignity,* St. Ecumenius gathers all the dignities together: "Kings, by dominion over our passions; priests, to immolate our bodies; *prophets,* in being initiated into the great mysteries."[24] St. Theophylactus adds: "prophet, because he sees what eye has not seen."[25] According to the Bible, a prophet is one who knows "the designs of God" in the world, one who grasps the providential course of history under the eyes of God. Eusebius of Caesarea, in his *Evangelical Demonstration,*[26] writes: "We burn the prophetic incense in every place and we sacrifice to him the fragrant fruit of a theology lived out." Here is a magnificent definition of the laity: by one's whole being, by one's whole existence, to become such a living theology—*theophanic*—the luminous place of the presence of the *Parousia,* God's coming again.

21 Rom 12:1.
22 *P.G.,* 12, 512-522.
23 *P.G.,* 35, 498.
24 *P.G.,* 118 932C-D.
25 *P.G.,* 124, 812.
26 *P.G.,* 22, 92-93.

In following the patristic tradition, we can outline in broad strokes a certain "type" of lay person. He is above all a person of prayer, a liturgical being, with the prayer of the *Sanctus* and the *Trisagion* in the heart: "holy, holy, holy," one who sums up his whole life in these words of the psalm: "I will sing praise to my God while I live." Abba Anthony[27] speaks of a man of great sanctity, a physician who practiced medicine in the world. He gave all that he did not need to the poor and sang the *Trisagion*, the thrice-holy hymn, every day, uniting himself to the choir of the angels. He makes us think of the type of saint called *anargyros*, "disinterested." He practiced his profession as a form of his priest-hood, as a priest. He makes us think also of "the good doctor" of Camus—but such as the author must see him now.

Today [1960s], in Communist countries where the Church is more than ever reduced to its liturgical life, this destitution be-comes a powerful appeal to center oneself on the one thing needful. Just recently, the Russian episcopate exhorted the laity, unable to participate regularly in liturgical life, to become a temple, to continue the liturgy in their existence, to present to those without faith a liturgical countenance and smile. In the tragic conditions of the utmost tension, the Church teaches above all how to pray, how to share in the struggle by a silent testimony, how "to listen to the silence of the Word" in order to render more powerful every compromised word. According to an old tradition, St. Michael offers on the altar on high "lambs of fire," the souls of martyrs. Their testimony is not necessarily spectacular. As a priest in the world, the lay person practices the discernment of spirits and says "no" to every demonic enterprise. The others, those who are "beneath the altar" cry, "How long, O Lord?"[28] The Church can create, with all its wealth of human culture, a splendid icon of

27 *P.G.,* 65, 84. *The Sayings of the Desert Fathers/The Desert Christian,* Benedicta Ward, trans. (New York: Macmillan, 1980), p. 6.
28 Rev 6:9.

the kingdom of God, but it can also be stripped even to the point of martyrdom and "naked, follow Christ naked."

During the liturgy, the bishop collects the prayers and the gifts of the faithful and bears this offering to the Father, and pronounces the epiklesis, the calling down of the Holy Spirit on behalf of all. But the presence of the lay person in the world is also a perpetuation of the *epiklesis*, which sanctifies every inch of the world, contributes to the peace of which the Gospel speaks, and gives to all the liturgical "kiss of peace." According to the liturgical litanies, our prayer is directed to the day ahead, to the earth and its fruits, to the efforts of all. In the immense cathedral, that is, the universe, we, the priests of this life, whether workers or scholars, make of everything a human offering, a hymn, a doxology.

A lay person is an *eyewitness* of the resurrection of Christ. Such is the teaching of the liturgy and the meaning of the service of Easter night. The liturgical mystery goes beyond the simple commemoration. It "re-presents" the event, even becomes the event. Before the people, the risen Christ appears, and this confers on every one of the faithful the apostolic dignity of a witness.

That is why a lay person is also an "apostolic being"[29] in his or her own way. According to the spiritual writers, such a person is described in the final words of St. Mark's Gospel: the one who will tread on serpents, cure all sickness, move mountains and raise the dead, if such is the will of God. If we live our faith simply, to the end, we will arrive at our goal unshaken.

Our attitude of recollected silence and humility must also be penetrated by passionate tenderness. St. Isaac and St. John Climacus say that we must love God as we would love our betrothed, and then to be in love with all of God's creation in order to discern the meaning of God in everything. According to Merleau-Ponty,[30] "man is condemned to meaning." We are invited to live our faith, to see what

29 St. Maximus the Confessor, *P.G.*, 90, 913. Cf. Lk 10:19.
30 *Phénoménologie de la Perception*, p. xiv.

is not seen, to contemplate the wisdom of God in the apparent absurdity of history, and to become light, revelation and prophecy.

Marveling thus at the existence of God, "the world is full of the Trinity," a lay person is also slightly mad, "foolish" with the "folly" of which St. Paul speaks, the paradoxical humor of "the fools for Christ," which alone is capable of shattering the many overly serious causes of our time and their devotees.

A lay person is also one who is freed by his faith from "the great fear" of the twentieth century, fear of the bomb, of cancer, of Communism, of death. The faith of such a person is always a way of loving the world, a way of following the Lord even into hell. This is certainly not a theological system, but perhaps it is only from the depths of hell that a dazzling and joyous hope can be born and assert itself.

Christianity, in the grandeur of its confessors and martyrs, in the dignity of every believer, is messianic, revolutionary, explosive. In the domain of Caesar, we are ordered to seek and therefore to find what is not found there—the Kingdom of God. This command signifies that we must transform the world, change it into the icon of the Kingdom. To change the world means to pass from what the world does not yet possess—for this reason it is still this world—to that in which it is transfigured, thus becoming something else—the Kingdom.

The central appeal of the Gospel is a call to the Christian violence that alone lays hold of the Kingdom. In reference to St. John the Baptist the Lord spoke of violence. Thus St. John is not only a witness of the Kingdom. He is already the place where the world is conquered and where the Kingdom is present. He is not only a voice that proclaims it. He is its voice. He is the friend of the Bridegroom, Christ; he is the one who decreases that the other, the divine Lover of mankind, may increase and appear. To be a true lay person is to be one who, by his entire life, by what is already present within him, proclaims him who is to come. It is to be one who, according to St. Gregory of Nyssa, full of "sober intoxication," cries out to every passerby: "Come and drink." It is to be the one who says with St. John Climacus these words already taking flight in their joyousness: "Thy love has wounded my soul, and my heart cannot endure thy flames; I go forward, singing to thee..."[31]

The Gospel speaks to us of the violent who take the Kingdom by force. One of the sure signs of its approach is the unity of the Christian world. In this expectation of the final fulfillment, hope, the great Christian hope, takes on life. The prayer of all the Churches ascends, formulating an *ecumenical epiklesis,* invoking the Holy Spirit to descend on the possible miracle of unity. This is our ardent desire, our ardent prayer. The destiny of the world depends on the Father's response, but this is dependent on our transparent sincerity and the purity of our hearts.

Jesus Christ, by the total gift of himself, has revealed the perfect priesthood. As the image of all perfections, he is the unique and supreme bishop. He is also the supreme and unique lay person. This is why his priestly prayer bears the desire of all the saints: to glorify the Holy Trinity with one heart and one soul and to unite all around the one and only chalice.

The divine Lover of mankind waits for us to share this joy, which no longer is only of this world. It already inaugurates the feast of the Kingdom.

31 *P.G.,* 88, 1160B.

6

The Mystical Ascent

St. Paul mentions his ecstasy very briefly and on this occasion presents the essence of the Christian life: "I know a man in Christ."[1] This ecstasy is only a special grace, by no means indispensable and never to be sought. On the other hand, every baptized person is "in Christ."

This Pauline expression indicates the mystical state, which means that no one is excluded, and that Christian mysticism is sacramental.[2] No one is a mystic apart from the Eucharist. Baptism indeed inaugurates it by the birth of God in the soul. "When the Redeemer was born, it was day in the middle of the night."[3] He takes possession of this place and never ceases deepening it. The *Letter to Diognetus* says: "The Logos who is always born in the heart of the saints is born and grows." St. Gregory of Nyssa is more precise: "The child Jesus grows in various ways according to the measure of each one. He manifests himself as a child, as an adolescent, as one fully grown."[4] According to St. Maximus the Confessor, a mystic is one in whom the birth of the Lord is best manifested. Likewise St. Ambrose writes: "Each soul that believes, conceives and brings forth the Word of God...According to the flesh there is but one mother of Christ, but according to faith, Christ is the fruit of us all."[5] In this way St. Paul defined his pastoral task: "In order that Christ be formed in you."[6]

1 2 Cor 12:2.
2 Nicholas Cabasilas called his treatise on the sacraments: *The Life in Christ.*
3 S. Kierkegaard, *Journals and Papers,* Howard V. and Edna H. Hong, trans., vol. I (Bloomington: Indiana University Press, 1967), p. 234: x-2, A283, 1849..
4 *P.G.,* 44, 82, 81.
5 *In Ev. S. Lucae,* II, 26.
6 Gal 4:19.

In following the progression described by St. Gregory of
Nyssa, Christ becomes "fully grown" in the human soul when
Baptism is followed by the Eucharist whose influence extends to
the whole life of the faithful Christian. "If anyone listens to my
voice and opens the door, I will come to him and eat with him,
and he with me."[7] It is more than a birth; it is a communion
whereby one "in Christ" becomes part of his body, a living member. By virtue of this communion one belongs to both tables (one
earthly, the other heavenly); the same guest is in both worlds:
above, the nuptial palace, here below, a progress toward the nuptial Kingdom, and at last to the Spouse. "Great is this mystery,"
wrote St. Paul, to exalt this union. For here is the mystical
marriage: the divine Spouse unites himself to his Church[8] and to
every human soul.

For the Pauline image of "the head," Cabasilas substitutes "the
triumphant and overflowing heart," the inexhaustible source of
the treasures of love. That is why the Eucharist contains the
biblical theme of the mystical marriage. "The man of sorrows"
reveals himself as "the man of desire," the eternal and divine Lover
of mankind. Christ alone is the one who attracts our love and
then enters into us in order that we may live again in him.
Cabasilas gives clear and simple evidence for this: "The soul
thirsts for the infinite. The eye was created for light, the ear for
sounds, everything for its end, and the desire of the soul to thrust
itself toward Christ."[9] The love of God inclines toward earth, and
espouses the impulse of the one who ascends.

In his ascent, the one "in Christ" learns the liturgical meaning
of history. It does away with every escape and leads him to the
hidden reality. The words of St. Paul that God acquired his people
"for the praise of his glory"[10] have a parallel in the Book of

7 Rev 3:20.
8 N. Cabasilas, *The Life in Christ*, p. 123.
9 *Ibid.*, p. 96
10 Eph 1:14.

good/mental/health — to live in the present

Revelation. Here, our only activity is "to fall down and worship." This is because all praise, every doxology, Eucharist and thanksgiving "redeems time." It opens upon "the eternal present."

"Give us this day our daily bread"[11] means that the gifts of salvation and of the Kingdom may be granted us even now, today, here below. It is not a hope for the future, but an immediate requirement, here and now. "We enter paradise *today* when we are poor and crucified," writes Léon Bloy.[12]

St. Matthew's Gospel, in speaking of the last judgment, stresses the decisive character of the present moment. As soon as time merges into eternity, all division is done away with, and with it the schizophrenia of syncopated time.

We understand the immense importance of this when we observe that in history we live outside time. Indeed by a strange kind of alienation, in this world we live in the past, in our memories, or in expectation of the future. As for the present moment we try to escape from it, and exercise our inventive spirit in order better "to kill time." We do not live in the here and now, but in dreams of which we are unconscious. An ascetic adage affirms: "The hour that you are living, the task that you are doing, the one you encounter in this moment, are the most important in your life." They are so because the past and the future in their abstract dislocation are non-existent and have no access to eternity. Eternity converges only toward the present moment and is given only to the one who makes himself totally present at that moment. It is only in these instants that one can attain it and live it under the guise of the eternal present. The liturgical "memorial" clearly teaches this. It suppresses the past that has gone by, makes the totality of history actual, and bears it before the face of the Father, introducing it into the dimension of the present that

11 More precisely "our bread of tomorrow." See J. Jeremias, *The Eucharistic Words of Jesus* (Philadelphia: Fortress, 1977).

12 *La Femme Pauvre.*

actualizes the before and after. In the "memory" of the Father, all is present, actual, vibrant with life.

The liturgy, freeing us from the weight of time, a weight caused by its non-existent dimensions, brings the divine presence into our souls and permits us to recognize it. It is because Mary Magdalen was looking for her God according to a fixed and established image within her, and therefore non-existent, that she did not at once recognize her Lord at the tomb.

A monk has written a book called *In Thy Presence.*[13] He tells of a day spent with Jesus, a simple day, yet one very different from a person's ordinary day. One can see in it a kind of osmosis and continuity between the human actions of our Lord and our own acts. Living the Gospel in the humblest things of daily life brings us amazingly close both to Jesus and at the same time to each other. A prayer springs forth spontaneously: "Do not let thy word to be in my soul as in a sanctuary that is isolated by iron railings from the house and the street."[14]

We perceive clearly that it is not at all a question of a "rule of life," often poorly adapted to real life, but of a "style of life," of a spirituality attentive to the mysterious and multiform presence of Christ who awaits us, and who expects from us a certain inventive genius so that we might recognize him and follow him even to hell and beyond. Such a day has the value of a Gospel parable that has been lived. It opens an infinite series, the actual eternity of present moments. If spiritual writers have spoken much of ladders, it is because on these ladders we descend toward our neighbors and then, all together, we ascend toward the One who awaits us.

The description of the last judgment is striking in its simplicity, but this does not make it less fearful. The sole accusation is that of being inattentive, insensitive to the presence of Christ in

13 A monk of the Eastern Church (Lev Gillet), *In Thy Presence,* (Crestwood, NY: SVS Press, 1977).
14 *In Thy Presence,* p. 96.

every suffering being, in every human person. It is therefore this recognition that Christ expects from us.

"After God, consider each person as God," spiritual teachers used to say. In place of the usual salutations, they knew how to salute the human face of God in everyone, in every unknown passerby. Abba Apollos would say to his disciples: "When a pilgrim or a guest comes to visit you, prostrate yourself before him. Not before the person, but before God. For it is said: 'You see your brother, you see your God.'"[15] Such an attitude is never a recipe or a rule, but a *style* that forms us from within and expresses an unquenchable thirst for Christ. One who (like St. Seraphim) knows how to say to each one, "my joy," speaks to each person as the dwelling place of God, and that is why his joy is perfect.

The Shepherd of Hermas reminds us that whoever refuses to help a person in distress will be held responsible for his loss.[16] St. Maximus the Confessor warns us that we shall have to render an account "of the evil we have done, but above all, for the good that we have neglected to do, and because we have not loved our neighbor."[17] While the Gospel condemns every idle word, the unwritten saying of Christ (*agraphon*) quoted by Didymus of Alexandria goes further: "Of every *good word* that they do not utter, they will render an account on the day of judgment."[18] "At the evening of life, we shall be judged by our love," notes St. John of the Cross.

We know that the piety of the Jews of the Old Testament was formed by hearing: "Hear, O Israel." The Word shapes history. But for the same Jews, at the time of the messianic restoration, eschatology replaced hearing with vision. It is no longer, "hear," but "lift your eyes and see." Likewise the Gospel has us hear the words of Jesus, invites us to listen to them, but as soon as history is

15 *Apophthegmata Patrum.*
16 *Simil.* X, 3, 4.
17 *P.G.,* 90, 936A-B.
18 Resch, *Agrapha,* 13.

transcended, "the pure of heart will *see* God." At the moment of his martyrdom, the deacon Stephen *saw* heaven open before his eyes on "the glory of God and of Jesus standing at the right hand of God."

G. Kittel[19] emphasizes that at the moment of the Resurrection hearing passed to vision and marked the beginning of the *Parousia* and entrance into eschatological time. A luminous cloud accompanied the Exodus, covered the tabernacle, filled the temple, and revealed the dwelling of the *Shekinah,* the glory of God, and the place of his manifest presence. That is why Moses and Elijah, the great visionaries of the Old Testament, accompanied the transfigured Christ, in order to testify to the same divine light. The light of Tabor anticipates that of the *Parousia* and of the world to come.

The spiritual life leads to ineffable contemplation where light is the object, but also the means of vision. In iconography, the halos of the saints show the luminosity of their bodies as ontologically normative. Although normal on icons, during the life of the saints such exterior manifestations are rare, extraordinary charisms. The spiritual remains interiorized, intense, centered in the heart and in the lifting up of the spirit, visible to God alone.

Seen from above, a saint is already clothed in light, but seen from below, such a person never ceases to struggle. "We shall not be accused of not working miracles," says St. John Climacus, "but we shall surely have to render an account to God because we have not ceaselessly wept over our sins."[20] St. Isaac declares: "Repentance is the trembling of the soul before the gates of the Kingdom."[21]

Not being satisfied with mediocre mimicry, the one who follows Christ reproduces his image in an interior manner. "Purity of heart is to love those who fall."[22] The mystical soul opens wide in

19 *Die Religionsgeschichte and das Urchristentum.*
20 *The Ladder of Divine Ascent,* step 7, p. 145.
21 Wensinck, *op. cit.,* p. 310.
22 St. Isaac, *Sayings.*

cosmic love, assumes universal evil, goes through the agony of Gethsemane, and rises to another vision stripped of all judgment. "The one who is purified sees the soul of his neighbor." Like sees like: "When one sees all as good and no one as impure, then we can say that he is truly pure of heart." "If you see your brother in the act of sinning, throw about his shoulders the mantle of your love."[23] Such a love is effective because it changes the very substance of things.[24]

It is no longer the passage from passion to continence, from sin to grace, but the passage from fear to love: "The perfect reject fear, disdain rewards, and love with their whole heart."[25]

The soul is elevated above every determined sign, every representation and every image. The complex gives way to the one and the simple. The soul, the image and mirror of God, becomes the dwelling place of God. The mystical elevation orients it toward the Kingdom. "If the characteristic of wisdom is knowledge of realities, no one can be called wise if he does not embrace also the things to come."[26] "A spiritual person of the latter days," says St. Isaac, "receives grace in his proper measure." This is the iconographic vision of "the divine liturgy." The heavenly choir of angels, where the "lost sheep," humanity, has its place, stands before the mystical Lamb of the Apocalypse, surrounded by the triple circle of spheres. On the whiteness of the celestial world, the royal purple of the passion stands out, tending toward the splendor of the day without end, the iconographic color of divine love clothed in humanity. This is the return of man to his heavenly dignity. At the moment of the ascension of Christ, the angels cried out: "Who is this king of glory?" Now the angels are in utter amazement before this ultimate mystery—the lost sheep become one with the Shepherd. The Song of Songs sings of the marriage of the

23 St. Isaac, *Sayings*, CXV.
24 St. John Chrysostom, *P.G.*, 61, 273.
25 St. Isaac, Wensinck, *op. cit.*, p. 341.
26 St. Gregory of Nyssa, *P.G.*, 45 580C.

Word and the Dove. Love is the magnet, and the soul, attracted always more powerfully, casts itself into the luminous darkness of God. One feels the powerlessness of words: luminous darkness, sober ecstasy, well of living water, motionless movement.

"You have become beautiful in approaching My light; your approach has drawn to you a share of My beauty." "Approaching the light, the soul becomes light."[27] At this level, it is not a question of learning about God, but of receiving him and being transformed in him. "The knowledge that has become love" is clearly of a eucharistic nature. "The wine that gladdens the heart is called, since the passion, the blood of the vine." "The mystical vine pours out sober intoxication."[28]

"Love is God who shoots his arrow, his only begotten Son, after having moistened its threefold point with the vivifying Spirit. The point is faith which not only introduces the arrow but the archer with it."[29]

The soul transformed into a dove mounts always higher—grace upon grace. "Having once put your foot on the ladder on which God has leaned, do not cease to go up...each rung leads to a further one."[30] It is Jacob's ladder.

To this encounter come "not only the angels, but the Lord of the angels." "But what can I say of what is ineffable, what the eye has not seen, what the ear has not heard, what has not entered into the heart of man to conceive, how can all that be expressed in words?"[31]

Every movement ceases. Prayer itself changes in nature. "The soul prays outside prayer."[32] It is hesychia, the silence of the spirit, its resting place that is beyond all prayer, the peace that surpasses all peace. It is the face-to-face vision extended over eternity, when

27 St. Gregory of Nyssa, *P.G.*, 44, 869A.
28 *Ibid.*, 828B-C.
29 *Ibid.*, 852A-B.
30 *Ibid.*, 401A-B.
31 St. Symeon the New Theologian, *Homélie*, XC.
32 St. Isaac, Wensinck, *op. cit.*, p. 118.

"God comes into the soul and the soul goes forth to God." In this direct encounter with the One who has already come, man finally becomes in himself such as divine eternity has changed him. Having arrived at "the most desirable end":

"He is separated from all, and united to all;
Impassible, and of a sovereign sensibility;
Deified, and he esteems himself the off-scouring of the world;
Above all, he is happy,
Divinely happy..."[33]

---

33 Evagrius, *Le Traité d'oraison.* See J. Hausherr, *Les leçons d'un contemplatif* (Paris, 1960), p. 187.

Very apparent in this
book — the emphasis
of the Eastern Church
on the divinity of Christ.
The Western Church has
an emphasis on the
humanity of Christ. While
I find the Eastern Church
very beautiful — I find
my greatest comfort in
the fact that the Christ
fully understood my
human nature.

Selected Bibliography

Paul Evdokimov

1942 *Dostoievsky et le problème du mal,* Lyon: Ed. du Livre français.

1947 "La culture et l'eschatologie," *Le Semeur,* 50: 358-369.

1950 "Message aux Églises," *Dieu vivant,* 15: 31-42.

1958 *La femme et le salut du monde,* Paris-Tournai: Casterman. [*Woman and the Salvation of the World,* Anthony P. Gythiel, trans., Crestwood NY: SVS Press, 1994).

1959 *L'orthodoxie,* Neuchâtel-Paris: Delachaux et Niestlé.

1961 *Gogol et Dostoievski,* Paris: Desclée de Brouwer.

1962 *Le sacrament de l'amour,* Paris: Ed. de l'Epi. [*The Sacrament of Love,* Anthony P. Gythiel and Victoria Steadman, trans. Crestwood NY: SVS Press, 1985).

1963 "Communicatio in sacris: une possibilité?" *Le messager orthodoxe,* 14, 25: 17-31.

1964 *Les âges de la vie spirituelle,* Paris: Desclée de Brouwer. *Ages of the Spiritual Life,* rev. trans. Michael Plekon and Alexis Vinogradov, Crestwood NY: SVS Press, 1998].

1966 *La prière de l'Église d'Orient,* Editions Salvator, Mulhouse.

1968 *La connaissance de Dieu selon la tradition orientale,* Lyon: Xavier-Mappus.

1969 *L'Esprit Saint dans la tradition orthodoxe,* Paris: Ed. du Cerf.

1970 *Art de l'icône: Théologie de la beauté,* Tournai: Desclée de Brouwer. [*The Art of the Icon, A Theology of Beauty,* Steven Bigham, trans., Torrance CA: Oakwood, 1990].

1970 *Le Christ dans la penseé russe,* Paris: Ed. du Cerf.

1972 *L'amour fou de Dieu,* Paris: ed. du Seuil. [anthology]

1977 *La nouveauté de l'esprit,* Begrolles: Abbaye de Bellefontaine. [anthology]

1977 *Le buisson ardent,* Paris: Ed. P. Lathielleux. [anthology]

Olivier Clément

1971 "Paul Evdokimov: Temoin de la beauté de Dieu," *Contacts* 73-74 (Special commemorative issue with biography, bibliography, remembrances, unpublished works).

1985 *Orient-Occident, Deux Passeurs: Vladimir Lossky, Paul Evdokimov,* Geneva: Labor et Fides.

1995 *Contacts,* 172 "Paul Evdokimov, Témoin de la beauté de Dieu," special 25th anniversay number with essays on him.

Peter C. Phan

1979 "Mariage, monachisme et eschatologie: Contribution de Paul Evdokimov à la spiritualité chrétienne," *Ephemerides Liturgicae,* 93: 352-380.

1981 "Evdokimov and the monk within," *Sobornost* 3, 1: 53-61.

1985 *Culture and Eschatology: The Iconographical Vision of Paul Evdokimov,* NY: Peter Lang. [Contains the most exhaustive bibliography of and about Paul Evdokimov].

Rowan Williams

1976 "Bread in the Wilderness: The Monastic Ideal in Thomas Merton and Paul Evdokimov," in M. Basil Pennington, ed., *Monastic Tradition, East and West, One Yet Two*: Kalamazoo MI: Cistercian Publications.

Michael Plekon

"Paul Evdokimov: Theologian of the Church and the World," *Modern Theology,* 12: 1, 1996, 85-107.

"Le Visage du Père en la Mère de Dieu," ["The Face of the Father in the Mother of God: Mary in Paul Evdokimov's Theology,"] Contacts, 172, 1995, 270-286.

"The God Whose Power is Weakness, Whose Love is Foolish: Divine Philanthropy, the Heart of Paul Evdokimov's Theology," *Sourozh*, 60, May, 1995, 15-26.

"A Liturgical Being, A Life of Service: Paul Evdokimov's Gift and Witness to the Church," *Sobornost*, 17: 2, 1995, 28-37.

"Interiorized Monasticism: Paul Evdokimov on the Spiritual Life," *The American Benedictine Review*, September, 1997.

Index

A

Abraham, 34, 46, 112
Absolute, the, 38, 40, 57, 44, 62
absolution, 172, 173, 174
accedia, 62, 176
Acts of Andrew, 97
agape, 139
agnostics, 24
Alexis, St, 122
alienation, 26, 29
almsgiving, 183
Ambrose, St, 102, 245
Ambrose of Optino, St, 217
angels, 128, 130
Anselm, St, 44
Anthony, St, 102, 121, 198, 199, 210
apatheia, 194
apocatastasis, 42, 218
Apophthegmata, 82
Arians, 236
art, 63, 193, 194, 195; abstract, 110
asceticism, 62, 64, 65, 68, 113,
    117-125, 127, 128, 130, 160, 163,
    170, 172, 175, 182, 184-187, 190,
    195, 203, 222. *See also* monasticism.
    versus mortification, 131, 179; and
    psychoanalysis, 192; and psychology,
    191; reparational, 181; and
    sublimation, 193; term, 159;
    Western, 180-181
ascetic literature, 160
Asen, Paul, 144
Athanasius, St, 82, 125, 223; *Life of St.
    Anthony,* 134
atheism, atheist(s), 13, 14, 16, 21-28,
    30, 33, 40, 42, 43, 45, 46, 47, 54, 83,
    84, 85, 87, 88, 108, 203
Augustine, St, 58, 85, 110, 155, 223

B

Balsamon, Theodore, 231
baptism, 67, 72, 73, 98, 99, 134, 185,
    199, 204, 231, 232, 245, 246
Barsanuphius, St, 213, 219
Basil of Ancyra, St, 113
Basil the Great, St, 100, 128, 152, 179,
    210
Baudelaire, 92
believer(s), 23, 46, 56, 57, 62. *See also*
    Christians, Christianity
Benedict, St, 114, 125, 126, 128, 179,
    208
Benedictines, 179
Berdyaev, N., 83
Bible, the, 89, 91, 155, 183, 190, 211,
    223, 225, 228
bishops, 228, 230, 231, 232, 236, 237,
    238, 241. *See also* episcopate
Bloy, L., 99, 209, 247
body, the, 149, 155
Boehme, J., 75
Bonaventure, St, 180
boredom, 92, 108
Bosch, H., 107, 124

C

Cabasilas, Nicholas, 60, 73, 222, 233,
    234, 237, 246
Camaldolese, 179
Camus, A., 36
Carthusians, 179
Cassian, St John, 69, 125, 127, 172, 179
causality, 31
celibacy, 113, 183
Chadaaev, 83
chastity, 139, 148-151, 155

chrismation, 74
Christ. *See* Jesus Christ
Christianity, Christians, 30, 45, 51, 58,
    86, 113, 169, 200, 233, 234, 238, 242
Christians, Christianity. *See also* believers
Chrysostom, St John, 135, 137, 146,
    214, 223, 225
Church, the, 27, 55, 73, 82, 85, 101,
    103, 110, 128, 142, 164, 169, 175,
    185, 233, 238; in Russia, 30
Cistercians, 179
civilization, 62, 63
Claudel, P., 206
Clement of Alexandria, St, 65, 99, 172,
    221, 223
Clement of Rome, St, 150
clergy, 227, 229, 238; term, 227
Climacus, St John, 13, 112, 115, 116,
    123, 189, 197, 198, 208, 211, 213,
    241, 243, 250; *Ladder of Divine
    Ascent,* 168
Columban, St, 179
Communism, 25, 26, 27, 29, 109
concupiscence, 150, 151, 172
confession, 124, 125, 172, 173, 174. *See
    also metanoia;* repentance
confirmation, 231. *See also* chrismation
conscience, 50, 109
consciousness, 25, 27, 29, 31, 123, 125,
    191
Constantine, Emperor, 142, 143
contemplation, 225
conversion, 76
Council of Ancyra, 127
creation, 241; of man, 25, 170
Creed, the, 54, 56, 58, 112, 193, 216.
    See also symbol of faith
cross, the, 51, 84, 111, 120, 185
Crusades, the, 180
Cyran, St, 181
Cyril of Jerusalem, St, 69, 189, 234
Cyril of Philea, 237

D

Damian, Peter, 179
Dante, 67, 103
death, 34, 35, 43, 52, 56, 58, 98, 155,
    167, 185, 200-205; fear of, 23
death of God, 38, 84
de Beauvoir, S., 201, 202
Decalogue, 151
de Groote, Gerard, 180
Deisis, 169
demons, 125, 126, 160. *See also* devil, the
denial of God, 26, 27, 109
descent into hell, 98-99, 112
despair, 110
destiny, human, 87, 104, 141
devil, the, 89-92. *See also* Satan
Diadochus of Photike, St, 126, 195,
    205, 211
dialectical materialism, 29
Didache, 83, 87
Didymus of Alexandria, 249
discernment, 91, 172, 189, 190
divine attributes, 28
divine love. *See* love, divine
divinization, 22
Dominicans, 180
Dosithesus, 113
Dostoyevski, F., 38, 39, 54, 65, 78, 84,
    87, 88, 92, 93, 111
dualism, 155

E

Eckhart, 60
ecstasy, 129, 196
Ecumenical Councils, 236
Ecumenius, St, 238, 239
ego, 35, 123, 170, 190, 191
Einstein, A., 32, 33
Ephrem the Syrian, St, 97, 115, 176
epiklesis, 55, 218, 224, 235
Epiphany, 97; icon of, 96, 97
episcopate, 230, 236. *See also* bishops

Epistle of Barnabas, 87

Erasmus, 205

Eros, 54, 190

erotic love, 85

Essenes, 183

Eucharist, 60, 73, 82, 98, 204, 214, 223, 230, 232, 245, 246

Eusebius of Caesarea, 239

Evagrius, 126, 130, 143, 160, 173, 182, 185, 189, 190, 191, 197, 221

evil, 21, 38, 43, 44, 62, 73, 76, 81, 82, 90, 91, 92, 101, 113, 124, 125, 155, 160, 171, 175, 184; manifestations, 89

existentialism, 33, 37, 39, 40, 47, 201

F

faith, 22, 23, 32, 34, 45, 46, 49, 50, 52, 53, 55, 56, 58, 65, 85, 87, 104, 108, 153, 164, 209, 210

fall, the, 171

fasting, 64, 137, 183, 189, 217

Father, the, 49, 51

Fathers, the, 54, 55, 69, 71, 89, 101, 108, 113, 117, 123, 124, 125, 137, 153, 186, 202, 223, 238

fear, 15

Feuerbach, 29

Florovsky, G., 135

"fools for Christ", 93, 116

forgiveness, 174

Francis, St, 180

Francis de Sales, St, 181

freedom, 25, 35, 36, 37, 39, 40, 41, 43, 44, 50, 51, 52, 101, 107, 111, 141, 142, 145, 148, 187

free will, 37

Freud, S., 39, 40, 61, 65, 191, 201

G

Gandhi, 199

Gide, A., 40

God, absence of, 43; existence of, 44, 53; experience of, 59

Gospel, the, 30, 43, 46, 47, 53, 58, 60, 65, 73, 74, 85, 90, 98, 107, 111, 119, 120, 124, 126; 128, 138, 146, 151, 160, 168, 180, 185, 193, 222, 233, 242, 243, 248, 249; of John, 72; of Luke, 146, 147, 224; of Mark, 241; of Matthew, 235

grace, 164, 183, 192, 238

Green, Julian, 201

Gregory Nazianzen, St, 51*n,* 54, 101, 128, 131, 170, 223, 239

Gregory of Nyssa, St, 13, 14, 23, 54, 87, 90, 91, 129, 156, 170, 171, 238, 243, 245, 246

Gregory the Sinaite, St, 130, 197

guilt, 38

H

healing, 184

heart, the, 156; purification of, 194

Hegel, M., 33

Heidegger, 33, 34, 35, 36, 37, 84, 200, 201

Heine, H., 25

hell, 44, 52, 81, 95, 97, 98, 100, 101, 102, 108, 110, 111, 113, 155, 160, 242; descent into, 98-99, 112

hesychasm, hesychast tradition, 121, 128, 182

Hinduism, 58

Hippolytus of Rome, 232

history, 25, 26, 30, 31, 39, 43, 44, 113, 126, 143, 202, 225, 242, 246, 247

holiness, 15, 62, 118, 155, 157, 229. *See also* sanctity; spiritual life; monastic, 134

Holy Spirit, 23, 51, 54, 55, 59, 67, 86, 103, 104, 111, 118, 134, 144, 147, 152, 167, 184, 209, 218, 228, 234, 236, 243; acquisition, 189

homologia, 56

human being, human person, 31, 157

humanism, 25, 26, 180
humility, 64, 65, 77, 78, 120, 131, 164,
    168, 169, 170, 199, 200, 241
humor, 93

I

icon(s), 95, 118, 119, 149, 158, 194,
    208, 250; crucifixion, 97; *Deisis,* 169;
    Epiphany, 96, 97; Nativity, 96;
    Pentecost, 99; the Resurrection, 97
Ignatius of Antioch, St, 82, 118, 133,
    184, 231
Ignatius of Loyola, St, 181
image of God, 91, 183, 192
images, 192, 193
imagination, 129, 149, 193
Imitation of Christ, 180
impassability, 195
Incarnation, the, 21, 50, 58, 60, 64, 71,
    72, 113, 125, 211
individual, the, 29, 161
insanity, 62
intellect, intelligence, 33, 180
Irenaeus, St, 72, 91, 140
Isaac of Syria, St, 84, 102, 116, 127,
    128, 161, 189, 195, 219, 222, 241,
    251
Isaiah, 49, 90
Islam, 58

J

James, St, 145
James of Saroug, 97
Janet, P., 62
Jansenism, 181
Jaspers, 41
Jerome, St, 223, 227
Jesus Christ, 21, 22, 29, 34, 42, 49, 50,
    52, 53, 55, 59, 67, 71, 78, 82, 84, 95,
    97, 98, 103, 125, 143, 144, 151, 154,
    160, 162, 163, 174, 180, 210, 224,
    243, 249, 250, 251; temptation of,
    140, 141, 147

Jesus Prayer. *See under* prayer
Jews, the, 49, 211, 249
Job, 43, 62, 202
John, St, 55, 56, 83, 161
John Chrysostom, St, 98
John Climacus, St, 150
John of Damascus, St, 194, 199
John of Kronstadt, St, 233
John of Lycopolis, 152, 194
John of Saroug, 52, 143
John of the Cross, St, 181
John the Baptist, St, 168, 169, 183, 242
Jouhandeau, M., 107
joy, 103, 149, 158, 185
Judaism, 58
judgment, 111; fear of, 23; of God, 34
Jung, C., 41, 42, 61, 62, 65, 187, 191,
    193
Justin Martyr, St, 140, 202, 223
    Apologies, 86

K

Kant, E., 193
kenosis, 101, 169
Kierkegaard, S., 33, 34, 205
Kittel, G., 250
knowledge, 49, 50, 141, 222, 252

L

Ladder of Divine Ascent, 168
Lagneau, J., 88
laity, lay persons, 137, 228, 231, 232,
    234, 236-243; term, 227, 229
Lavelle, L., 33, 60
LeSenne, R., 33
Letter to Diognetus, 245
Life of St. Anthony, 134
light and darkness, 95, 96, 98, 111
liturgical prayer. *See under* prayer
liturgical texts, 95, 96, 134

liturgy, 56, 101, 105, 107, 119, 120, 130, 160, 194, 215, 216, 224, 237, 238, 240, 241, 247, 248

love, 14, 21, 52, 55, 56, 68, 101, 103, 104, 111, 131, 149, 164, 168, 187, 195, 230, 251, 252; divine, 47, 88, 102; erotic, 102; of God, 50, 51, 199; of neighbor, 161

lying, lies, 90

M

Macarius of Egypt, St, 68, 69, 114, 116, 127, 131, 159, 198, 211, 238; *Homilies,* 121, 126

Macarius the Elder, 82

Malraux, 40

mandorla, 98

marriage, 148, 149, 233

martyrs, martyrdom, 55, 56, 85, 104, 114, 121, 133, 134, 145, 200

Marx, K., 28

Marxism, 25—28, 31, 37, 39

materialism, 32, 88

matter, 27, 28, 29, 31, 39, 71, 145

Maximus the Confessor, St, 128, 245

Meletius of Antioch, Patriarch, 127

Merleau-Ponty, 40, 241

messalians, 159

metanoia, 72, 134, 145, 168. *See also* repentance

modernism, 63

monastic communities, 114, 115

monasticism, 65, 114, 119, 126, 128, 135, 137, 138, 142, 144, 145, 159, 161, 182. *See also* asceticism. interiorized, 135, 139, 233; and the laity, 136-137; and ordination, 237; origins, 133; salvific character, 143; Western, 136, 179-181

Monastic Rules, 128

monastic vows, 139, 153

monism, 28

mortification, 179, 180, 181

Moschus, John, 127

Motovilov, N., 138

Mount Athos, 115, 130, 136, 211

mysterium tremendum, 15

mystery, 33, 42, 47, 50, 54; divine, 14

mysticism, 57; Western, 180

myth, 22, 33

N

nature, 30, 43, 167, 172, 203, 230

neurosis, collective, 39

Nicodemus the Hagiorite, 223

Nietzsche, F., 39, 84, 87, 169

Nilus of Sinai, St, 137, 157

Nonnus of Edessa, Bishop, 150

O

obedience, 139, 151, 152, 153

ordination, 232, 233, 237; episcopal, 236

Origen, 65, 86, 124, 133, 148, 162, 193, 198, 203, 217, 221, 223, 224, 239

P

Pachomius, St, 115, 185, 186, 222

Palamas, St Gregory, 128, 144, 158, 191

Paphnutius, 127

Parousia, 34, 65, 82, 112, 113, 129, 131, 154, 230, 233, 239, 250

Pascal, B., 32, 43, 57, 62, 205

Pascha, 98, 203, 230

passion, 88, 91, 92, 123, 148, 176, 185, 189, 190, 191, 195, 251

patristic tradition, 14

Paul, St, 16, 21, 46, 50, 52, 54, 56, 60, 62, 71, 72, 73, 77, 82, 85, 86, 95, 125, 144, 149, 159, 174, 190, 193, 202, 205, 209, 218, 225, 239, 245, 246

Peguy, 45, 103, 208

Pelagia, St, 150

Pentecost, 46, 78, 100, 103, 105, 108, 110, 112, 113, 129, 185, 234; icon, 99

pessimism, 108, 128, 201

Peter, St, 14, 16, 49, 97, 104, 228

phenomenology, 32

Philemon, Abbot, 194

pilgrimage, 180

Plato, 20, 86, 90, 124, 202

poetry, 207

Polycarp, St, 133

positivism, 88

poverty, 139, 146

praxis, 26, 29, 123

prayer, 33, 64, 102, 121, 127, 130, 137, 153, 180, 183, 189, 196, 197, 206-211, 219, 222, 235, 252; forms, 210; Jesus Prayer, 118*n*, 128, 211-213; liturgical, 213-216; obstacles, 216—217

pride, 163, 170

priesthood, 227, 231, 239, 240; universal, 228, 229, 235

Prodigal Son, 69

psalms, 217

psychoanalysis, 36, 173; and asceticism, 192

psychologism, 41, 42

psychology, 31, 34, 59, 61, 62, 64, 190; and asceticism, 191

purification, 72, 73

Q

quietism, 181, 185, 197

R

rationalism, 32

reading, 224-225

reason, 14, 21, 34, 37, 50, 52, 54, 172

religion, 17, 26, 32, 41, 86; criticism of, 28; organized religion, 25

religious attitude, 42

religious experience, 59, 60

religious life, 17, 62. *See also* spiritual life

Renaissance, the, 180

reparational ascetism, 181

repentance, 72, 115, 168, 198, 199. *See also* confession; *metanoia*

responsibility, and freedom, 37

Resurrection, the, 49, 84, 85, 86, 95, 98; icon, 97

revelation, 17, 50, 60

ritual, 63

romanticism, 28

Rostand, J., 45

Russia, 27, 30, 233, 236

S

sacraments, 63

sacred, the, 16

saints, sainthood, 16, 42, 47, 56, 59, 64, 102, 129, 153, 229, 250

salvation, 22, 34, 51, 98, 123, 161, 164, 183

sanctity, 16, 17. *See also* holiness; spiritual life

Sartre, J.-P., 36, 37, 38, 39, 40, 111

Satan, 67, 90, 111, 142, 143. *See also* devil, the

science, 21, 24, 30, 32, 33, 42, 45, 52, 109, 195

scientism, 30

Scriptures, the, 16, 91, 221, 222

Second Coming, 34. *See also Parousia*

Seraphim of Sarov, St, 138, 158, 189, 196, 205, 207, 209, 218, 249

The Shepherd of Hermas, 99, 130 249

sickness, 61

silence, 60, 64, 67, 116, 118, 196, 206, 207, 241

Silouan of Athos, St, 103

Simon the Stylite, St, 127

sin, 52, 62, 76, 83, 84, 101, 123, 155, 160, 163, 164, 167, 170, 251; and the mind, 191

Sixth Ecumenical Council, 62, 189

skepticism, 16
Socrates, 44, 167, 202
solitude, 29, 61, 77, 122, 131, 168
Soloviev, V., 109, 170
soul, the, 30, 31, 61, 121, 131, 149,
    155, 187, 193, 251, 252, 253
Spinoza, 75
spiritual father(s), 151-153, 232, 238
spiritualism, 57
spiritual life, 14, 23, 57-60, 62, 64, 67,
    71, 72, 73, 75, 167, 175, 183, 189,
    197, 250. *See also* religious life
The Spiritual Meadow, 127
Stirner, M., 108
Stoics, 36
sublimation, 193
suffering, 38, 43, 61, 64, 87
Suso, Henry, 180
symbol, symbolism, 17, 41, 81; of
    baptism, 73-74; liturgical, 63
symbol of faith, 54. *See also* Creed
Symeon the New Theologian, St, 60,
    104, 122, 129, 147, 154, 175, 211
syncretism, 60

T

Tauler, 56
tears, 198, 199
telos, 26
temptation, 62, 142, 147, 171, 175,
    190; of Christ, 140, 141, 147
Teresa of Avila, St, 181, 195
Tertullian, 120
The Testament of XII Patriarchs, 87

theism, 26
theocracies, 136
Theodore of Cyrus, St, 83
Theodore of Studion, St, 137
Theodulus the Stylite, 127
Theognostus, 152
theology, 42, 43, 86, 95, 103, 130, 153,
    180, 182, 239; teaching of, 237
Theophilus of Antioch, St, 14
Therese of Lisieux, St, 64
Thomas a Kempis, 180
Tikhon of Zadonsk, St, 139
tonsure, 74, 234, 235
totalitarianism, 28
transcendence, 34, 201, 202
transcendent, the, 16, 32, 41
Transfiguration, the, 129
Trinity, the, 73, 100, 212, 215, 235,
    242, 243
truth, 31, 34, 41, 44, 139; and freedom,
    37

U

Urcy, H., 109

V

Valensin, 43
Virgin Mary, the, 147, 148, 168, 169

W

Weil, S., 46, 47, 108
Whitehead, 29
woman, 148
Word, the, 22, 53, 71, 221, 222, 224